D1461614

# RAILWAYS IN THE BRITISH ISLES

*Adam & Charles Black · London*

# Railways in the British Isles

## LANDSCAPE, LAND USE AND SOCIETY

### David Turnock

First published 1982
A & C Black (Publishers) Ltd
35, Bedford Row, London WC1R 4JH

© 1982 David Turnock

ISBN 0–7136–2281–4

British Library Cataloguing in Publication Data

Turnock, David
Railways in the British Isles.
1. Railroads – Great Britain – History
I. Title
385′.0941      HE3018
ISBN 0–7136–2281–4

Filmset in Monophoto Ehrhardt by
Latimer Trend & Company Ltd, Plymouth
Printed in Great Britain

# Contents

List of illustrations and maps     vii
Introduction     ix

### 1   The development of the railway system

1   Some early railways     3
2   A basic railway system     11
3   Competition between railway companies     20
4   The selection of railway routes     27
5   The influence of landowners on railway development     33
6   Later railway development especially in Ireland, Scotland and Wales     40
7   Redevelopment of plateway routes: The Forest of Dean     48
8   Railway layouts in cities     56
9   Railway architecture with particular reference to stations     64
10   Railway station locations     76

### 2   The significance of the railways for economic and social development

11   Some general perspectives     85
12   The railways and suburban development     91
13   The railway town     96
14   The impact of railways on canals     102
15   Railways and the ports     112
16   Railways for the slate quarries of North Wales     121
17   Railways for the iron industry     128
18   Railways and distilleries in North Scotland     136
19   Railways and farming     143
20   Railways for recreation     148

*Contents*

### 3  The contemporary scene

| | | |
|---|---|---|
| 21 | A changing railway industry | 157 |
| 22 | The run-down of cross-country services | 164 |
| 23 | Selective development of railways | 172 |
| 24 | The resurgence of suburban railways | 178 |
| 25 | Irish narrow gauge with particular reference to peat workings | 185 |
| 26 | The problem of derelict railways | 194 |
| 27 | Conversion of railways into roads | 203 |
| 28 | Recreational uses for derelict railways | 207 |
| 29 | Preserved railways | 214 |
| 30 | Railways preservation in North Wales | 224 |
| | Bibliography | 229 |
| | Index | 245 |

# List of Illustrations

PHOTOGRAPHS

| | | |
|---|---|---|
| 1 | Dandy car at York Museum | 4 |
| 2 | Electrified west coast main line north of Wigan | 13 |
| 3 | Lord Harborough's Curve, at Saxby, Leicestershire | 34 |
| 4 | Railway landscape in the Brecon Beacons | 43 |
| 5 | Redbrook in the Wye Valley | 54 |
| 6 | Suburban train at Wigan | 59 |
| 7 | Local services on Clydeside | 62 |
| 8 | Crossing the Tweed | 65 |
| 9 | Conwy in North Wales | 66 |
| 10 | The Forth Bridge | 67 |
| 11 | Ashby de la Zouch, Leicestershire | 70 |
| 12 | Oundle, Northamptonshire | 72 |
| 13 | Portrush, Co. Antrim | 74 |
| 14 | The Great Central in Leicester | 89 |
| 15 | Leicester's London Road Station | 93 |
| 16 | Derby Locomotive Works | 100 |
| 17 | Ticknall Tramway | 106 |
| 18 | The main street at Ticknall in Derbyshire | 107 |
| 19 | Railway revival at Shackerstone | 109 |
| 20 | Railway reopening with a difference | 110 |
| 21 | A Fairlie on the Festiniog | 125 |
| 22 | Railways in the service of the iron industry | 134 |
| 23 | Preservation at the ironstone quarries | 135 |
| 24 | Distillery landscape | 140 |
| 25 | Station overhaul at Tamdhu, on Speyside | 141 |
| 26 | Hill farming in the Grampians | 146 |
| 27 | The Antrim coast | 153 |
| 28 | Crossing the Border | 162 |
| 29 | Railways and road transport | 165 |
| 30 | The most northerly railway route in Britain | 167 |
| 31 | Scotland's mountain railway? | 169 |
| 32 | Stopping train at Selby | 170 |

| | | |
|---|---|---|
| 33 | A special freight service for the Trawsfynydd power station | 173 |
| 34 | Tyneside's new Metro | 182 |
| 35 | Railway arch at Carnlough, Co. Antrim | 189 |
| 36 | Working the peat bogs in Donegal | 191 |
| 37 | A bridge without a purpose | 195 |
| 38 | The changing landscape at Walsingham, Norfolk | 198 |
| 39 | Railways in the memory | 199 |
| 40 | Welsh Highland | 212 |
| 41 | Severn Valley scene | 216 |
| 42 | Main Line Steam action | 217 |
| 43 | Snowdon Mountain Railway | 220 |
| 44 | Reconstruction on the Festiniog Railway | 226 |

## MAPS

| | | |
|---|---|---|
| 1 | Early railway development in the Coalbrookdale Ironbridge area of East Shropshire | 7 |
| 2 | The Cromford & High Peak Railway and its connections | 8 |
| 3 | Main line railway development to 1854 | 12 |
| 4 | Railway development in north-east England | 15 |
| 5 | Stages in the development of the railway system of Leicestershire | 24 |
| 6 | Railways in the Forest of Dean | 50 |
| 7 | Railway stations of particular architectural merit | 68 |
| 8 | Station sites in Bedford, Carlisle, Macclesfield and Shrewsbury | 80 |
| 9 | Railways and canals in West Leicestershire | 105 |
| 10 | Railway developments in relation to the docks of Barrow-in-Furness and Bristol | 117 |
| 11 | Railways and slate quarries in North Wales | 123 |
| 12 | Railways and ironstone quarrying in the East Midlands | 131 |
| 13 | Railways and whisky distilleries on Speyside | 139 |
| 14 | The present railway network | 161 |
| 15 | Suburban railway developments in Glasgow, Liverpool and Newcastle | 181 |
| 16 | Narrow-gauge railways in Ireland, past and present | 187 |
| 17 | Rationalisation of railways in Cork, Dublin, Edinburgh and Hull | 196 |
| 18 | Some derelict railways in Ulster | 200 |
| 19 | Railway conversion to roads in East Anglia | 205 |
| 20a | Railway conversion for recreation: footpaths and bridleways | 209 |
| 20b | Railway conversion for recreation: long-distance footpaths | 211 |
| 21 | Aspects of railway preservation | 219 |

# Introduction

The brisk tempo of publishing in railway matters makes it difficult to find new ground. Yet the extensive coverage of technical details and company history has left the themes of landscape, land use and society relatively untouched. Perhaps this is because they are not topics that concern the railway specialist: rather, they occupy a borderland between several fields of study including landscape history, industrial archaeology, historical geography and architecture. 'Landscape' is used here in the broadest sense. This book considers first the scenic impact made by the railways which is dramatically evident in deep trench-like cuttings and towering viaducts but also more subtly reflected in the sylvan setting of a rural station or the mature stonework of a simple 'accommodation' bridge. These qualities can be appreciated at their different scales and intensities on the working railway, but also, as many are finding in our more leisured days, on the preserved lines or indeed on derelict tracks where railway operation is but a memory. Walking an old railway can be a pleasurable occupation in itself but it also provides a clearer understanding of the engineering problems involved in railway building and the difficulties of selecting the best route. It is worth remembering that separate railways were part of an overall system which has grown, and contracted, over the years. How did the network develop to assume such a complex and irregular form—and to what extent was the whole structure affected by the fact that many separate companies were seeking to develop their own particular empires? At the local level too it is worth pondering the problems of route selection which often required the reconciliation of conflicting objectives. It is not necessary to have detailed knowledge of engineering or mathematics to appreciate that the layout of railways has a particular form or 'morphology' and whatever the scale of enquiry from local to national there are interesting stories to be told. All this leads on to 'land use' and 'society'. For the railways were built to make economic and social intercourse more efficient and it is a fascinating exercise, attempted in the second section of this book, to unravel the functional links between the railway and its users. In the second half of the nineteenth century, of course, the railway was the dominant form of transport in Britain and the whole process of economic and social development, while not 'caused' by the railway, must be associated organically with the prime haulier. The third and final section relates the various themes to the modernisation of the railways in an age of competition from road and air transport. Selective development of the system, by improved track and signalling and new locomotives and rolling stock, has been complemented by extensive closures of secondary routes. The need for railways has changed and public attitudes have changed as well. The landscapes of derelict railways thus require study as do those of the several preserved railways which steam enthusiasts have taken over.

There is no suggestion that the topics summarised above have not been dealt with in previous publications. W. G. Hoskins in his classic work on *The Making of the English Landscape* has given the railways due emphasis. J. A. Appleton has studied the problem of derelict railways and considered various options for reclamation, including conversion to recreational use, while the same author has contributed a valuable morphological study. C. Hamilton Ellis is renowned for his aesthetic appreciation of railways while G. Biddle has contributed to a growing volume of work on railway architecture. And although the economic and social impact of the railway has received scant consideration, J. R. Kellett's book on *Railways and Victorian Cities* is a most notable contribution. However, much of this work is comparatively little known and the objective of this book is to combine these various approaches into a single volume that may, hopefully, serve to make railways a more profitable topic for environmental studies. To assist in this direction a substantial bibliography is included, graded to separate general railway histories from more detailed studies available in the form of pamphlets and articles in learned journals.

It is something of a problem to decide just what constitutues a railway. Although there is no doubt that the main focus must attach to the network of British Rail (and the two Irish companies), as well as their illustrious ancestors, there are a good many private lines which can be followed backwards through history to reveal the full technological evolution which really begins back in the ancient world when the idea of a track for wheeled vehicles finds rudimentary expression in ruts that were deliberately cut into road surfaces. In the late medieval period it is known from the writings of Georg Bauer that a number of mines in Central Europe improved efficiency by laying boardways so that loaded wagons could negotiate narrow underground passages more easily. Under this remarkable system, which must have called for great skill on the part of the 'drivers', smooth wheels ran on smooth surfaces. But there are no records of such a system being used in Britain and the first evidence of anything remotely resembling a railway appears only in 1555 when parallel baulks of timber were laid down near Barnard Castle (Co. Durham) so that horses could pull heavier loads. The first written mention of a 'railway' appears in a document relating to Sir

Francis Willoughby's estate at Wollaton near Nottingham. It seems that a short coal-carrying line was built between 1603 and 1604, about the same time as another was laid to connect pits at Broseley in Shropshire with the navigable Severn. And it may be that the idea of running wagons with flanged wheels on edge rails originated at one of these two places. A continental origin is possible but an eighteenth-century reference to an 'Englischer Kohlenweg' in the Ruhr does not support such a view. But there is no doubt that it was during the eighteenth century that the railway was first used on a significant scale, because during the canal age it was a suitable means of connecting coal mines with navigable water. It is with such systems that the book begins.

DAVID TURNOCK

# Acknowledgements

Many people have helped in the preparation of this book but I would particularly like to acknowledge the excellent cartographic work done by Katie Moore and Ruth Rowell and the very careful editing by Philip Harris. I also thank my wife who typed the final draft and my children who joined me on many of the field investigations.

Last but not least I am grateful for the interest of many fellow enthusiasts, especially those encountered at University Extra-Mural and W.E.A. classes throughout the Midlands: it is largely from evening classes on the 'Railway Age' that the idea for this book emerged.

*For Andrew*

# I

# The Development of the
# Railway System

# Some Early Railways

During the eighteenth century the most active coalfields in the British Isles lay in north-east England. The coal seams lay in close proximity to navigable water on the Tyne and Wear and this meant that coal could be carried coastwise to London at relatively low cost. The railway was an ideal means of transport to connect the pits with the riverside staithes (from which coal was discharged into ships) and the 'English Waggonway' with flanged-wheeled trucks running on edge rails, although adopted widely across Europe, was nowhere more popular than in the Newcastle area. The typical Tyneside 'doubleway' consisted of a foundation of fir or oak capped with beech (which hardened when wet); eventually iron cappings were used to allow longer life (and some evidence of this dates back to 1716) yet some unaltered wooden railways survived up to the 1820s. The early wagons were variable in size and shape but by the late eighteenth century there was considerable standardisation and the 'chaldron' wagon (holding 2.7 t. or 53 cwts) was widely adopted. With downhill runs to the staithes the loaded wagons could run by gravity. The main problem was not traction but efficient braking and it was the better performance of wooden wheels in this respect that slowed the use of iron; many chaldron wagons would have one pair of iron wheels and another pair of wooden wheels through which the brakesman would retain control.

Horse power would be used only to draw the empty wagons back to the colliery although at Wylam, where a waggonway was built along the riverside for several kilometres until navigable water was reached at Lemington Staithes, the need for horse traction in both directions meant relatively high transport costs. It is no accident that it was on this Tyneside railway where the first experiments were conducted with steam locomotives – at a time of fodder scarcity during the Napoleonic Wars. An engine was built at Newcastle in 1805 to Richard Trevithick's design but it proved too heavy for the fragile track. But maybe the effort was significant because George Stephenson, who went on to design many successful engines, lived at Wylam at the time (before moving to Killingworth) and became personally acquainted with both Trevithick and his locomotive. Also, William Hedley designed his 'Puffing Billy' for use at Wylam in 1813.

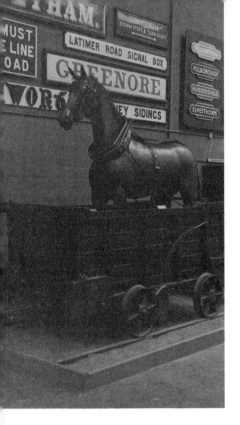

1. *Dandy car at York Museum* A feature of some gravity-worked lines, connecting mineral workings with navigable water, to allow horses to concentrate their energy on hauling empty wagons back to the mine or quarry.

The advantages of the locomotive were marginal at first on the gravity-worked lines and later additions to the waggonway system, for example at Backworth (1818) and Cramlington (1823) used horse traction at their inception. The Newcastle Waggonways were fundamental to the prosperity of the region and the network was remarkably well-developed, taking the form of parallel lines along the valley slopes to integrate with the staithes like veins on a leaf. Sometimes several collieries would feed into one system but the need to secure continuous downhill gradients would complicate matters while divisions of ownership would lead to duplication, so jealously did each company guard its wayleaves. Traces of the waggonways can still be seen, as at the small harbour of Seaton Sluice, destination of the waggonway built from Hartley in 1758. Particularly interesting is the line built in 1725 which used to connect Dunston Staithes in Gateshead with collieries at Tanfield, near Stanley. The bridge over the Beamish Burn at Causey (the celebrated Causey Arch) is an excellent structure for its period and is still *in situ*. It is interesting to record that not only are remnants of the waggonway era preserved at Beamish Hall nearby but an industrial steam society is based at an old colliery locomotive depot at Marley Hill with plans to operate over five kilometres of the old line between Sunniside and Tanfield.

It must not be supposed that north-east England had a monopoly of the new form of transport. The total route length was distributed widely throughout Britain. One of the areas closely involved in the initial stages of development at the beginning of the seventeenth century, the Coalbrookdale area of east Shropshire, made good use of the railway to deliver coal and ore to the blast furnaces and transport finished products to riverside wharfs. The Severn was one of the busiest waterways of Europe and the ease of transport made the east Shropshire coalfield the most productive in Britain after the north-east of England. Large *trows* of up to eighty tons could negotiate the river from Bristol as far as Ironbridge, while the smaller wherries could get a good deal further. Although the first line was built from Broseley (1605) on the southern side of Ironbridge Gorge (with another development at Willey in 1745) it is the northern side which became most heavily developed with the most important initiatives being taken by the Coalbrookdale Company, associated for many years with the Darby family. Abraham Darby I succeeded in smelting iron with coke at the furnace he purchased in Coalbrookdale in 1709. The production of cast iron increased and additional premises were acquired at Horsehay and Ketley during the 1750s. It was during this decade that the works were linked with the Severn at Ironbridge by a railway. The first section was built in 1750 and ran from the Coalbrookdale works to pits at Coalmoor. Four years later a branch was completed through to Ketley and Donnington Wood and in 1757 the section between Coalbrookdale and the Severn was finished. With a line extending from Ironbridge to Donnington it was much easier to supply raw materials to the works and move heavy castings such as steam-engine cylinders which had previously been carried in carts along unsurfaced roads.

It is probable that the rails were made of oak wood, strong enough to bear flanged iron wheels which were certainly manufactured locally by 1727 and also likely that the gauge was fairly broad (1.1–1.6 m) like the Newcastle waggonways. However, Shropshire had the advantage of cheap iron and the conversion to iron rails came relatively early: between 1768 and 1773 the line to Ketley was relaid (using a different alignment in places) using wooden rails with an iron capping and, according to R. A. Mott, 'there is no doubt this was the earliest use of iron rails'. However, it was not long before rails made entirely of iron were being made, although the innovation in this case was apparently pioneered in the Sheffield area by J. Curr, mineral agent for the Duke of Norfolk's collieries. An iron plate-way was built about 1774 and it was in the 1790s that Coalbrookdale adopted this new technology. The new rails were quite different from what had gone before because they were L-shaped in section: plates, rather than edge rails, so that the wheels of wagons using them did not need to be flanged. It seems that plates were cheaper to manufacture and were generally more serviceable than edge rails, but they attracted dirt and gravel, thereby increasing friction, and all-iron edge rails, thought to have been introduced first on the railways of the Charnwood Forest Canal in Leicestershire, eventually proved more satisfactory. It seems likely that wrought iron edge rails were used in Shropshire during the 1820s. A further technical change concerns the gauge, which seems to have narrowed considerably (to 0.5–0.7 m or 20–30 in.) as conveyance of iron rather than coal became more prominent: iron is heavier than coal per unit of volume and was best handled in small wagons which would not require a gauge as generous as the Newcastle chaldron wagons.

However, interesting changes were taking place in the layout of the system in the Ironbridge area arising from the completion of the Shropshire Canal. The canal was built through quite steeply undulating country and changes in level were effected by means of inclined planes. The first was built at Ketley in 1787 (the first incline plane to be employed successfully on a British canal) but the Hay Incline at Blists Hill (1793) is better known. A section of canal was built to Brierley Hill above Coalbrookdale and another incline plunged down into the valley to meet the railway (a short spur gave access to the foot of the incline). It seems that the link between Coalbrookdale and Horsehay was provided by a realigned track following the canal bank northwards from the top of the incline, but only for this arrangement of 1803 to be altered yet again in the 1820s when the Lightmoor Valley diversion avoided the incline altogether. This railway was quickly overtaken by the 'main line' railways but the Coalbrookdale–Horsehay line persisted for many years as a private industrial railway and sections of the trackbed are still very clear today. Thus Coalbrookdale offers a fine example therefore of the way in which a gradually advancing railway technology was applied to a particular area to fit its topographical characteristics and traffic requirements. A final twist might be added to the story in respect of the Coalport branch of the London & North Western Railway. This line made use of the old Shropshire Canal, but as with the Lightmoor diversion already mentioned, incline working was not acceptable and some new alignment was inevitable. It is avoidance of the Hay Incline by a gradually descending path from Madeley that results in the incline, and a short section of canal above it, being abandoned (last in use in *c.*1894) and therefore available for preservation as part of the Blists Hill complex. The Coalport railway has also closed (1960) and is now used as a public footpath: in the vicinity of Blists Hill as it negotiates Lee Dingle it passes under an elegant wrought-iron truss built in 1872 to carry a plateway from Blists Hill to Meadowpit Colliery – another element in a complex picture of economic and technical change.

Map 1. (*Opposite*)   Early railway development in the Coalbrookdale/Ironbridge area of East Shropshire.

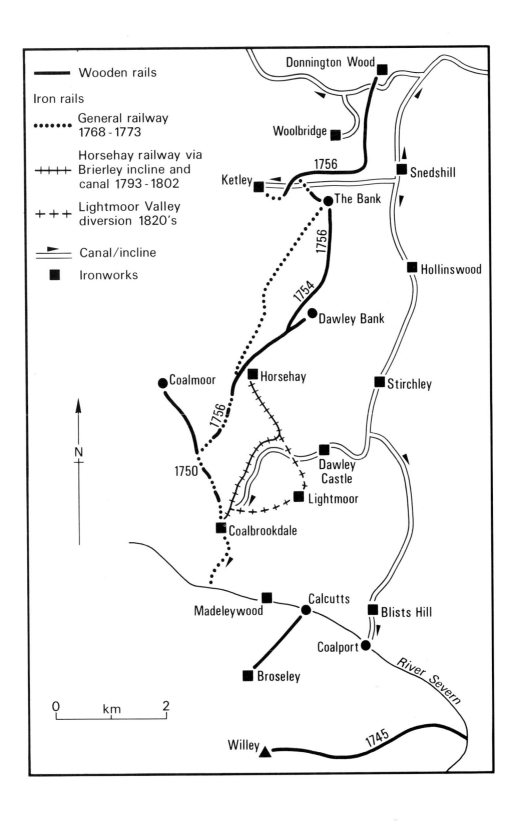

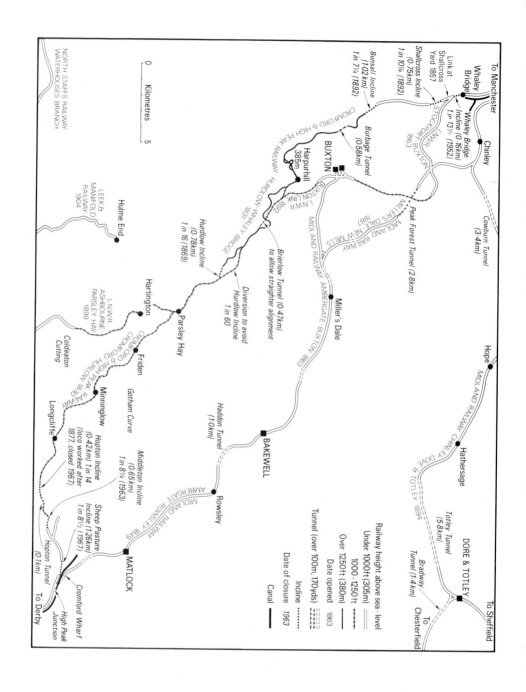

To Manchester

Whaley Bridge

Whaley Bridge Incline (0.16km) 1 in 13½ (1952)

Chinley

Link at Shallcross Yard 1857

Shallcross Incline (0.75km) 1 in 10¼ (1892)

Bunsall Incline (1.02km) 1 in 7¼ (1892)

CROMFORD & HIGH PEAK RAILWAY

STOCKPORT–BUXTON 1863

Cowburn Tunnel (3.4km)

Burbage Tunnel (0.58km)

Harpurhill 385m

BUXTON

HURDLOW–WHALEY BRIDGE

LNWR BUXTON LINK 1892

Peak Forest Tunnel (2.8km)

MIDLAND RAILWAY MILLER'S DALE–NEW MILLS 1867

LNWR

Hurdlow Incline (0.78km) 1 in 16 (1869)

Brierlow Tunnel (0.47km) to allow straighter alignment

Diversion to avoid Hurdlow Incline 1 in 60

Miller's Dale

MIDLAND RAILWAY AMBERGATE–BUXTON

Hulme End

LEEK & MANIFOLD RAILWAY 1904

Hope

MIDLAND RAILWAY CHINLEY–DOVE & TOTLEY 1894

Hathersage

Hartington

LNWR ASHBOURNE–PARSLEY HAY 1899

Coldeaton Cutting

Parsley Hay

CROMFORD & HIGH PEAK RAILWAY 1830

Friden

Gotham Curve

Minninglow

Longcliffe

Hopton Incline (0.42km) 1 in 14 (loco worked after 1877, closed 1967)

Middleton Incline (0.65km) 1 in 8¼ (1963)

Haddon Tunnel (1.0km)

1863

BAKEWELL

Rowsley

MIDLAND RAILWAY AMBERGATE–ROWSLEY 1849

Sheep Pasture Incline (1.26km) 1 in 8½ (1967)

Hopton Tunnel (0.1km)

Cromford Wharf

High Peak Junction

MATLOCK

To Derby

DORE & TOTLEY

Totley Tunnel (5.8km)

Bradway Tunnel (1.4km)

To Chesterfield

To Sheffield

NORTH STAFFS RAILWAY WATERHOUSES BRANCH

0  Kilometres  5

Railway height above sea-level

Under 1000ft (305m)

1000–1250 ft

Over 1250ft (380m)

Date opened    1863

Tunnel (over 100m, 170yds)

Incline

Date of closure    1963

Canal

The view presented so far suggests that the early railways were found in coalmining areas where they connected collieries with sea-ports or navigable rivers. However, the Coalbrookdale example hints at a further rôle in association with canals when branches had to be provided under circumstances of terrain and traffic that ruled out orthodox canal building. This involved the canal companies in railway ownership, first exemplified by the Caldon Canal of 1777 which terminated at Froghall but gained liaison with limestone quarries at Caldon Low by a mineral railway. Two decades later came the short-lived Charnwood Forest Canal which consisted of a short contour canal between Nanpantan and Thringstone in Leicestershire flanked by railways that gave access to the coal pits at Swannington to the west and the river port of Loughborough to the east (1794). Rather more durable was the Ashby Canal which spawned the Ticknall Tramways (1803) as a twenty kilometre system of branches from Willesley Basin to the limestone quarries at Ticknall. It included a 0.4 km tunnel at Old Parks near Ashby, and a shorter cut and cover tunnel of 0.1 km at Ticknall to avoid disturbing the drive to Calke Park. Using plates, in contrast to edge rails on the Charnwood system, the Ticknall line survived until the First World War. But in the early nineteenth century the canal companies were installing railways on a much grander scale: there was, for example, a railway extending 58.5 km along the Wye Valley as far as Hay. This is a fine example of a canal (the Brecon Canal) increasing its 'catchment' by installing a relatively cheap means of transport to open up sparsely-populated countryside. The Hay Railway was built between 1816 and 1818 at 1.08 m (3 ft 6½ in.) gauge and the Kington Railway of 1820–5 provided an extension to New Radnor. An interesting feature were the stone and cast iron bridges at Afon Llynfi and Kington respectively.

A much more dramatic example concerns the Cromford & High Peak Railway which was engineered across a high limestone plateau by Josias Jessop to forge a link between the Peak Forest Canal at Whaley Bridge and the Cromford Canal in the Derwent Valley. At the time the act was obtained in 1825 the company had a larger capital (£164 000) than any other railway company. The aim of the 52.8 km line (opened in 1831) was to connect the Cromford and Peak Forest canals: it was a development, on a permanent and larger scale basis, of the concept of the temporary railway of 1800–5 linking sections of the Grand Junction Canal pending the completion of Blisworth Tunnel. The highest point of 380 m is only 60 m above the level of the Peak Forest Tunnel on the Midland Railway main line, but in the style of construction the two lines could hardly be more different. The Midland

Map 2. (*Opposite*)   The Cromford & High Peak Railway and its connections.

Railway route involves long climbs at gentle gradients (averaging 1 in 115 for the 24.5 km from Rowsley to the tunnel) while the C.H.P.R. follows the contour for long distances and makes contact with the canals on either side of the Peak by means of inclines which plunge steeply into the valleys: the installations at the Cromford end are particularly dramatic with Sheep Pasture, Middleton and Hopton inclines in close succession lifting the tracks from 84 m to 340 m within a distance of only 6.7 km (average gradient 1 in 26). For the next 20.5 km the line climbs only 40 m more (average gradient 1 in 512), mainly by means of a further incline at Hurdlow. The explanation for the difference lies simply in the steam locomotive which gradually transformed the whole railway concept from the rôle of feeder to a more exalted function of prime haulier. If there is any way in which the early railways can be grouped together as a single 'innovation' then it is through the persistence of horse traction (in association with gravity working and manpower) whatever the differences over rails, gauge, function and ownership.

It is possible that without the locomotive a national network of railways might have developed. After all, the very first public railway, the Surrey Iron Railway which obtained its act in 1801, was envisaged as the first stage of a line from London to Portsmouth, while working in the reverse direction the Stratford and Moreton line (27 km) was conceived as the start of a line to London. The Cromford & High Peak was eventually integrated with other railways (at Cromford 1853 and Whaley Bridge 1855), but in the mid-1820s there were plans to use the line as the penultimate stage of London–Manchester route approaching from the south via Cambridge, Peterborough and Loughborough or Northampton, Leicester and Derby. The locomotive alone did not create the railway age but it stimulated a great increase of interest in a transport system which would otherwise have evolved slowly and uncertainly. Nevertheless the entire horse system by 1830 must have exceeded 2400 km, a significant achievement despite the high level of concentration in the coalfields.

## 2

# A Basic Railway System

It will be clear from the previous section that railways did not begin with the celebrated Liverpool & Manchester Railway 1830 nor with auspicious events like the Rainhill Trials held in the preceding year (and re-enacted with considerable pomp and ceremony in 1980). But the L.M.R. is a convenient marker for the beginning of an age when railways played a dominant role in the growth of the nation: the railways did not produce the corn, the cloth or the iron on which the country depended but efficient transport is so crucial to economic and social progress and so prominent in everyday life that there was good reason to use the label 'Railway Age' as a synonym for Victorian prosperity. Several criteria have been advanced to distinguish the developments of these halcyon days from all that went before. First there was the emphasis on providing a *public* service for both freight and passengers, which in turn necessitated a degree of government control and supervision. Government scrutinised bills but did not attempt to lay down an 'ideal' network. But safety standards were enforced in the 1840s with maximum charges laid down to prevent abuse of monopoly and a Clearing House was set up to deal with the problem of through journeys. Government initiatives helped incidentally consolidate a 'railway interest' to watch proceedings in parliament. Second, there was the use of the locomotive and the need, in the interest of safety, to have the track bed fenced off from adjacent land and used only for railway operation. Thirdly, there has been reference to a genuinely *national* system with standard gauge and adequate connecting facilities between the networks of different companies. If all these criteria are rigidly applied then the railway age would begin only in the late nineteenth century when the remoter regions of Ireland and Scotland enjoyed rail communication. On the other hand the theme of public service and parliamentary sanction originates in the Surrey Iron Railway of 1801, although the extension of public control through more rigorous safety procedures, minimum services for third-class passengers and provision for forwarding (through the Railway Clearing House), date to mid-century. The Liverpool & Manchester Railway is however an accurate marker as regards *exclusive* use of steam locomotives.

Steam locomotives had been in use for several years before 1830. Richard

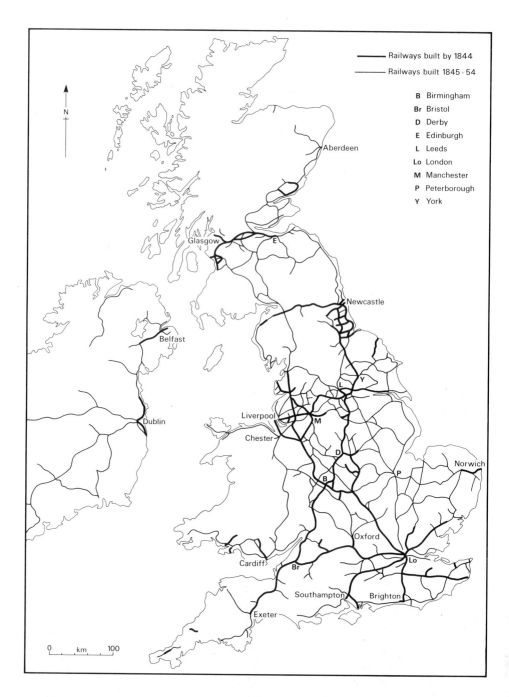

Map 3. Main line railway development to 1854.

Trevithick's experiments at Wylam form part of a series of initiatives on plateways which also found colourful expression on the Penydarren Tramroad in South Wales (1804), and in London (1808) when the locomotive *Catch me who Can* was proudly displayed. However, the first successful locomotive for use on mineral railways came in 1814 when Stephenson's 'travelling engine' hauled wagons at 6.4 km or four miles per hour on the line built in 1761 from Killingworth Colliery to Willington, near Newcastle. The stimulus to invention came through employment with the Grand Allies, a Tyneside coalmining consortium which owned the Killingworth and other railways. It led to a number of orders for similar locomotives for use on coal carrying lines built with horse traction in mind – like the Kilmarnock & Troon Railway in Scotland which opened in 1808 but made use of a Stephenson locomotive in 1817. The Stockton & Darlington used Stephenson locomotives from the start, as is brought out so forcibly by the famous painting by John Dobbin which shows *Locomotion* at work crossing Skerne Bridge on the opening day in 1825. But there was no exclusive dependence on locomotives and when the L.M.R. was being built there were grave doubts about the feasibility of using them at all. Heavy traffic was anticipated, for the interaction between the two cities was already intense, and locomotives were not thought to be sufficiently reliable. Frequent breakdowns were reported and it seemed that an engine of adequate power would be too heavy for the rather fragile track. The challenge was therefore to improve reliability and achieve higher steam-

2.   *Electrified west coast main line north of Wigan* The main line through central Lancashire, developed out of branches thrown off the Liverpool & Manchester Railway. Springs Branch, later extended to Preston and Carlisle, now carries Anglo-Scottish traffic.

raising capacity per unit of weight. It was in this atmosphere that the Rainhill Trials were held. A system of stationary engines, with cable haulage, was proposed, but the costs of equipping the whole line with such engines before any through working was possible was disturbing. Hence the novel formula of locomotive tests to see if any designs could meet the stringent criteria laid down. As is well known Stephenson's *Rocket* was successful. Its great merit was the use of a multi-tube boiler which made steam-raising much more efficient.

The L.M.R. was a great success in both technical and financial terms. Stephenson's locomotives realised their promise in regular service and substantial dividends were paid by the company. With hindsight it seems quite inevitable. Yet there was an element of doubt because the rate of economic growth (and therefore of transport demand) could not be accurately predicted and it could not be assumed that inter-city railways would all meet with the same success of the L.M.R. However, the railway did prove itself – probably more incredibly than its early supporters could ever have imagined. The first railways attracted investment in other schemes in the next trade cycle upswing. Public confidence was so strong as to trigger an investment boom in the 1840s – the railway mania – which effectively completed the basic system. There was a solid case to be made because passenger traffic developed very briskly indeed while the effectiveness of the railway in tapping new minerals and raw materials yielded secure traffics like the Midlands–London coal trade.

Moreover the success of the new railway was won in the teeth of competition from water transport: it was not just a case of the railway catering for an area where no satisfactory transport facilities existed. Although the canals and navigable rivers may have seemed far more established they were in no position to exploit the advantages of the steam engine. Even where canals had been straightened and distances shortened there were difficulties in the way of rapid increases in speed: the canal was not so well integrated as a business unit while the danger to canal banks arising from more active wash was a source of difficulty. Of course, the canals could still remain in business as freight carriers where speed was not essential and it was because of their considerable potential that the railways often went all out to weaken them. But as the distribution of industry became more closely tied up with railways there was less scope for the canal to provide 'door to door' services.

The growth of the system is therefore a result of the railway's value viewed in relation to the British economy and the availability of capital. But what of the layout of the railways by the mid-nineteenth century? The railway geography was not a matter of chance. It was a rational response to the demands of the time. First there was a growth of relatively short lines which had local or regional significance and represented a

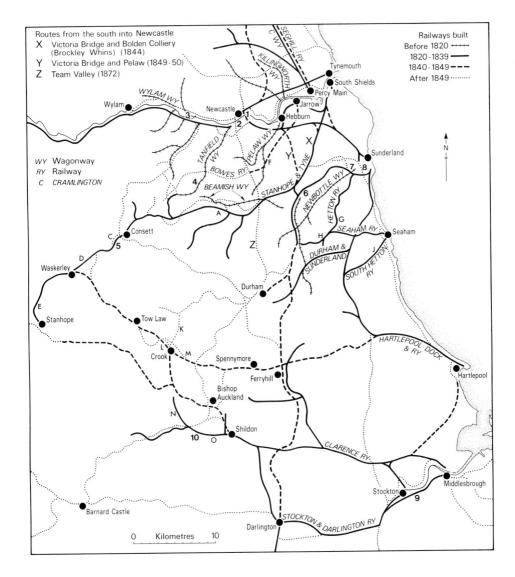

Map 4. Railway development in north-east England.

Letters refer to principal inclines: a. Stanley–Edenhill–Waldridge; b. Loud Hill; c. Hownes Gill; d. Nanny Mayors; e. Weatherhill–Crawley; f. Kibblesworth; g. Warton Law; h. Byer-Copthill; i. Cold Hesleden; k. Stanley; l. Sunniside; m. Helmington; n. Etherley; o. Brusselton.

Numbers refer to major bridges: 1. Newcastle High Level 1849; 2. Newcastle King Edward 1906; 3. Newcastle Scotswood 1868; 4. Causey Arch 1727; 5. Hownes Gill Viaduct 1858; 6. Victoria Bridge 1838; 7. Queen Alexandra Bridge 1876; 8. Sunderland 1879; 9. Tees Bridge 1830 (replaced 1841); 10. Gaunless Bridge 1825.

continuation of trends evident earlier in the nineteenth century. The coal carrying Stockton & Darlington Railway of 1825 was extended to Middlesbrough in 1831 and in 1833 a branch opened from Shildon to Port Clarence, on the opposite (northern) side of the Tees from Middlesbrough. Further north lines pushed inland from Hartlepool in 1835 and Sunderland in 1836, but most impressive was the Stanhope & Tyne Railway which ran from South Shields deep into the Durham Coalfield. It was essentially a coal carrying line and there was no need to engineer the line so as to allow fast running. Sections of locomotive working were separated by inclines, some of them worked on a compensatory basis, others with the help of a stationary steam engine. Horse power was used as well. It was in many respects a carbon copy of the Stockton & Darlington Railway which began not at Darlington as the name suggests but much further inland near Bishop Auckland. Two hill ridges, separated by the Gaunless Valley, lay between the collieries and the coastal plain at Shildon. Pairs of inclines were therefore installed at Etherley and Brusselton and stationary engines provided. So as regards the local mineral railway it is clear that the locomotive did not induce any revolutionary change. The approach adopted on the Cromford & High Peak Railway, with no prospect of locomotives, was the same as on the Stockton & Darlington where partial use was made of them. The Bowes Railway (Pontop and Jarrow) of 1826 was similar, while the Stanhope & Tyne continued this approach five years after the Rainhill Trials. In other parts of the country the same conservative approach was taken. In Scotland the Dundee & Newtyle opened in 1831 with three inclines connecting fairly level sections where horses could be used (locomotives in 1833). In the Midlands the Leicester & Swannington Railway of 1832 was built to deliver coal to Leicester after the failure of the Charnwood Forest Canal and the proven success of the railway. There is a clear link with George Stephenson through the local M.P., John Ellis, who had agricultural interests in Lancashire when Stephenson received his first commission as a railway engineer. In Leicestershire Stephenson surveyed almost level sections where locomotives could operate efficiently, with links provided by inclines where stationary steam engines would be installed. The Bagworth and Swannington inclines resulted – as did a tunnel which ensured that the gradient would remain moderate.

Why should there have been such conservatism from an engineering family that made revolutionary progress? Basically the locomotive did not appear quite as momentous a development at the time as it now seems looking back with hindsight. George Stephenson enjoyed considerable respect and influence. He saw railway development essentially as an extension of colliery systems where locomotives had played only an incidental role. He advised the coalfield gauge of 1.435 m (used for the chaldron wagons of north-east England) and although I. K. Brunel adopted

2.12 m (7 ft) parliament decreed the former in 1846 and the existing Brunel broad gauge was eventually converted in 1892. Despite the success with *Rocket* it was obvious that locomotives were still rather fragile and delicate machines: with stiff gradients their efficiency was gravely impaired. Hence, even on lines where locomotives were going to be used from the outset, there was no justification for an immediate abandonment of canal principles. It was not anticipated that the locomotive would be improved so quickly that routes which had originally necessitated inclines could be built for through locomotive running. Given more efficient locomotives, inclines became inconvenient interruptions to through running and it was necessary to remove them. Frequently, therefore, the landscape of early local railway building shows the first phase of construction in canal principles followed quickly by a second phase in which various measures are applied to bypass the inclines. Sometimes this can be done by a modest realignment with cuttings and embankments so that the railway follows a long gentle gradient instead of a short steep pull. At Bagworth in Leicestershire, where part of the original Leicester & Swannington Railway is still used as a coal carrier, the present alignment (Thornton Deviation 1848) with a gradient of about 1 in 100 for two kilometres lies immediately adjacent to the incline with 0.2 km at 1 in 29. But frequently the alterations were more substantial with entirely new routes being followed, like the Stockton & Darlington's Tunnel Branch from Shildon to St Helen's and West Auckland (1856) or the Dundee & Newtyle Railway which followed a new course via Lochee in 1861.

These short railways, whether equipped with steam locomotives or not, fit in with the continued predominance of canals and coastal shipping. What brought the railways into its *predominant* stage as a transport mode (and simultaneously reduced the canals to an auxiliary rôle) was the construction of a network of long distance lines which connected the major cities by the early 1850s. Although no 'ideal' network was laid down the lines which were proposed for parliamentary approval inevitably carried expectations of profitable working and constituted the best business propositions of the time. Hence private enterprise very quickly completed a network of basic inter-regional links which might have been anticipated under a centrally-controlled investment programme. The line from London to Lancashire (completed by the London & Birmingham Railway and by the Grand Junction in 1838) crossed in the Midlands with another series of railways connecting Yorkshire with Bristol. This simple X-shaped network was rounded off by an east-west line between London and Bristol and between Lancashire and Yorkshire. London spawned a radial system of lines – Colchester, Dover, Brighton and Portsmouth – while construction reached from Bristol into the West Country and from Lancashire and Yorkshire into Scotland with further cross links in the Central Belt of Scotland and the

Tyne Valley. In Ireland the Dublin–Cork axis was quickly revealed. So it is arguable that in general outline the emerging network was a rational one. Of course, the routes selected would reflect the technical requirements laid down and an element of chance would arise through the standards laid down by the engineer and the attitudes of landowners to the sale of land. Strong demand for a railway from a particular town could be important: contrary to popular belief that the railway speculator George Hudson brought the railway through York, it seems that the idea came from city businessmen who wanted cheap coal. There was also an influence on the morphology coming from the sphere of influence of the various companies and the understandings reached between them. Thus the Dover line took off from the London & Brighton at Redhill (it simplified the amount of new construction although the total distance from London to Dover was greater than by a direct line). Background research into the decision over the Grand Junction route in Lancashire shows clearly the financially attractive option of linkage with the Warrington Branch under conditions of difficult money supply. A more direct line into Liverpool would have avoided contact with the Liverpool & Manchester, including its steeply graded sections at Sutton and Whiston, but bridging the Mersey (achieved at Runcorn in 1869) would have been costly and strong opposition from the Bridgwater Canal (in respect of the Preston Brook–Runcorn section) would have been inevitable. And Peterborough was first reached in 1843 by a branch from the London & Birmingham at Blisworth and not by the direct route later provided by the Great Northern. Yet the railway to Portsmouth originated in London, although it might well have branched from the Bristol line at Reading.

So the conclusion must be that, while the network bears the stamp of the structure private enterprise that created it, it is not fundamentally irrational. What is worth considering however is the difference between *economic* and *social* approaches to railway building. Construction must begin somewhere and the network must spread gradually by development from the centre of the innovation to the peripheral regions. Every region cannot benefit immediately. But whereas economic considerations led to proliferation of lines in some areas before other regions had gained any railway at all, a social approach would have placed more emphasis on the completion of a basic network throughout the country. Reallocation of route length on social grounds would have meant more railway to East Anglia where only Norwich and Yarmouth were linked in 1844. It is fairly clear that private enterprise took an economic approach. Thus while much of Ireland, Scotland and Wales still lacked railways, work went ahead in Lancashire and Cheshire to build direct lines from Crewe (established as a junction by the Chester line in 1840) to Manchester (1842) and Liverpool (1869), although these two cities could be reached by the original Grand Junction line which joined the L.M.R. at Newton-le-Willows. It does not follow that central planning of the railway system would have given more attention to social considerations and it is idle to speculate on what might have happened had the rules of the game been different. One can only interpret the actual system in relation to the forces moulding it.

# 3

# Competition Between Railway Companies

Here the aim is to develop the themes introduced in the previous section on the structure of the network as a product of inter-company rivalry rather than central planning and control. Although it is widely believed that monopoly is harmful to the consumer, through the lack of any competitive spur to efficiency and slim profit margins, the myth of an irrational railway system created by warring companies has proved hard to resist. The view is nourished by well-documented cases of duplication of services and by the existence of thousands of kilometres of derelict trackbed which has become redundant in an age of nationalisation. It is easily overlooked that there was a considerable degree of standardisation. Once it was clear that the railway would become a national institution and long distance routes were joining end-on at places like Gloucester, steps were taken to prevent proliferation of gauges and a businesslike conduct of through traffic was arranged through the Railway Clearing House which started to function in 1842. It also provided a forum for discussion of minimum safety procedures and more efficient administration, as with the adoption of the ticket system devised by T. Edmondson on the Newcastle & Carlisle Railway. Parliament laid down certain requirements in the public interest and the companies underlined the value of this means of coordination by having certain members who reflected their interests. However, some competition was inevitable once the network developed because the provision of links between towns and cities would result in alternate routes being available between distant cities – just as with a well-developed road system today there are more and more alternative routes the greater the distance between two places. Competitive services would have arisen inevitably even it they were not planned for at the outset.

While the L.N.W.R. had a direct route from Manchester to London it transpired that with keen schedules and comfortable rolling stock the Manchester Sheffield & Lincolnshire could maintain a competitive service in collaboration with the Great Northern, who took over the trains at Retford. The Great Northern may be considered to have started the trend towards stiff competition because the line from London to York, via Peterborough and Doncaster, duplicated the one already available via

Rugby and Chesterfield. Yet returning to the concept of an X-shaped layout in the heart of England it was surely inevitable that just as horizontal lines had appeared early on the top and bottom of the figure so, in time, there would be vertical lines, reducing the distance from London to York and from Bristol to Liverpool. George Hudson, the 'railway king' who controlled the companies interested in the Rugby–York route tried to prevent the G.N.R. scheme by proposing his own direct line to the north (via Cambridge and Lincoln) but his bill failed. Had it succeeded the competition between the new and old routes would have emerged – only the separate company organisation would have been avoided. The consequences might not have been very different: Hudson would have been obliged to run services on the new line and starve the older route of through passenger traffic, obliging it at the same time to fall back more heavily on its freight business, based on the lucrative coal traffic.

A further point which is often obscured is the quite justified expectation of a growth in traffic: the economy was expanding and therefore, in addition to extending the network into the remoter areas, further capacity was needed in areas where services already existed. Extra tracks might be provided: a single line could be doubled or a double track line might be quadrupled, as happened on most of the principal routes out of London by the end of the nineteenth century. However, a new route might be preferred if the old alignment was indirect or technically inadequate. Direct lines to Liverpool and Manchester from Crewe were built to shorten the distance involved over the original Grand Junction line to join the Liverpool & Manchester Railway at Newton. Later in the century a new route was built through the southern approaches to Manchester to avoid the line through Stockport. Further capacity was needed and the cost of quadrupling track over the old route was excessive because of the long viaduct over the Mersey at Stockport. In the Newcastle area it is evident that on two occasions, 1850 and 1872, the main route from the south was adjusted to allow more direct access to the city for the fastest trains at times when capacity had to be increased anyway. If separate companies were involved then inevitably the lines would be duplicated but it should not be assumed that it would not otherwise occur. Redundant trackbed is a feature of all railway systems that have encountered competition from road transport and countries with a history of central planning of railways are not exempt. The most that can be said is that with a single national company in Britain there might have been more contraction through the reduction in the number of tracks rather than the closure of routes.

The thrust of the argument therefore is that extra capacity was needed and the need to increase tracks provided the option of selecting a new route which could allow higher speeds and/or a reduced distance. It would also allow a service to be provided to a considerable number of people who had no railway communication within easy reach. Although travellers from London to Birmingham might well have a choice between the Euston–New Street and Paddington–Snow Hill routes (L.N.W.R. and G.W.R. respectively) there was no real alternative for people living along either route. Thus the spirit of competition was nourished by pressures from communities and industries that wanted better rail services. The political drive at national level to discourage monopoly was backed up locally where people stood to gain from the opening of a duplicate route. When a railway from Glasgow to Carlisle was being constructed it was considered that only one route could be justified. After much discussion the route along the Clyde and Annan valleys (crossing the watershed at Beattock Summit, 313 m) was preferred to the line through Kilmarnock and over the Ayr–Nith watershed to Dumfries. However, when it became clear that a second route was needed there was no question of rejecting the Nith route in preference of quadrupling over Beattock.

Another interesting case concerns the Cornish town of Launceston which was subject to rival railway proposals in the early 1860s: should there be a broad gauge line by the G.W.R. from Plymouth and Tavistock or a standard gauge line from Okehampton? It so happened that the political parties were divided with Liberal support for the G.W.R. and Conservative interest in the standard gauge line, and the success of the former inevitably brought the Liberal Party into the ascendency in the town after the line opened in 1865. But the important point is Launceston's desire for standard gauge connection as well and so there was support for any initiatives that were taken to achieve this objective. After several abortive schemes the North Cornwall Railway Act was passed in 1882 for a line from the London & South Western Railway at Halwill to the coastal town of Padstow and four years later the line was opened to Launceston. Arguably, therefore, tolerance of competition was one way of ensuring that a good 'spread' of rail services emerged so that large sections of the population were not denied access to the benefits of the railway – for personal travel, cheaper freight movement and scope for employment in the railway service and in enterprises which it stimulated.

In the second part of this section the discussion moves on from general issues to consider how the pattern of railway companies evolved in parallel with the growth of the network. Was the evolution harmonious and rational or not? Two simple examples may be considered at the outset. First, in the East Midlands there were two companies operating by 1840: the Midland Counties Railway comprised a line from Long Eaton in the Erewash Valley south through Leicester to Rugby, with a link between Derby and

Nottingham, while the North Midland Railway (Birmingham & Derby Junction) connected Derby with the London & Birmingham at Hampton and the North Midland extended from Derby northwards to Chesterfield and Rotherham. Functions overlapped because two connections with the London & Birmingham were offered and there was stiff competition in the early 1840s before the 1844 amalgamation which created the Midland Railway. Subsequent growth of the system created even more alternative routes than had existed in the area before: this was the inevitable consequence of improving the services for each individual city. One of the developments took the form of a link between the two erstwhile competitors running from Leicester to Burton upon Trent. Use was made of the Leicester & Swannington Railway absorbed in 1846. The Midland Counties Railway had selected a route through Leicester that followed the eastern side of the Soar Valley and so avoided any physical contact with the L.S.R., so anxious were the Nottinghamshire coal interests (strong supporters of the Midland Counties Railway) to avoid giving Leicestershire coal masters opportunity for a wider distribution of the rival product. But wider perspectives eased local rivalries and a link became mutually advantageous: the Midland's expansion was simplified while Swannington Incline was avoided by taking off the new construction towards Burton immediately before it. The link between the two railways in Leicester was also designed in such a way as to cope with the deficiencies of the original L.S.R. route. The new line from Knighton to Desford meant that the narrow 1.6 km Glenfield Tunnel did not have to be negotiated by through traffic (though local goods services to the West Bridge terminus in Leicester continued until 1966).

The second example shows the rational way in which the Cromford & High Peak Railway was integrated into the national system which grew up around it. Improved locomotives made the inclines unacceptable for a long-distance route and the extent of the climb at both the Cromford and Whaley Bridge ends made it impossible to replace the inclines with orthodox railway. So neither of the railways that were being built into Buxton (one from Derby and another from Manchester) could make any use of the C.H.P.R. However, the old mineral line was connected with the former at Cromford in 1853 and the latter at Whaley Bridge in 1857. This provided some scope for competitive through services but the C.H.P.R. wisely decided that the technical deficiencies could never be adequately overcome and the auxiliary rôle of feeder to local industries in the Peak District was accepted. Takeover by the L.N.W.R. in an outright amalgamation in 1887 led to a modified section of the line at Hurdlow being used for the company's Buxton–Ashbourne line of 1899. This meant that the summit section of the line had been captured and theoretically it would have been possible to have closed both sets of inclines. This in fact happened at the northern end in

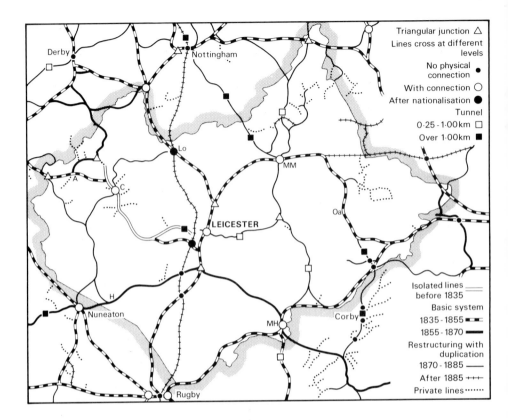

Map 5. Stages in the development of the railway system of Leicestershire. A. Ashby; C. Coalville; H. Hinckley; Lo. Loughborough; MH. Market Harborough; MM. Melton Mowbray; Oa. Oakham.

1894 since there was virtually no traffic north of Ladmanlow: freight traffic at the Cromford end justified retention of the inclines until 1967.

The examples show that the growth in the scale of the railway business and improvements in technical efficiency induced logical structures on the ground. Companies increased in size to embrace first local and then regional interests. They tended to absorb, or cooperate with, small companies which might consolidate their interests. They had a clear sense of 'territory' and the threat of intervention by a rival concern was always a strong stimulus to develop territory even though the financial results might not always justify this. Characteristically it was in border zones where different company networks touched that some of the sharpest rivalry emerged. The Great Eastern emerged out of a grouping of smaller companies and maintained a quite solid regional monopoly until the Midland & Great Northern Joint Railway launched an assault on the Norfolk coast: it had a tremendous tourist potential and yet had attracted only limited rail services. Likewise the North Eastern Railway became dominant in the Tyne-Tees area. A formidable regional railway monopoly emerged as the initial grouping of 1854 was enlarged by the Newcastle & Carlisle in 1862, the Stockton & Darlington in 1863 and the West Hartlepool in 1865. These companies preferred to join the core of the North Eastern and keep out intruders rather than assist outside companies to compete. But there was no guarantee that rivals would not emerge: this is clearly shown by several important developments. The lack of complete control over the main source of traffic, the Leeds area, meant a highly competitive approach for both freight (for which the Aire & Calder Navigation was able to compete) and tourist passengers who could be seduced by rival railway companies to west coast resorts. Also in the north the North British challenged for a stake in north Northumberland. Branches were built and eventually these enabled an independent service to be run from Edinburgh to Newcastle. through Hawick, Riccarton, Scots Gap and Morpeth, in conjunction with the Blythe & Tyne Railway (not amalgamated with the North Eastern until 1874). And a belief in Hull that the local docks were getting an inadequate service gave rise to the Hull & Barnsley Railway and a duplication of links with the Yorkshire coalfield.

Competition was a fact of life – a force which powered the whole development of the railway system as regards both the network and the company structure. Companies had no option but to play by the rules that parliament laid down on the nation's behalf. Jack Simmons is quite forthright about the 'confusion of railway policy or rather the absence of any fixed policy at all'. Yet it must always be a value judgment how far parliament came up with the right formula. If politicians 'failed' to exercise tighter control and compel closer collaboration between rival companies (as was envisaged in some abortive clauses of the Railway & Canal Traffic Act of 1854 – requiring forwarding without partiality or unreasonable delay) perhaps they simultaneously 'succeeded' in balancing conflicting interests. And there seems no intrinsic objection to pragmatism over amalgamations: a parliamentary report of 1853 counselled against the L.N.W.R./Midland/North Staffordshire amalgamation, yet this did not prevent approval of regional groupings in the north-east and East Anglia the following year.

Individual cases may be judged on their merits and there is good evidence to suppose that in some cases competition involved a tremendous waste of resources with duplication of services to the point where neither the public nor the companies could benefit. The rivalry in Kent between the South Eastern Railway and the London Chatham & Dover comes most readily to mind: the companies wasted their money on a bitter rivalry to provide double services to every town of any importance in the county. The origin of the trouble lay in the failure of the South Eastern to shorten the route to Dover by a direct line from London to Sevenoaks and Tonbridge, eliminating the original route along the Brighton line as far as Redhill. By 1861 a shorter route had been provided by a separate company using the route through Chatham and only in the following year the South Eastern gained sanction for a direct line to Tonbridge (opened in 1868). However, the excessive competition gave way to a working union in 1899 and when the railways went into the grouping after the First World War there was a single company for Kent: the South Eastern & Chatham. In Devon and Cornwall, again, the marks of competition appear indelible. Competition sometimes led to rivalry for its own sake without concern for the interests of the customer or the investor. Furthermore, as Simmons has argued, 'it could and undoubtedly did lead to an overdevelopment of services beyond the point at which they were remunerative'.

# 4

# The Selection of Railway Routes

The previous section examined the influence of the companies in deciding what railways would be built. Here the discussion deals with the more detailed question of the particular line that a railway would follow. Several influences would be effective here but the first and most significant would be the technical requirements. The railway would have to be planned economically, yet have in mind how the locomotive's performance would be affected by particular gradients and curvatures. Where there was a conflict between low construction costs and simplified operation then a decision would have to be taken as to how far the costs could be justified in terms of higher receipts through greater usage of the railway if it operated more efficiently. By the 1850s it was becoming clear what kind of action was appropriate: standards were being set on main lines so that new builders could ill-afford to install very steep gradients (except in very special circumstances) and winding courses, following contours, were to be avoided unless the countryside was extremely sparsely populated with a traffic potential that could never justify expensive engineering works. In the Scottish Highlands the 'through-valleys' that connect the principal drainage systems have been used by the railways despite the deviation involved, for as J. H. Appleton says, 'it is doubtful whether the expectation of traffic from this lean countryside could ever have justified the expense of making the long tunnels which would otherwise have been unavoidable'. On the other hand, improved locomotive performance made testing gradients more acceptable. Yet between 1830 and 1850 there was considerable controversy over the ingredients of an ideal route. It was a time when the incline mentality was being gradually shaken off, along with the cautious attitudes that accompanied the early years of the steam locomotive. It has already been shown how inclines were often regarded as inescapable on some of the shorter local lines built before 1830. But what of the longer distance inter-regional lines?

The London & Birmingham Railway affords an interesting example. Robert Stephenson undertook the survey work and a bill was presented to parliament in 1832. There was much hostility to the scheme, as L. T. C. Rolt tells us, 'to the support of the opposing landowners rallied those whose profits or livelihood depended on roads or canals'. There were very powerful interests involved in the road-coach and fly-boat trades and Stephenson was subjected to sustained cross-examination over the feasibility of his route, which involved a great cutting through the chalk scarp at Tring. An effective form of opposition from vested interests always lay in seeking to demonstrate the impracticability of a rival project. The bill failed in the Lords in 1832 but the following year it gained speedy acceptance as much of the opposition had by then been bought off. Stephenson then moved to the next phase of the campaign, the building of the railway. And here the annals give full expression to the difficulties encountered in Kilsby Tunnel – a four-year battle against subterranean quicksands which had unfortunately not been revealed in the trial borings. Against this tremendous challenge, overcome by herculean physical efforts and installation of pumping equipment which cleared 1800 gallons per minute, the crumbling rock and water springs encountered in the Roade-Blisworth were almost insignificant. Yet there is a further aspect of the London & Birmingham Railway which is worthy of mention, though it is frequently overlooked by the more dramatic events of the parliamentary hearing and the great building sites. It concerns the decision to take the railway through Northamptonshire by way of Watford Gap between Blisworth and Rugby, thereby avoiding the town of Northampton which merited a railway service and offered a considerable potential traffic to the railway company. The situation is particularly anomalous since at its nearest point (Blisworth) the London & Birmingham Railway is only seven kilometres from the town. And furthermore, when the decision was taken to quadruple the tracks as far as Rugby, the additional capacity north of Roade was in fact provided by a new line to Rugby via Northampton.

An argument frequently advanced in the past claimed that Stephenson's route was selected in response to opposition from the town. One historian, T. Roscoe, claimed in 1839 that Stephenson had worked out a route through Northampton but 'so great however was the opposition which certain parties in authority entertained to it that a most determined opposition was raised to the project and the bill was consequently lost'. The point was copied by subsequent writers. J. C. Jefferson, writing in 1864 on the life of Robert Stephenson, claims that Northampton lay on the original route, 'but the inhabitants of Northampton raised so effectual an opposition to the scheme that the engineer was necessitated to choose a route along which adverse influence was less powerful'. And as S. Smiles explained in an earlier history of George Stephenson, dated 1857, 'the necessity was thus involved of distorting the line, by which the enormous expense of constructing the Kilsby Tunnel was incurred'. Another historian in 1888 described the mood as one of 'barbarous fury'. Yet examination of the local records shows that an important and influential section of the townspeople were anxious to have the railway built through Northampton. The only reservations were expressed by an unrepresentative Corporation concerned about the adverse effect on their Bugbrooke estate – and this had nothing to do with the failure of the 1832 bill when the country landowners like the Duke of Grafton were actively obstructive. Furthermore, this bill was no different from the successful bill of 1833 as regards this critical question of avoiding Northampton, for although Stephenson made some minor accommodations Kilsby Tunnel was envisaged from the start. The reason lies in a rigid insistence of a maximum gradient of 1 in 330 (16 ft per mile). Following the chosen line such a requirement could be met provided a tunnel of 2.2 km was cut through the ridge. Although this was a longer tunnel than any previously envisaged for locomotive working (and it prompted claims that passengers would inevitably be suffocated) the canal age had generated even longer tunnels and there was little reason to doubt the technical feasibility. Had a line been taken through Northampton the amount of tunnelling through the ridge would have increased to an unacceptable degree, because the level of the Nene at Northampton is 40 m below the level at Long Buckby where the Kilsby route swings away. When the 1879 route was opened the tunnel, at Crick, was 0.5 km (compared with 2.2 km at Kilsby) because by this time stiffer maximum gradients were tolerated and the line was allowed to climb out of Northampton at 1 in 230. The Northampton route was now positively attractive since the town was at last endowed with a main line and the duplication of Kilsby Tunnel was avoided.

Actually, the railway first arrived at Northampton in 1845, en route for Peterborough, though it served the suburb of Cotton End, south of the Nene, rather than the town centre. Incredibly this success followed a second 'near miss' when the Midland Counties Railway proposed a junction with the London & Birmingham at Rugby in preference to the original plan to meet at Blisworth. This was done on the grounds that it would mean less new railway and a more direct link with Birmingham at the cost of a slight increase in the distance to London. The revised plan of 1835 went unnoticed for some time in Northampton because the advertisement was placed in a local paper (the *Northampton Free Press*) that was little read by influential people. Although a rival (South Midland) project was hastily put forward to coerce the Midland Counties to revert to the Blisworth line it did not succeed in denying the Midland Counties their act in 1836.

This is not the only example of Stephenson engineering leading to the avoidance of important towns. The North Midland Railway was built through Chesterfield and Rotherham because the approach to Sheffield was considered unsuitable in 1840 and it was not until 1870 that a direct line was taken from Chesterfield to Sheffield through Dronfield and Bradway Tunnel. The reason for the cautious attitude lay quite logically in the argument that the power of a steam locomotive should be used for hauling maximum loads and not exhausted in coping with severe gradients. If gradients were steepened beyond 1 in 330 the train would have to be significantly lightened. Stephenson was aware of difficulties of steam locomotive operation on the Canterbury & Whitstable Railway of 1830, and also on L.M.R. where in addition to the 1 in 40 incline out of Liverpool Crown St (involving rope haulage for 0.3 km – before Lime St was built in 1836) there were steep climbs to the Rainhill Summit: 2.6 km of Whiston Incline (1 in 96) and 2.4 km of Sutton Plane at 1 in 89.

Such a philosophy was scorned by Joseph Locke and other protagonists of 'direct railways'. They insisted that an undulating railway could be worked almost as economically as a level one because adverse and favourable gradients would cancel each other out. But such an argument could not overcome the fact that a more powerful locomotive would be needed to haul a train of given weight over an undulating railway than over an almost level track. Supporters of 'direct railways' inevitably exaggerated their case as a reaction to the rather dogmatic stand adopted by the Stephensons, who enjoyed very strong support through Liverpool merchants and City bankers like the Gurneys. Financial backing for railways depended to a considerable degree on the attitude of such elements of the business community and L. T. C. Rolt makes the point that Liverpool merchants followed their successful speculation in the L.M.R. with support for other railways provided the works were executed in accordance with the Stephenson approach. To promote a more enlightened view must inevitably have required a good deal of rhetoric. Important towns were not going to accept denial of direct railways on the grounds that the terrain was unsuitable. Higher costs might be involved in building and/or in operating but provided the traffic would justify them there was no problem.

Several early main lines involved very steep gradients. Charles Vignoles went from the Midland Counties Railway to tackle the Sheffield Ashton-under-Lyne & Manchester project, which involved gradients of 1 in 100 up Longdendale between the Mottram Viaduct and Woodhead Tunnel. The line continued to climb at 1 in 129 for the first half of a 4.8 km tunnel which was completed at the end of 1845 and allowed the opening of the whole line. The Pennines had been likened by Defoe to the barrier of the Apennines which divided Italy, but Vignoles was not overawed and considered that the difficulties 'are not greater than have been overcome in other places with facility and success'. Then there is the famous Lickey Incline on the Birmingham–Bristol line near Bromsgrove with a gradient of 1 in 38 for some three kilometres. This was tackled by locomotives from the very day the line opened in 1840, though banking assistance was of course necessary. Captain Moorsom was the engineer who built the line in defiance of advice from both Stephenson and Brunel: a line further east would have allowed easier gradients but at the expense of taking the railway even further away from important towns like Worcester. It is not clear if locomotive working of the incline was envisaged from the start but certainly when work was well advanced Moorsom was able to draw on American experience which was favourable to locomotives in such circumstances. Branch lines also might involve steep climbs like the short line from the Calder Valley main line which climbed Werneth Incline to reach Oldham in 1842: the steepest section involved approximately one kilometre at 1 in 27. An easier alternative route via Hollinwood opened in 1880 and Werneth Incline was closed in 1963, but the two main lines mentioned continue to handle heavy traffic: the Manchester–Sheffield line is a major coal carrier and has been electrified as a means of accelerating the traffic. Against such a background it is rather surprising that Stephenson should have insisted on keeping within the limit of 1 in 330 so much so that when a gradient of 1 in 70 was unavoidable between Camden and the Euston terminus (on account of the decision to take the line underneath the Regents Canal), incline working was adopted. In the bill of 1833 Camden Town was the proposed terminus but authority was given in the amending act of 1835 to extend as far as Euston Grove and it was here that the station opened two years later, embellished by the famous Doric Arch. Hamilton Ellis has given colourful descriptions of the approach to Euston: 'incoming trains tobogganed solemnly down at an absolute maximum of ten miles per hour in the charge of special brakesmen. Their advent was announced by a siren connected by an air pipe with the top of the incline and producing in action a low melancholic moaning'. The assistance of a stationary steam engine for northbound trains was needed until 1844, when more powerful locomotives were introduced. Glasgow Queen St was, incidentally, another city terminus where such assistance was necessary and cable working on the 1 in 42 to Cowlairs survived until the present century.

Stephenson railway concepts thus came under increasing scrutiny. As early as 1836 there was a setback when Robert Stephenson's proposal for the London–Brighton railway, making use of the Mole and Adur valleys, lost out to Sir John Rennie's more direct route with its long tunnels at Balcombe and Claydon. Even more spectacular was the conflicting advice over the route for a railway from Lancashire over the border to Scotland. Just as the Grand Junction had led south from the L.M.R. to Birmingham, so building proceeded northwards to Wigan (Springs Branch) in 1830, to Preston in 1831, to Wyre in 1834 and finally to Fleetwood in 1840. Because of the barrier of the Cumbrian Hills it was considered prudent to institute a combined rail-steamer route. In 1841 a steamer service connected the railheads of Ardrossan and Fleetwood. For an all-rail route George Stephenson recommended in 1839 that the builders should follow the Cumbrian coast through Whitehaven and Maryport, starting off across

Morecambe Bay by a great embankment that would allow a large area of land to be reclaimed. Such a railway was built to serve Barrow-in-Furness, Whitehaven and Workington but the route was excessively devious for Scottish traffic and Joseph Locke engineered the route over Shap Fell (rising to 290 m and involving maximum gradients of 1 in 75) although George Stephenson considered such a route to be out of the question. There was some delay, for the Lancaster & Carlisle was only authorised in 1845, five years after the railway had reached Lancaster from Preston. Locke relied confidently on the developing power of the locomotive while the Stephensons, who had championed the locomotive so stoutly in the 1820s, seemed distinctly conservative. The reluctance to accept the Shap route as feasible in 1845 is curious since the previous year the Euston Incline (shorter than Shap though equally steep) had been converted to locomotive operation. In 1846 the line opened and the following year a railway extended all the way from London to Glasgow (for the Caledonian had built south to meet the Lancaster & Carlisle). Some minor improvements were made shortly after: a direct line avoiding Coventry, Birmingham and Wolverhampton was taken from Rugby through Nuneaton and Tamworth to Stafford in 1847, while further north in Lancashire the switch-back at Newton-le-Willows arising from the fact that the Grand Junction and Springs Branch took off from the L.M.R. at slightly different points (Earlestown and Lowton respectively) was overcome in 1864 by a new line which burrowed under the L.M.R. and gave a straighter course while simultaneously avoiding the complication to Liverpool–Manchester running. Otherwise the line is identical to the inter-city route that was electrified in 1974.

# 5

# The Influence of Landowners on Railway Development

The influence of the landowners is a prominent theme in railway history with considerable evidence advanced to show that there was sustained opposition to some of the early schemes. A view has developed of intransigent landowners hounding trespassing surveyors and opposing railway bills out of fear of depredations by immoral construction gangs. Also there were perceived adverse consequences of the completed line for the agricultural and sporting efficiency of the estate as well as for canal and turnpike incomes with which many proprietors were concerned. Sir George Armytage resisted the Huddersfield & Manchester plan to build across Kirklees Park and the first proposal for a railway to connect the Liverpool & Manchester Railway with Birmingham involved George Stephenson in controversy when surveying a route through Sandbach. Opposition from the Marquis of Stafford resulted in the selection of a different route passing well to the west of Sandbach by way of Crewe Hall, where a great railway town was destined to emerge. In other cases it was not so easy to give a wide berth to a likely centre of opposition. When the Syston and Peterborough line was being surveyed through Leicestershire it was found that the most feasible route lay through the Wreake Valley and on into the Vale of Catmose: a somewhat devious route but one which involved only minimal gradients and secured access to the towns of Melton Mowbray and Oakham. The Earl of Harborough's estates at Stapleford, near Saxby, was inevitably affected and a hostile reception was given to the railway surveyors, leading to the celebrated Battle of Saxby Bridge. The result was a compromise which tolerated the railway but only on the understanding that it kept well clear of the mansion house. This necessitated a very sharp curve which involved a speed restriction, one which was particularly irksome later in the century when the Manton–Melton section of the railway was used by express trains from London to Nottingham via Corby. In 1892 a realignment was allowed and the present route was opened, involving a new station at Saxby. However, Lord Harborough's Curve remains a prominent landscape feature and is just one of several relict features in the local landscape: the

3. *Lord Harborough's Curve, at Saxby, Leicestershire* This sharp curve, which arose out of a landowner's objections to the proposed route of the Syston & Peterborough Railway, was realigned in the 1890s to allow faster running. The original line ran beside the house seen in the distance on the right-hand side of the picture.

meanders of the Wreake Valley Canal and the trackbed of the Midland & Great Northern Joint Line which took off from Saxby Junction in 1893 are also plain to see.

Anyone familiar with the route of the Newcastle–Carlisle railway may wonder why it resists the temptation to follow the Irthing Valley down from Gilsland towards Carlisle and instead takes a route to the south through hilly country, avoiding the little town of Brampton, and the principal villages in the area as well, while burrowing in a deep cutting through the Cowran Hills south of Hayton. The main reason for the anomaly lies in the insistence by Lord Carlisle that his support for the project would be conditional on an intersection with his private waggonway from the Naworth Coalfield to Brampton Staith (opened in 1799). But the deviation south of Hayton was made to take account of objections from Sir Hew Ross, one of the local landowners. The deep cutting on the amended route arose out of the need to ensure a steady downhill gradient to Carlisle, because the original plans of the 1820s envisaged horse traction and Lord Carlisle was anxious that one team of horses should suffice to take a rake of loaded wagons into town and return with the empties within the day. As it happened, the use of locomotives was approved by the time the line opened in 1836 and some of the engineering work was thereby rendered superfluous.

An interesting and well-documented study has been made of the Gifford & Garvald Light Railway in Lothian. A line was proposed in 1890 to extend from the railhead of Ormiston to serve a string of rural communities situated along the northern edge of the Lammermuir Hills. The project had the enthusiastic support of the majority of the landed proprietors: not unnaturally, since their agricultural produce could be more easily marketed and their various requirements more readily satisfied. Particularly crucial to the original route was the goodwill of Fletcher of Saltoun, whose estate would be bisected by the railway. It soon became clear that there was a conflict of interest between the landowners who saw the railway as a local amenity ('a proprietors' line') and the North British Railway Company who had agreed to operate the service but who wished to control the line as a ramification of their network. The assertive policy of the N.B.R. led to a withdrawal of goodwill by Fletcher of Saltoun and a completely new line had now to be planned. The Deviation Bill of 1893 allowed for a swing through Humbie, well to the south of the original direct line from Ormiston to Gifford: it meant that only a minor incursion would be made across Fletcher's estate and instead the Marquess of Tweeddale, a powerful force in N.B.R. circles, would be the principal host. The line opened in 1901 and survived for thirty-two years. With no large centres of population from which to attract passengers and no potential mineral traffic there was little chance of prosperity and it is unfortunate that its main claim to fame should lie in the decade of wrangling that preceded construction.

However, the case of the Gifford & Garvald Light Railway, while demonstrating the influence of landowners as important decision makers, does not support the view that they were stubbornly obstructive. Quite the reverse. There was general support for the railway and the change in route followed simply from political rivalry. For that matter the notorious case of Lord Harborough's Curve does not prove that landowners were opposed to railways in the 1840s: rather it demonstrates a certain sensitivity towards privacy and amenity that required the railway to compromise. In the same way the building of the railway from Rowsley in the Derwent Valley towards Manchester involved a cut and cover tunnel through the grounds of Haddon Hall so that the pastoral calm of the estate would not be disturbed. The same technique had been applied in 1803 on the Ticknall Tramway (where a short cut and cover tunnel was installed across the drive to Calke Park) and it was also used at Parlington, near Aberford, to conceal both the coal road from Garforth Collieries and the railway which followed it. A late nineteenth-century example comes from Wigan when the Whelley Loop line was pushed through the Haigh Plantations (though in this case the cover was subsequently removed).

Another interesting accommodation was made at Guthrie Castle where the Arbroath & Forfar Railway had to find a compromise against the twin evils of conflict with either the estate or the local turnpike trust. In the end the railway was allowed to pass the castle drive provided that a bridge would incorporate an entrance gate and porter's lodge. Since this part of the railway eventually became part of the Caledonian main line to Aberdeen the arrangement achieved considerable fame. Again, when the Trent Valley line was projected across Shugborough Park the Earl of Lichfield insisted that the railway should harmonise with the existing buildings, including the mansion house and various ornamental buildings put up in commemoration of the naval successes of Admiral Anson, whose brother owned the estate. So Hamilton Ellis describes how 'Shugborough Tunnel's gloomy condition was enlivened at the northern end with towers and battlements and crenellations and a Norman arch. Generations of enginemen have called the place the Gates of Jerusalem'. In Ireland the Dublin & Kingstown Railway overcame opposition from Lord Cloncurry by agreeing to conceal the line in a cutting at Blackbrook with the entrance marked by flanking Italianate lodges and with an overbridge 'of handsome design' to give the owner access to a maritime promenade.

It has been claimed that some landowners exploited the railway companies by demanding excessively high prices for land. M. Robbins cites the case of Lord Petre of Ingatestone Hall in Essex who received more than twenty times the normal price of land on which the Eastern Counties line was built. But he concludes that on the whole the cost of land involved in railway construction between 1825 and 1850 was a not unreasonable fourteen percent and that 'the somewhat eager or excessive payments so often quoted were singular and not characteristic'. And of course there were good reasons why this should have been so. The railway may at first have been perceived as a noisy intrusion but there was an economic value to be set against any loss of amenity, even in purely agricultural country. Landowners like the Duke of Bedford who fundamentally disliked the railway and objected to its early progress came to accept it as a necessity. The Duke of Bedford played a prominent rôle in bringing the railway into Bedford from Bletchley. And the Kerry branch on the Cambrian system was built thanks to a prosperous local farmer, John Wilkes who, incidentally, founded the Kerry Mountain Sheep. The line opened in 1863 and ran from Abermule over five kilometres at gradients as stiff as 1 in 43 to end at Glanmule, more than a kilometre from Kerry, at which point narrow gauge tramways fanned out to outlying sheep farms and plantations in the Kerry Hills. On the other hand Llanfair Caereinion did not enjoy such formidable patronage and only in 1901 did work begin on a narrow gauge railway to meet the Cambrian at Welshpool.

Deference to noble families might be shown through the selection of harmonious *cottage orne* architectural styles for the country stations. The Duke of Devonshire was influential in Derbyshire in promoting an extension of the Rowsley branch (serving Chatsworth) through to Buxton in 1862. Architecturally there is a strong link because of the work of the Duke's gardener, Joseph Paxton, who designed a famous greenhouse (finished in 1840). This greenhouse was an inspiration not only for the Crystal Palace (1850) which ensured Paxton's fame, but for a generation of all-over arched roofs for major railway stations. On a more modest scale however it is almost certain that Paxton designed the old terminus of Rowsley of 1849 (superseded in 1860) and the oldest part of Matlock Station is similar. The new Rowsley Station of 1860 (also Bakewell in the same year) did not involve Paxton, but he was certainly influential in the iron tracery erected at Buxton (1862) while his assistant, G. H. Stokes, is associated with the attractive little station at Cromford.

Landowner influence is also evident in the Midland Railway project for an independent line to London, in preference to the link with the L.N.W.R. at Rugby. The opening of St Pancras Station in 1868 was, however, preceded by a transitionary solution under which a connection was made with the G.N.R. at Hitchin. A line from Wigston, near Leicester, to Bedford and Hitchin was authorised in 1847. Abandonment of the scheme after George Hudson's downfall did not go unchallenged by landowners: William Whitbread of Southill led a deputation to Derby which threatened an approach to the G.N.R. if the Midland would not honour its obligation. They backed up their case by offering to sell land for no more than its agricultural value. That the Duke of Bedford was among those who displayed generosity is a telling indication of how quickly initial belligerancy was tempered by a more realistic branch of self interest. Hence J. T. Ward concludes that 'certainly the landed interest could not be accused of apathy or hostility towards railway promotion by the mid-century'. His remarks are based on research in Yorkshire but there is no reason to suppose that the comment does not have wider validity. Some examples from Scotland may be mentioned. It has been shown that the Caledonian Railway's plan for a basic system of railways focusing on Carstairs, with lines to Glasgow, Edinburgh, Kelso, Carlisle, Dumfries and Ayr was crucially dependent on landowner support. The value of the railways in the rural areas was immediately perceived and demands for accommodations to preserve amenity were generally more moderate than in the towns. A very strong lead in the construction of the Arbroath & Forfar Railway was given by W. F. L.

Carnegie, described by S. G. E. Lythe as 'a local proprietor of outstanding vigour and enterprise with financial interest in the local quarrying business'. He surveyed the route at his own expense and acted as chairman of the company throughout its independent existence. The line was opened in 1838, the same year as the Arbroath & Dundee line: like its neighbour it was built at 5 ft 6 in. gauge, but converted to standard in 1847. Caught up in the expansion of long-distance railways during the 1840s its management was taken over in 1848 by one of the constituent companies of the Caledonian Railway. Lord Wharncliffe was an active promoter of the Dundee & Newtyle Railway, which carried considerable potential benefits for his Tayside estates. The family remained consistently interested in railways both as parliamentarians and as private individuals. Inevitably therefore, landowners were prominent in railway decision-making and inevitably their approach was largely one of self-interest.

When the Highland Railway was being planned the Seafield estates insisted that the line be carried through Grantown and Forres, in preference to the direct line through Carr Bridge, so that timber could be exploited more economically. Still more impressive is the initiative of the Duke of Sutherland in financing the entire railway project along the Sutherland coast from Golspie to Helmsdale. Investment in a railway was seen as a means of improving the potential of a whole region in which the Duke had an interest by virtue of his vast estates in the county. The railway from Inverness reached Golspie in 1868 but financial difficulties prevented further progress immediately and it was at this juncture that the Duke stepped in. It is claimed by O. S. Nock that he took 'a step without parallel in British railway history' in building his own line. And he took an extremely rare action in commencing work before the act had been obtained. Consequently, when the royal assent was given in June 1870 the line was already well on the way to completion with the first train running the following October. It was not until June 1871 that a physical connection with the Inverness line was made at Golspie. But when this happened the temporary terminus at Dunrobin became a private station serving the mansion house and the first rolling stock was also reserved for the private use of the Duke. However, in Sutherland the Duke could be fairly confident that his plans would not encounter vigorous opposition. The family also made a generous contribution to the extension of the railway beyond Helmsdale and the influence of the Dowager Duchess was expressed in a successful petition for a station at Culrain, opened in 1870: people living near her mansion house of Carbisdale Castle had to make a long detour to reach Invershin on the other side of the Kyle of Sutherland. The opening of a station on the opposite side of the railway bridge meant that people could cross the bridge by train and shorten their journey considerably.

Since railways were seen as being so fundamental to the prosperity of landed estates it is not surprising that landowners were often prominent as buyers of stock and members of provisional committees while many were elected to company boards. This may sometimes have been for reasons of social prestige but certainly not always. The Duke of Sutherland occupied a hereditary seat on the L.N.W.R. – he was much involved in the company through his Staffordshire estates and the noble architecture of Trentham Station projected the link into the landscape. Similarly, the chairmanship of the Manchester Sheffield & Lincolnshire, held through the 1850s by the progressive Lincolnshire landowner the Earl of Yarborough, is brought out by a fine Jacobean station at Brocklesby in 1848, close to the earl's country seat.

Not that landowner policy was restricted to the countryside. At Abingdon the decision to revise the route of the Oxford line so that the town was served by a branch from Radley meant a more direct path to the London–Bristol main line at Didcot, but it was taken primarily because of objections by Captain Pechell to the intrusion of the railway into his estates. On the other hand at Huddersfield a main line railway was taken through the heart of the town despite the fact that all the urban land was owned as one estate by the Ramsden Trustees. In D. Whomsley's words, policy ensured that the railway 'served Huddersfield without bruising it', for the approaches by tunnel and viaduct minimised both demolition and disruption of the road system while the station site allowed for the development of a New Town on the fringe of the historic core, thereby resulting in a big increase in the estate rental. The station building was also significant in setting an architectural standard for subsequent urban development. At Bedford the Duke of Bedford used his influence to ensure that a station would be found on the south side of the river: land he donated for the railway terminus was not conveniently situated in relation to the centre of the town but it was attractive in stimulating the profitable development of other parts of the Bedford estate.

# 6

# Later Railway Development especially in Ireland, Scotland and Wales

The further development of the railway system after the initial mania was impressive. Any detailed review of the development would require many volumes and this essay is concerned only with the basic geographical aspects. Later in the century the network expanded in all parts of the British Isles: even the area most affected in the mania years shows up with considerable prominence. This is because the growth of population at the time was most marked in the cities of England and greater capacity was needed. Track was quadrupled on some existing lines while the opportunity was also taken to find easier and more direct approaches to some urban centres: for example the L.B.S.C. to London (avoiding Redhill) in 1900 and both the L.N.W.R. and Midland Railway to Manchester (avoiding Stockport in 1909 and 1902 respectively). At the same time there was a rapidly increasing interest in seaside holidays and railways to the coasts were considerably improved (while the branch lines in such rural areas as Cornwall and Norfolk increased at this time).

Two lines are worth picking out for comment. The first comprises the new main line opened in 1899 by the Great Central Railway. It ran from Annesley, near Nottingham, to the new London terminus of Marylebone and represented a successful attempt by a provincial railway, the Manchester Sheffield & Lincolnshire, to gain independent access to the capital. It thus followed the Midland Railway's example – though whereas the Midland advanced in stages (first to Bedford and Hitchin in 1857 and later, in 1868, to St Pancras) and was already established in Midland towns, the G.C.R. undertook a single mammoth programme which involved heavy outlays in Nottingham and Leicester as well as further south. This last main line to London has been carefully scrutinised by those who consider that the railway system was over-developed by the turn of the century and that the London Extension was an unpardonable extravagance. Certainly the financial results were disastrous and hence the sarcastic dismissal of M.S.L. tactics by the catch-phrase 'money sunk and lost': the poor loadings of its lavishly-appointed trains seem to clinch the argument that this railway was superfluous. Yet it was beautifully engineered for high-speed running (despite the fact that the ruling gradient of 1 in 264 was slightly steeper than Stephenson's standard of 1838) and could be regarded as the first of a new generation of main lines through its ability to accommodate continental rolling stock.

In fact the project is associated with Sir Edward Watkin, who was prominent in the Metropolitan Railway and South Eastern Railway as well as the M.S.L.R. He envisaged a link-up between the three companies and also a Channel Tunnel that would allow through running to and from the Continent. During the late 1880s Watkin envisaged an extension of Metropolitan influence through the Aylesbury & Buckingham complemented by M.S.L.R. penetration south into Shropshire through the Mersey and Wirral railways. A step to fill the gap as far as Worcester was frustrated when a separate company received approval for a railway from Buckingham to Towcester. But this did demonstrate parliament's willingness to sanction new lines and in the early 1890s a link with the M.S.L.R. in Nottinghamshire was gaining support. But Watkin retired in 1894 and there was deterioration in relationships between the Metropolitan and the M.S.L.R. which meant that the continental dimension was not a major issue at the time the line was being built. Most places along the route already had satisfactory railway services and hence there is room for genuine surprise that such a costly investment was implemented.

The fate of the Great Central was dismal enough for ordinary shareholders to receive no dividend from the company at all during the years between the opening of the London line in 1899 and the amalgamation to form the L.N.E.R. in 1923. This does not however mean that all new lines were suspect, for in some instances it was possible to open up new long-distance routes with only minimal construction. An excellent example concerns the route developed for the 'Cornish Riviera Express' which spearheaded the G.W.R. campaign in support of tourism in the West Country. The rival L.S.W.R. had already improved its access to Plymouth in 1890 and built new lines in north Cornwall, reaching Wadebridge (1895), Bude (1898) and Padstow (1899). For travellers to Devon and Cornwall 'G.W.R.' had for many years been interpreted as 'Great Way Round' because the distance to Exeter via Bristol and Taunton was 312.6 km, compared with 276.6 km by the L.S.W.R. But the G.W.R. had a simple solution. There were already branches from Taunton to Yeovil (1853), from Chippenham to Yeovil (1857) and from Reading to Devizes (1862). It required only short connections at Devizes (1900) and Castle Cary (1906) to provide a direct route to Exeter only two kilometres longer than the rival route. Of course there were difficulties arising from the lack of consistently high engineering standards throughout, but heavy investment was avoided and the new link did not undermine the company's finances. The same policy is seen in the 1903 cut off between Swindon and the Severn Tunnel which enabled South Wales expresses to avoid Bristol. This followed the seven kilometre Severn Tunnel of 1886 and led on to a line to Fishguard Harbour through new construction from Clarbeston Road in 1906 and a bypass at Swansea (0.5 km, opened in 1913). Work started on a better alignment for the Letterston area (between Clarbeston Road and Fishguard) but the scheme was abandoned during the First World War. The Great Western also shortened their Birmingham line through a cut off at Bicester. Bypasses may be noted at Spalding (1894) and Boston (1913).

However, there is no doubt that the greatest relative expansion to the railway system came in the remoter parts of Ireland, Scotland and Wales. The delay in building railways arose partly because these areas lay furthest away from the places where the railway system first developed. Yet this simple argument is patently inadequate when it is noted that the West Highland Extension to Mallaig took that line to the West Highland coast, 264 km from Glasgow in 1901, when on the east coast of Scotland Aberdeen (246 km from Glasgow) was reached in 1850. Additional factors lie in the sparse population, mainly employed in hill farming, combined with rugged terrain which tended to increase construction costs. The situation in Wales is interesting in the early completion of the lines along the north and south coasts to Holyhead (1850) and Neyland (1856) respectively and the Chester–Newport line, through the Welsh Marches in 1853. This frame provided a base line from which several thrusts were launched on the interior heartland of Wales. One emerged in 1860 as the Manchester & Milford Railway which envisaged a long tunnel under Plynlimon to connect relatively straightforward lines along the Severn Valley to Oswestry and by 1852 to Carmarthen. The under-capitalised project was abandoned but there is clear legacy in the landscape with the 1863 earthworks at Llangurig (showing where the line would have swung away from the branch that later meandered through Llanidloes) and the abrupt change of direction at Strata Florida where the line from Carmarthen (1866) swung westwards towards Aberystwyth (reached in 1867). The history is quite complicated because the Plynlimon route was also being seriously considered by the Mid Wales Railway (eventually part of the Cambrian Railways) seeking a connection between Llanidloes and Rhayader and Aberystwyth. Both companies agreed to cooperate in 1865 with the Mid Wales building over the mountains to meet the Manchester & Milford who would now concentrate on reaching Aberystwyth. There would be a triangular junction at Trawscoed, Yspytty Ystwyth and Ystrad Meurig (Strata Florida). However, the Mid Wales line was never built and the M. & M. line to Aberystwyth, though always seriously contemplated as part of their programme, took an anomalous course. According to the 1860 act the T-junction would have been at Devil's Bridge (suggested by the earthworks at Llangurig).

Progress was more substantial in the late 1860s: the line from Craven Arms to Llanelli was ready in 1868 and this is the sole remaining line outside the 'frame', apart from the Cambrian line from Shrewsbury to Aberystwyth/Barmouth and Pwllheli. Delays in completing the Welsh network meant that the local lines built, like the canals, to integrate with coastal shipping, went unchallenged for many years. The Festiniog Railway opened in 1836 to convey slate down to the new harbour of Porthmadog. Even the contact with the Cambrian at Penrhyndeudraeth in 1872 did not sever the coastal link, nourished by the opening of an additional feeder, the Croesor Tramway, in 1863. Arguably, the 'maritime phase' survives to the present since the Festiniog is very much alive as one of the 'Great Little Trains' of Wales. The majority of the latter are, however, narrow gauge branches associated with the national railway system, like the Talyllyn and Welshpool & Llanfair, or represent narrow gauge conversions as between Pant and Pontsticill on the Brecon–Merthyr line.

Scotland's industrialised Central Belt stimulated early demand for

4. *Railway landscape in the Brecon Beacons* The trackbed of the Brecon & Merthyr Railway seen climbing northwards towards Torpantau Tunnel in the Brecon Beacons National Park. This picturesque route once linked the South Wales coalfield with rural counties to the north.

railway links with the south and it has already been explained how the Annandale route was developed for the first Anglo-Scottish main line, opened in 1847. Short local works in Lanarkshire were now absorbed by the emergent main line companies. The Caledonian Railway built the line to Carlisle, taking off southwards from the Wishaw & Coltness Railway (1833), which in turn connected in Coatbridge with the Glasgow & Garnkirk Railway of 1831. This latter railway provided an alternative route into Glasgow for the Monkland coalmasters who had previously used the Monkland Canal. Equally, when the Caledonian expanded northwards to Stirling and Perth the Garnkirk line provided the start, with new construction beginning at Coatbridge. As traffic expanded it became necessary to build more direct lines into Glasgow: hence the Clyde Valley line through Motherwell in 1849 and the extension of the original Garnkirk terminus of St Rollox into the heart of Glasgow at Buchanan Street in the same year. But Central Scotland provides a neat example of the economical way in which railways evolved in importance to become carriers of national and not simply regional significance. The simple absorption and upgrading of early railways did however have limitations where inclines were involved because such equipment had only limited capacity and involved long delays. Hence, while the Edinburgh & Glasgow Railway (eventually part of the North British) absorbed the Ballochney and Slamannan Railways the combined line which led from Coatbridge over to the Union Canal at Causewayend (1840) could not be used for the new main line between the two great cities and a route through Falkirk and Lenzie was used instead in 1842. However, the inclines were eventually bypassed and the Slamannan line played a useful rôle in the continuing industrial development of Central Scotland.

The further development of railways in Scotland involves several interesting themes, including the furious expansion of suburban lines in Glasgow (particularly those which gave access to the dockland and shipyards) and the reorganisation in Fife as a result of the building of the Tay and Forth bridges in 1887 and 1890 respectively, the former of course associated with the disaster of 1879 when the first Tay Bridge collapsed under strong winds as a train was crossing it. But the topic that perhaps has greatest appeal concerns the building of railways in the Highlands. As one of Scotland's leading cities it was logical that Aberdeen would be reached in the mania years. It was equally logical that Inverness would be connected initially through Aberdeen. The additional distance from Aberdeen was 174 km, through well-settled and intensively-farmed lowland countryside, whereas the distance northwards from Perth to Inverness 190 km across terrain teeming with engineering problems and stubbornly unrewarding in terms of traffic, especially in the wilds of Drumochter Pass (450 m). When the new line to Inverness was built in 1863 it took an indirect course from

Aviemore through Grantown and Forres which meant a slightly lower length of new railway and a better service for the Spey Valley and Moray Firth towns. The Seafield estate was a strong supporter of the railway and was anxious to have the easterly route followed so that the export of its timber would be expedited. It was only in 1898 that the claims of Inverness and the towns further north for a truly direct railway were satisfied with the opening of the surviving line by way of Carr Bridge and Slochd Summit (380 m).

In the meantime there had been much discussion of railway schemes in the West Highlands. The Oban line had opened in 1880 in the form of a branch from Stirling which served the upper Tay Valley and continued into Strathfillan and by a glacially-breached watershed to the Lochy Valley, leading thence to Loch Awe, Loch Etive and the Sound of Mull. But the entire coastal strip northwards to Sutherland had no railway service (apart from the line from Inverness to Strome Ferry – 1870) and, as in the Hebrides, the population depended largely on the steamer services based on Glasgow or Oban. During the 1880s there was much public concern about the condition of the Highland crofting population and it was accepted that the smallholders should enjoy security of tenure on their tiny farms and also have better opportunities for ancillary employment. It seemed that the railway was crucial for the reinvigoration of the Highland economy, yet a grandiose scheme for a 272 km railway from Glasgow to Inverness via Fort William and the Great Glen was considered inappropriate because there was insufficient traffic (although it was 62 km shorter than the existing route through Aviemore and Forres and even 20 km shorter than the line subsequently opened over Slochd Summit). So the act was refused and the Great Glen, despite providing a fine natural routeway to the north, was never exploited for rail communication except for a branch line from Spean Bridge to Fort Augustus. This was a development of the Glasgow–Fort William railway opened in 1894. With government encouragement (similar to the Strome Ferry–Kyle of Lochalsh extension in 1897) the line was also extended to Mallaig in 1901 to provide better access to southern markets for Hebridean fishermen. But railways were never built on the islands themselves and many projected branches to the west coast from the Kyle and Wick lines were overtaken by the growth of bus services. Thus places such as Garve and Lairg became interchange points rather than railway junctions.

The Highland case is interesting because it does, belatedly, involve a measure of government assistance. This is quite exceptional for Great Britain because, apart from nineteen loans to railway companies by the Public Works Loan Commissioners between 1837 and 1842 (totalling almost half a million pounds), there was no subsequent government support. It might seem that the government's readiness to assist the

Liverpool & Manchester and Newcastle & Carlisle companies, among others, while withholding assistance in remoter parts of the country indicates a further case of blatant inconsistency. But arguably, support dried up once it became clear (during the mania) that private capital was capable of doing the job and over-readiness to grant favours to the Highlands as a special case might have discouraged proprietors from taking initiatives which, as the Duke of Sutherland showed, were frequently within their financial capacities. Hence help given to the Highlands was applied only belatedly and only in the more difficult west coast areas. Nevertheless, the fact remains that in Ireland the insularity of this part of the United Kingdom made it easier geographically for government to recognise a special case. Not only did Ireland adopt a different gauge as standard: 1.60 m or 5 ft 3 in. in 1846 (this would involve the least amount of conversion) – but government financial support was substantial with twelve percent of the capital supplied by the government between 1831 and 1852. The second report of the Irish Railway Commissioners (1838) had proposed the development of a modest system under strong state direction. Since the economy was less dynamic than in Britain it was felt that the benefits of the railway might not be fully obtained under private enterprise. Also it was argued that the investment in canals should be protected and railways built to complement the waterways rather than compete with them. The proposed system was to be based on Dublin (on which steamer services would concentrate), provide links south to Cork (also Kilkenny, Limerick and Waterford) and north to Enniskillen, Belfast (via Armagh) and Newry. However, such an element of public involvement was unfamiliar to British politicians and private enterprise was a dominant influence. The system was eventually far more elaborate than the Commissioners had envisaged and canal links were duplicated. One result of this was that a greater number of ports were able to develop a hinterland. Instead of simply concentrating traffic at Dublin (and Waterford, which had a proposed cross-country rail link with Limerick) the emerging railway system emphasised the nodality of Belfast and Londonderry: it was from the latter port rather than Dublin that the first railway reached Enniskillen and penetration was continued into Connaught.

Later in the century under the Light Railways and Tramways Act of 1883 the local authorities (or baronies) were empowered to provide financial guarantees – hence the 'Baronial Railways' of County Galway (Attymon Junction–Loughrea and Claremorris–Ballinrobe) – while the recognition of some western areas as 'Congested Districts', subject to the attentions of a special authority endowed with central government funds, led to the further development of narrow gauge railways such as the remarkable County Donegal system which threw off branches to various places on the west coast including Glenties, Killybegs, Ballyshannon and Letterkenny (the latter built as a 'government railway' and opened in 1909). Sparse traffic in many parts of Ireland also led to considerable variety on the theme of economy. The Donegal railways made early progress with railbuses, but before this a monorail (of the Lartigue type) was installed over 14.9 km between Listowel and Ballybunion (County Kerry) in 1888 while the 12.9 km tramway to Giant's Causeway (1883) exploited the hydro-electricity potential of an old waulkmill site on the Bush river at Bushmills: these interesting lines survived until 1924 and 1949 respectively and abundant traces of the latter can still be seen, both the trackbed and hydro-electric installations.

# 7

# Redevelopment of Plateway Routes:
## The Forest of Dean

It has been shown how some of the early railways of the locomotive period were quickly integrated into a national pattern. Almost immediately branches were laid off the Liverpool & Manchester Railway and while some of these remained as secondary links, like the Bolton line which took off from Kenyon Junction in 1831, other ramifications extended eventually into the London–Glasgow main line: until a bypass was opened in 1864 trains on the west coast main line continued to negotiate a short section of the L.M.R. between the points where the original Wigan and Warrington branches led off at Lowton and Earlestown respectively. And in Central Scotland the structure of main lines built by the Caledonian Railway is basically determined by the local railways of the 1820s and 1830s which served the coalmines and ironworks of north Lanarkshire and linked this booming industrial region with Glasgow. Despite subsequent refinements, such as the direct route from Wishaw (Law Junction) to Glasgow in 1849, the network inevitably bears the indelible impression of the original 'base line': trains from Perth to Carlisle still avoid Glasgow by following part of the original Wishaw & Coltness Railway, and some services heading into the city still negotiate the Glasgow & Garnkirk route. But how did the technically more historic plateway systems adapt to the era of nationwide railway systems operated by locomotives? Even where inclines were involved, as on the Cromford & High Peak Railway, the line could still adapt to a changing technological environment, although the 'main line' function envisaged in the canal age when the line connected two important waterways that formed links in a Manchester–London chain had to be set aside in favour of local services. The Forest of Dean is an interesting example.

The Forest of Dean lies within a triangle between the rivers Severn and Wye and comprises an area of bold relief extending sixteen kilometres from Mitcheldean in the north to Lydney in the south and twelve kilometres from Cinderford in the east to Coleford in the west. Much of this area was set aside by Edward the Confessor as a royal forest where deer and wild boar could be hunted and despite substantial clearance of woodland to make way for agriculture there was an interest in conservation because of the special value of the timber for shipbuilding. These interests helped to check the extent of clearance for agriculture but there were strong pressures exerted by the iron industry demanding copious supplies of charcoal for smelting. Iron ore was mined from early times: simple bloomeries and forges were set up throughout the area, a situation which continued until the early seventeenth century when the blast furnace was introduced from Sussex and water power sites in the main valleys of the forest were used to work the bellows and hammers. Exploitation of the timber resources to fuel the voracious blast furnaces was at its peak during the seventeenth and eighteenth centuries: there seems to have been a reduced concern for conservation, arising from the collapse of forest administration in the first years of Hanoverian rule and the availability of alternative supplies of timber for shipbuilding. In 1788 Dean was the country's leading charcoal iron producer. The introduction of coke smelting, beginning at Cinderford in 1795, stimulated the coal mining industry. This had long been important, for the coal miners became a privileged community and eventually attained the status of 'Free Miners', but only now was there a close functional link with iron production and deeper mines were sunk to reach more inaccessible deposits of both coal and iron ore. This association of local resources supported a vigorous industry but momentum was lost in the late nineteenth century when the iron ores were found unsuitable for Bessemer steel-making and lost the premium they had previously enjoyed. The last ironworks to close was at Cinderford in 1894 though some iron ore working continued until 1945 and deep coal mining continued for a further twenty years.

It will be apparent that in the early stages of the industrial revolution Dean was a thriving centre of industry with diversification from the basic coal and iron combination into wire production and tin plating. A key to the success of the industries which were dispersed among the small centres of population in this somewhat remote district lay in the provision of efficient transport services. The link between forest and river port was for long provided by pack mules negotiating primitive tracks. Between 1761 and 1786 the Crown spent more than £11 000 in road improvements but since the work was geared largely to the convenience of travellers on the route between Gloucester and South Wales it could not benefit the local industry very greatly – and, moreover, the fact that the roads became impassable in winter by the end of the century (and always dangerous for the coal carts which required large teams of horses) the market for Dean coal was limited by the high distribution cost. But the proven unsuitability of the transport available and the equally clear evidence of valuable minerals in the forest at a time of industrial growth led irresistibly to the installation of a tramway system. In 1799 it was resolved that railways from the Dean collieries to the

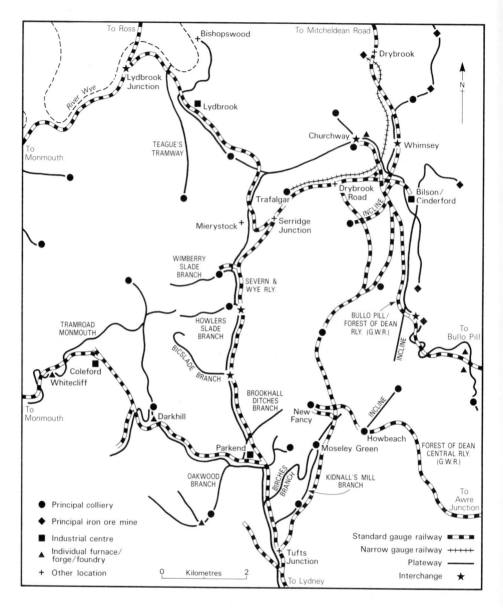

Map 6.   Railways in the Forest of Dean.

Severn and Wye rivers would be highly advantageous to Gloucester and Hereford respectively. Links to Lydbrook on the Wye and Lydney on the Severn were proposed in 1801 and a further review of the possibilities in 1807 suggested a railway from the Blakeney area of the Severn estuary to serve the eastern part of the forest. It so happened that in 1808 an act was passed re-affirming the power of the Crown to enclose up to 4450 ha. or 11 000 acres of forest. Plantations were to be laid out and it was appreciated that the work could be funded in part from the rentals that the railway schemes could generate.

In 1809 the Severn and Wye project was approved (Lydbrook to Lydney) and also shorter lines from Bullo Pill and Monmouth to Cinderford and Coleford respectively. Construction went ahead quickly and all the lines were working by 1812 (the first coal using the Bullo Pill plateway had reached Gloucester in 1810). Although traffic was depressed for a few years by the slackening of demand at the end of the Napoleonic Wars the lines were undoubtedly successful projects. They must mark the last case of extensive use of L-section plates, first evolved in the Sheffield area in the 1770s by John Curr. Edge rails were becoming popular in the early nineteenth century but Benjamin Outram, who strongly favoured plate-ways, had his judgment confirmed by John Rennie who had favourable experiences with tramways at Caldon Low in 1803. The plates were set into stone blocks with a gauge of 1.07 m (3 ft 6 in.) and then the lines were opened to private users subject to the payment of tolls and observance of the regulations: wagons had to conform to certain specifications because narrow wheel rims grooved the plates while 'dangerous driving' had to be discouraged by insisting that horses were to proceed with their 'trams' at walking pace. Numerous 'turn-outs' or passing loops were needed. For many years through the middle decades of the century the plateways remained hard at work and the system extended through the opening of various branches, particularly along the slades to the north of Parkend on the Severn & Wye line. The gauge was altered slightly, first to 1.09 m (3 ft 7 in.) in 1840 and then to 1.12 m (3 ft 8 in.) in 1843 but this seems to have been done simply to keep pace with the gradual spreading of the stone blocks.

It is quite remarkable that the tramways persisted for so long, considering that even before 1830 there had been a challenge from steam (through the abortive Purton project). But the cost of conversion for the whole of the complex Severn & Wye system meant that the company clung to old ways despite much strong criticism. This was especially true after the Dean Forest Mines Act of 1838 which established mining commissions to regulate the industry which conflicting ownership claims had reduced to chaos. By 1846 the various mines and quarries had been assigned to claimants who began to develop their properties now that their rights had been established.

Hence improved transport became a pressing necessity but important developments were only slowly initiated. The Bullo Pill line (renamed the Forest of Dean Railway in 1826) was replaced by a conventional broad gauge railway in 1854 (standard 1872): it was taken over by the Great Western who extended the original plateway through to Mitcheldean Road. Thus a plateway which had originally linked forest industries with the harbour of Bullo Pill was transformed into a railway which, while retaining the link with the harbour on the Severn, was basically part of the Great Western system through connections with the main lines from Gloucester to both Hereford and Newport. It is evident that the railway replacement followed basically the same course as the Bullo Pill plateway, including the use of Haie Hill Tunnel (but with new tunnels at Blue Rock and Bradlet Hill). But the requirements of gentle curves for locomotive operation required a relatively straight line and hence the cutting through of many of the meanders which existed in the original alignment. The railway plan was launched as the Mitcheldean Road & Forest of Dean Junction Railway and authorised in 1871. It was to include new construction from Whimsey to Drybrook and then through Euroclydon Tunnel (0.5 km) to meet the Hereford–Ross–Gloucester railway at Mitcheldean Road down a gradient of 1 in 38. However, since the Lydbrook route was better for access to South Wales the section north of Speedwell sidings was never opened and the rails heading beyond to Mitcheldean Road were eventually lifted in 1917. Meanwhile Bullo Pill harbour was fading away. There had always been disadvantages, for barges often had to wait high and dry on the Arlingham shore for the tide (with only limited accommodation at the deep water wharf). Up to five days was needed for coal to reach Gloucester. The railway was obviously quicker.

In addition, the G.W.R. installed a new branch from the Gloucester–Newport line (at Awre Junction) to New Fancy Colliery. This void between the Bullo Pill and Severn & Wye plateways was to have been filled by a steam railway to Purton Pill but the activity between 1826 and 1832 did not have a successful outcome. The Forest of Dean Central Railway was authorised in 1856, but it faced many problems and the line was eventually opened in 1868 by the Great Western as far as Howbeach (for New Fancy). The Severn & Wye system was more difficult to convert because there were a large number of branches and many private operators involved. Complete reorganisation was not practical although mineral output was increasing. As early as 1834 permission had been sought to use a steam locomotive on the Forest of Dean plateway but this was not forthcoming for another thirty years. However, the introduction of locomotives in 1864 was not successful because the plates tended to become clogged with stones and this prevented smooth running. It became clear that two systems (plateway and railway) would have to operate side by side and by 1868 a broad gauge railway was opened from Lydney on the Gloucester–Newport main line along the line of the Severn & Wye plateway as far as Mierystock (soon converted to standard 1872). Land on the eastern side of the plateway was used so that traffic on the plateway branches like Bicslade, Howler's Slade and Oakwood (which were overwhelmingly on the western side of the valley) would not be impeded. The minor branches were never converted. But as well as extending the line through to Lydbrook in 1874 the Severn & Wye did install a branch to Cinderford from Serridge Junction along with a mineral loop from Drybrook Road round to Moseley Green and back to Lydney line at Tufts Junction. Once again it can be seen that there were some significant departures from the plateway alignment although the favourable conditions of the Cannop (or Lyd) Valley meant that the original plateway line had been fairly straight. But Mierystock Tunnel was opened out and an extra line built to Churchway to accommodate locomotives. Clear differences in alignment can be seen at Mierystock while the liaison with the Ross-on-Wye & Monmouth Railway at Lydbrook Junction in preference to riverside quays at Bishopswood created another variation.

As already noted, the Severn & Wye plateway branch to Churchway was eventually complemented by a railway branch to Cinderford. For some years the only *railway* access to Churchway was provided by the rival Forest of Dean (G.W.R.) line from Bullo Pill. Some interesting scenes must have been witnessed in the transitionary period when the railway had reached Cinderford from Bullo Pill while ironworks in the area continued to draw coal (from Wimberry) and iron ore through the Severn & Wye plateways – for the best iron was found to come from a mixture of ores from eastern and western parts of the forest and there were transverse flows of ore across the forest to service the Cinderford and Parkend furnaces (both established in the 1820s). This exchange led to the Severn & Wye retaining the plateway to Churchway for a few years until a railway spur to Bilson on the outskirts of Cinderford gave a link with the Bullo Pill line in 1873 (overtaking a proposal of 1867 to place tram wagons on broad gauge flat wagons). The plateway to Churchway closed in 1877. The Severn & Wye retained its independence from the major companies for many years: in 1879 the company amalgamated with the Severn Bridge Company which had opened its bridge between Gatcombe and Sharpness in that year: a railway was built along the coast from Lydney parallel with the Great Western to gain access to the bridge and to docks at Sharpness on the other side. This enabled a link up with the Midland Railway at Berkeley Road between Gloucester and Bristol in addition to the connections with the G.W.R. at Lydbrook and Lydney. It was therefore logical that the company should be taken over by a joint committee of the two railways in 1894. Private lines were associated with the basic system. There were private narrow gauge steam railways, 800 mm (2 ft

5. *Redbrook in the Wye Valley* One of the small industrial communities which grew up on the edge of the Forest of Dean. The bridge taking the Monmouth–Chepstow line across the river can be seen. The first railway to serve Redbrook was the Coleford branch which climbed through the woodlands into the Newland Valley and connected with Redbrook by means of an incline.

$7\frac{1}{2}$ in.) gauge, built to connect Trafalgar Colliery with Bilson (*c.*1865) and tap Drybrook (Golden Valley) iron mines (*c.*1870). But the Bilson traffic from Trafalgar was captured by the Severn & Wye Railway who laid out a junction from Drybrook Road 1890. There was land sale of coal from Trafalgar to Nailbridge wharves (horse power after 1906), but production had ceased and the railway had been removed by 1928.

The final element in the picture concerns the Coleford line which was converted in 1883. The Monmouth tramway was in a poor shape in 1872 and it is doubtful if any traffic was carried subsequently. Like the Bullo Pill line it shows very clearly how a straighter alignment was driven through the loops negotiated by the original tramway. In some cases the cut-offs could only be achieved by short tunnels. Tunnels were needed at Redbrook and

Whitecliff in addition to Newland. Both sets of earthworks are still quite fresh in many cases and can be studied in detail in the field to show the different technical requirements of the two stages in railway development. In the case of the Monmouth–Coleford line an incline was eliminated. The existence of a railway along the Wye Valley (1876) meant that Redbrook could be served directly without the need for a branch from the Coleford line. So steep was the Newland Valley that any railway negotiating it had to start climbing the side of the Wye Valley at Wyesham almost immediately after leaving Monmouth: the result was that at the confluence of the Newland Valley with the Wye the railway was high on the hillside and a link with the industrial centre of Redbrook, famous for its tinplate works, could only be provided by incline. Coleford, like Cinderford, was also served by the Severn & Wye system (1875).

Forest industry was in decline after 1870, without the compensation of an increased coal output. Railway development continued until 1900 (Severn & Wye Cinderford extension) and 1908 (G.W.R. Cinderford loop) but subsequent emphasis has been on contraction. Indeed, all the railways in the forest have closed. Passenger trains on the Severn & Wye disappeared in 1929 and on the Forest of Dean Railway in 1958. Freight closure came as early as 1916 on the Monmouth line (west of Whitecliff). In 1949 the Howbeach line closed (after heavy wartime charcoal traffic) as did the Severn & Wye Cinderford branch. The last freight on the Pillowell–Tufts mineral loop ran in 1957 and on the Forest of Dean Cinderford line in 1967. The Parkend–Coleford line closed in the same year and the last freight from Lydney to Parkend ran in 1970. Some plateways lasted almost as long with the Bicslade branch, in use until 1946. The line from Lydney to Parkend was to have been taken over by the Dean Forest Railway Preservation Society (founded when closure of this last line was announced) but the section is being retained on a care and maintenance basis in case it is needed to transport stone from Whitecliff Quarry. The preservation society meanwhile are confining their attention to a site at Norchard.

# 8

# Railway Layouts in Cities

The most complicated railway layouts are encountered in cities. Although the railway has almost invariably contributed to their growth such places would tend to attract railway building in the first place through being already large centres of population and industry. While small towns en route between two cities could be overlooked if connection involved too lengthy a deviation or unacceptably severe engineering problems, there could be no avoiding the cities. Problems of land acquisition or technical difficulties had to be accepted. They would be minimised by such strategies as taking a railway round the edge of a town or city until the point was reached where the distance through the built-up areas to the proposed terminus was minimised, or by tunnelling to overcome topographical problems. But the railway had to find a way somehow and the result of the forced adaptation by the railway to the urban topography is seen in some of the steepest gradients on the entire system. This point has already been made in connection with Liverpool Crown Street, London Euston and Glasgow Queen Street. And it is worth recalling that in the link between Central and St David's stations in Exeter (1862) over one kilometre is as steep as 1 in 37. But the railway network in cities is complex on account of an intricate layout, quite apart from technical problems. The demand for services would require that the railways radiate out from the city centre like spokes on a wheel, while further complications would arise from the need to provide for through running and for the suburban traveller. In theory, therefore, the spokes would be connected to a hub at the centre and would be interconnected at intervals by circular or semi-circular lines. Complete symmetry would not be expected because of piecemeal development taking place in the context of both lively competition between railway companies, and a highly diversified 'landscape' as regards both physical conditions and land ownership. It is proposed to look at the development of railways in Manchester and then to identify the key points which may then apply to other cities.

In 1842 the system was quite simple. Five lines radiated out from four terminal stations, each situated close to the edge of the built-up area. The Liverpool & Manchester had arrived at Liverpool Road Station in 1830 and a second line was built from Salford to Bolton in 1836. Then by 1840 the

Leeds railway, originating from Oldham Road Station, was complete and finally in 1842 Store Street found itself the host of both the Sheffield, Ashton-under-Lyne & Manchester and the Manchester & Birmingham. Although there was an element of competition in the sense that Birmingham passengers could travel from Liverpool Road to Warrington and Crewe by the longer Liverpool & Manchester/Grand Junction route of 1837 the various trunk routes were basically non-competitive. The approaches in some cases involved significant gradients and it is curious to find that the steepest gradient on the Sheffield line was the 1 in 93 on the approach to Manchester at Guide Bridge. By 1850 another important main line had opened: this being a more direct line to Leeds via Huddersfield which was opened as far as Stalybridge in 1846 and towards the Standedge Tunnel in 1849. The shorter route to Leeds was gained at the expense of steeper gradients and a longer summit tunnel (5.0 km at Standedge compared with 2.7 km at Littleborough). There was also a new line to Macclesfield opened in 1849: it was linked with the North Staffordshire Railway through the Potteries and provided a further route to the south. It is also worth noting the line from Patricroft, on the Liverpool & Manchester, to Bury, which was an attempt by the L.M.R. to compete with a rival company for Bury traffic, by linking up with a line which the East Lancashire Railway was building from the Bolton line at Clifton Junction. However, by the time the lines were open the company organisation had changed drastically: the Manchester & Bolton had become part of the Lancashire & Yorkshire (along with the company building the direct Liverpool–Bury line) and naturally opposed the East Lancashire Railway (until amalgamation in 1859) while good relations between the L.Y.R. and L.N.W.R. ruled out a rival Liverpool–Bury service via Patricroft which closed after only three months (though the line remained available for freight until 1953).

But the main feature of the decade was the connection of the spokes to the hub, for it was becoming increasingly necessary to provide for through traffic, between Liverpool and Leeds for example. Direct links between the existing termini would have been impossible because the lines would have cut through the core of the city. So connecting loops were built round the edge of the built-up area and joined up with the original lines some distance 'downstream' of the terminals. It was in 1844 that an east-west route was provided in this way. The new line went through Hunt's Bank where a new station was opened (Victoria) to replace Liverpool Road, Oldham Road and Salford. The line involved considerable engineering problems and even with costly viaduct building the climb up to the junction with the Leeds lines at Miles Platting was 1 in 47, more than twice as steep as any other gradient on either line. By 1849 two further connections were complete. One ran along the southern edge of Manchester and gave the Sheffield and Birmingham companies a direct link with the Liverpool line while the other was built much further out to connect Stalybridge with Guide Bridge and Stockport and allow movement of freight between two parts of what was now the London & North Western Railway (after the amalgamations of 1846). It marks the first development of an 'outer belt' line. But it did not, however, upset terminal facilities to the same extent for Store Street remained in use for passengers, though its name was changed to London Road (and again, recently, to Piccadilly). Overall, by 1850 the railway mileage had increased considerably but there had been some rationalisation through the process of amalgamation, followed in the 1850s by a commercial agreement which reduced the competition between the three big companies then active in the area. The agreement was short-lived in the case of the Manchester Sheffield & Lincolnshire for in 1857 it refused to respect the L.N.W.R. monopoly on London traffic and offered its own services in conjunction with the Great Northern Railway via Retford.

Of course, railway politics are never far from the scene and the apparently logical sequence of events in Manchester masks a considerable element of controversy. The Hunt's Bank scheme was much debated between 1838 and 1842. Initially contrived by the Liverpool & Manchester as a gambit to corner land in a strategically important part of the city (and thereby prevent the Leeds company from promoting a rival line to Liverpool) it was for some years overshadowed by a rival southern route to connect up with the Oldham Road line via Store Street. However, the link between Store Street and Oldham Road would have been very difficult to build and a tunnel would have been inevitable. Furthermore, the connection between Liverpool Road and Store Street was successfully opposed by those shareholders of the L.M.R. with interests in the Grand Junction which would not be furthered by a physical link-up with a rival Birmingham railway.

But further complications arose through the desire of the Midland Railway to gain access to Manchester. The Sheffield company was building from Guide Bridge towards Marple and Stockport in the early 1860s and the Midland came over from Rowsley via Peak Forest to meet at New Mills in 1867: access to the centre of Manchester via Guide Bridge was made more direct when the line from Romiley to Ashburys was opened in 1875, while 1880 saw a second option available in the shape of a line from Romiley through Stockport (Tiviot Dale) and Heaton Mersey to a new terminus at Manchester Central. Central Station assured the Midland Railway the space that was lacking at London Road but, equally important, provided a connection with Liverpool that had been opened up by the Cheshire Lines Committee. The C.L.C. was backed by the G.N.R., M.S.L.R. and M.R., all of whom had an interest in access to Liverpool and competition with the L.N.W.R. The new Liverpool line served Irlam, Warrington and Widnes, and at Irlam there was a link from Stockport which had opened in 1873. The Sheffield company was also concerned to get good access to Central Station

6. *Suburban train at Wigan* A train consisting of diesel multiple units enters Wigan's Wallgate Station on the line from Manchester (Victoria).

and a link from Fairfield to Chorlton was ready in 1892. Finally it is important to mention the improvement in access to Manchester made by the Midland and L.N.W.R. to accelerate their London trains. The Midland built a line from Heaton Mersey to New Mills in 1902 (avoiding Stockport and Romiley). This included the 3.5 km Disley Tunnel. Then in 1909 the L.N.W.R. built a more direct line to Wilmslow and Crewe, again avoiding Stockport.

These lines had considerable value for suburban services which contributed to the great increase in traffic in the late Victorian period. On the northern side of Manchester more direct lines to Bury and Rochdale were opened by the Lancashire & Yorkshire Railway in 1879 and 1880 respectively. A direct line to Wigan, avoiding Bolton, followed in 1888 and gave a faster journey to Southport (and, by the Amberswood Loop in Wigan, to Liverpool as well). And of course the Altrincham line built in

1849 had a tremendous value for commuter services. The original idea seems to have been to convert the Bridgwater Canal into a railway from Manchester to Runcorn but the scheme was modified and a purely local line was built as far as Altrincham, running parallel to the canal. The efficiency of the suburban services was increased by electrification: Altrincham in 1915 and Bury in 1931 (followed by several main lines in the post-war period). But long before this the increase in the number of trains had necessitated an enlargement of the principal stations. Bigger stations were needed, even with the opening of Central in 1880 and the earlier extension of London Road in 1866. Victoria was enlarged on two occasions, in 1864 and 1884, while the L.N.W.R. removed its traffic to the adjacent station of Exchange. Additional space for goods stations and warehouses made the railway a potent force in the whole process of late nineteenth-century urban redevelopment. A final element in the picture is provided by the growth of the docks, through the opening of the Manchester Ship Canal in 1894. A large private dock railway developed along the canal between Manchester, Trafford Park and Irlam but links were quickly established with the main line companies at Irlam, Manchester Docks and Weaste: only short spurs were necessary however and the emergence of the docks as a major industrial area has not involved any major restructuring of the railway system.

Manchester therefore provides a good example of the way in which a simple system with a number of radial lines gradually develops a hub at the centre (avoiding the main built-up area) and then spawns an increasing number of radials, some of them to provide direct links with places that previously connected with main lines only through branches. Some additional links accommodated rival companies while others accelerated inter-city services. Manchester also shows the development of outer belt lines through the Fairfield–Chorlton, Stalybridge–Stockport and Godley–Stockport–Irlam lines. But while these lines had some suburban function it is noticeable that they all lie on the southern side of the city (where railway builders faced fewer physical constraints) and were primarily concerned with the efforts of three companies to extend their influence eastwards across Manchester and on to Liverpool. This grouping, reflected in the C.L.C., proved a stable set of interests, pitted against the L.N.W.R./L.Y.R. whose close association stopped only just short of outright amalgamation. Rather different was the shifting pattern of company alignments which produced the railway from Patricroft to Clifton Junction and then reduced it to obscurity very soon after it had opened. Finally there are short branches to connect with docks and major industrial installations.

These characteristics may be seen in other major cities. Perhaps the most famous monument to changes in company alignments is to be seen in Birmingham where the Duddeston Viaduct was built to provide a link between the Grand Junction and the Birmingham & Oxford. The projected Oxford line was sought in order to break the London & Birmingham's monopoly. Formation of the L.N.W.R. of course put paid to the idea and the viaduct was never used. The projected Oxford route opened in 1852 and ran into Snow Hill, while two years later the trains of both L.N.W.R. and Midland were using New Street. As happened in Manchester when the original termini were superseded, Curzon Street and Lawley Street became goods depots. Yet because relationships between the companies quickly stabilised into rivalry between the New Street and Snow Hill interests there was little need for the growth of any elaborate hub (merely a simple cross-roads with the two main lines driven straight through the heart of the city) let alone any growth of outer belt lines.

Glasgow shows further variations on some of these themes. Here there was brisk competition between the Caledonian and North British north of the Clyde and between the Caledonian and Glasgow & South Western south of the river. But the development of the hub came very slowly, mainly because of difficulties in bridging the Clyde. However, in 1875 the G.S.W.R. crossed the Clyde and linked with the North British at Springburn – and the following year it transferred its terminus from Bridge Street south of the Clyde to St Enoch. In 1879 the Caledonian Railway moved over the river to a new Central Station, but there was no link through the centre with its other terminus of Buchanan Street (used for services to the Highlands) because a south-north connection was provided through Coatbridge by the old Coltness Railway. Indeed, until the line was opened through Motherwell to Bridge Street all Caledonian trains were routed into Glasgow through Coatbridge. So by a historical accident the Glasgow area produced an outer belt railway from the earliest days of development. But more exciting developments were to follow because the rapid growth of Glasgow's docks and shipyards led to branch line building on a remarkable scale, especially on the northern side of the river. The North British line to Helensburgh (1858) was a springboard for a branch to Stobcross (1873), extended subsequently to Clydebank (1882). The Caledonian looped round the northern edge of Glasgow to get iron and steel from Lanarkshire into the Clydebank shipyards. But then the growth of settlement in the West End of Glasgow and a very large amount of commuting across Glasgow to Clydebank factories led to both companies taking their Clydebank lines straight through the heart of Glasgow to join up the other side with lines to Coatbridge and Airdrie. These steam operated lines were partially underground – hence the Low Level sections at two stations: Queen Street (1886) and Central (1896).

Following the experience with Hunt's Bank it is worth noting that at Ayr the extension of the railway southwards through the town led to a semi-circular path round the edge of the built-up area. The railway arrived at

7.  *Local services on Clydeside* A Glasgow–Gourock electric train leaves Greenock. The line was built by the Caledonian Railway and complemented the Glasgow & South Western Railway's service to Greenock (Princes Pier).

Newton on the northern side of the river but when the extension southwards was projected the new construction began well to the north of Newton and, according to W. Dodd, 'curved through fields well to the east of Newton and Ayr, crossing the river by a high viaduct but running in cuttings elsewhere so as not to interrupt the road pattern and possibly to screen views of the line from the estates of Blackhouse and Craigie'. Thus the railway reinforced the eastern limits of the favoured residential belt. A new station was built south of the river (on the edge of the commercial core) while the original station in Newton became a goods depot.

These further examples show that hub, radial and belt lines are found in the large cities. The radials tend to increase gradually in complexity but the evolution of the hub and belt elements is subject to great variation as the railway companies each perceived opportunities to exploit the potential, against a background of the local terrain. Suburban branches were built but elaborate schemes were comparatively rare and the companies were mainly interested in attracting suburban traffic to lines that were built primarily for other purposes. Special commuter belt lines did not emerge, not least because journeys would be indirect and subject to competition from the electric tramways which were a powerful force at the beginning of the twentieth century.

# 9

# Railway Architecture with particular reference to Stations

Once the era of inclined planes had passed the railways settled down to a long period of development with fairly standard engineering norms. The railway would naturally keep to the level of the surrounding land wherever possible, but on most lines the need to minimise distance and provide for high-speed running meant that embankments and cuttings would be quite readily accepted, with the two basic earthwork types being planned so as to balance out in terms of the volume of material involved: this avoided the problem of finding extra material or of dumping surplus. Frequently roads, tracks and streams would have to be crossed and here there was a simple carryover of canal practice with simple homely stone-arched bridges, sometimes giving way later in the century to girder bridges resting on stone or brick piers. Much the same applied to the longer bridges or viaducts where a series of arches would be placed side by side. Thus it has been argued that the greatest memorial to George Stephenson is to be found near Earlestown where the Liverpool & Manchester Railway crossed the Sankey Brook by a nine-arch viaduct, considered by N. Morgan to be 'a prototype for a form of structure which was to be repeated a thousand times over before the end of the century . . . and which remains as characteristic of the English landscape as do her church spires and last hedgerows'. An early copy of Earlestown came in 1842 with the twenty-two arches of Stockport Viaduct (0.5 km long and 33 m high) on the Manchester–Crewe line. Stephenson's merit lay not in the design of the bridge, which was well-established on canals and had also been used on waggonways as early as 1727 in the case of the Causey Arch, but in the adoption of a familiar style for main line railways.

As with the single arches there would be differences in style and in building materials with considerable use of brick and some recourse to concrete, as on the Lyme Regis branch in 1903. For the Mallaig Extension of the West Highland Railway there was neither brick nor stone available economically in the area and so the various bridges, including the curving viaduct of twenty-one arches (up to 27 m high) at Glenfinnan, were built in concrete – yet still perpetuating the traditional form of the Stephensons. Even the temporary timber bridges built by I. K. Brunel in Devon and Cornwall included traditional elements with fans of timber ribs springing from the masonry piers to support the deck. There were some great iron bridges like Thomas Kennard's 0.5 km Crumlin Viaduct (1857) where the line from Pontypool Road to Neath soars 63 m high across the Ebbw Vale valley using castings from Falkirk and wrought iron from Blaenavon. Sections of the viaduct were fabricated on site. The nature of the ground called for a lighter structure than masonry piers and arches, but iron was found to be cheaper in any case. With wrought iron now acceptable in bridge building equally lofty structures were built at Belah and Deepdale, designed by R. H. Bow for the Stockton & Darlington's line from Barnard Castle to Penrith. And early examples of iron decks resting on widely spaced stone piers appear at Conwy and Menai (1849) where 140 m tubes were used. Just as Stephenson built Conwy as a preliminary to Menai, so Brunel used the 91 m bridge at Chepstow as a preparation for the Royal Albert Bridge, Saltash (near Plymouth) in 1859, where 142 m tubes were needed. Brunel envisaged a timber bridge over the Tamar at Saltash but Admiralty insistence on a 30 m headroom for shipping meant that only iron would serve.

Equally distinctive is the High Level Bridge at Newcastle (1849) with its close succession of bowstring arches and Runcorn Bridge of 1863 where the

8. *Crossing the Tweed* The graceful columns of this stone-built viaduct still march across the Tweed, between Newtown St Boswells and Melrose, although the trains which once made for Earlston and Duns no longer run.

9.    *Conwy in North Wales* The railway bridge here was designed to harmonise with the adjacent castle and also to provide a testing ground for the tubular girders being considered for use on a grander scale on the Menai Strait.

wrought iron lattice girder spans are 92 m long. Suspension bridges were considered unsuitable after the Stockton & Darlington's bridge over the Tees to Middlesbrough had failed, while the cantilever structure posed problems in ensuring a solid base for each truss which must then be built up in a balanced fashion. However, the system was employed with distinction for the Forth Bridge of 1890, where cantilever spans of 517 m contribute to a total length of 2.3 km and make a formidable impact in terms of sheer power and strength which would be absent in a smaller scale version. The Forth Bridge incidentally represents the first large scale use of open hearth steel (until 1877 the Board of Trade would not consider proposals for railway bridges in steel under any circumstances and it is the only large bridge that can be used at speeds of 96.6 km or 60 miles per hour). However, these examples are a mere handful of special cases with particular problems (like clearances of shipping lanes) to be set against hundreds of more anonymous structures that can be seen up and down the country.

If the railway landscape did not contain great variety in terms of basic engineering this was amply compensated for in other ways. Locomotives and rolling stock (not given close attention in this book) were distinctively embellished in important details of style and colour (and even sound, if the tones of engine whistles are considered). Then come the various buildings ranging from humble mile posts, lamp stores, platelayers' huts and signal boxes through to large warehouses and workshops, where each company could project a particular architectural style. It is perhaps the railway station that provides the greatest scope for the enthusiast because it was through its passenger stations more than anything else that the railway projected itself to the public. The station had to be functional, providing basic facilities for booking tickets, partaking of refreshment and boarding trains, but the buildings had to inspire confidence and promote rail travel as a safe and pleasurable activity. Although the railway was considered by some people to

10. *The Forth Bridge* Although duplicated now by the Forth Road Bridge the cantilevered railway bridge of 1890 is still awe-inspiring, as viewed here from behind the commuter suburb of North Queensferry.

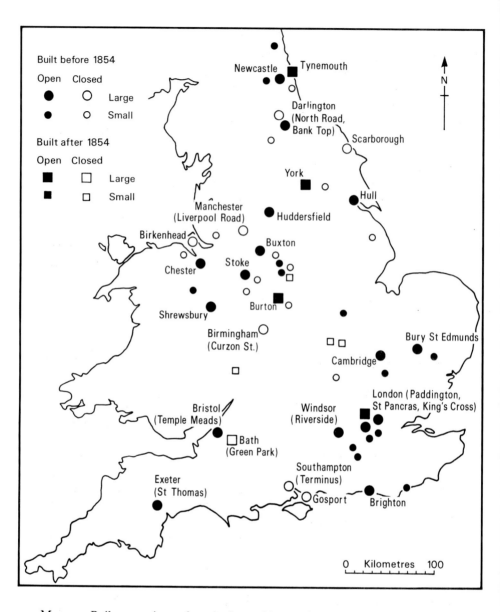

Map 7. Railway stations of particular architectural merit.
As listed in D. Lloyd 1967, Railway station architecture, *Industrial Archaeology 4*,
185–205.

be an unwarranted intrusion in the landscape it is arguable that for the majority it was merely one more change after the building of canals and enclosing of the fields. But sensitivity over aesthetic issues of design and appearance certainly helped to marshall support for the railway over and above the sheer social and economic implications. M. Robbins emphasises that the style of the railway companies was worthy of great public undertakings: 'The whole railway system was something more than a commercial transaction: it was a public improvement'. The change in attitude was swift during the 1830s. There was a tendency to use stagecoach methods at first and issue tickets from inns near stopping places on the railway: thus initially the Leicester & Swannington hired a room in the Ashby Road Hotel to serve as a station for Bardon Hill, while at Thornton it was the Stag & Castle Inn that provided facilities. But when the future of the passenger business seemed assured purpose-built stations were inevitable. The Liverpool & Manchester clearly expressed a sense of achievement in the matching sandstone buildings standing on either side of tracks at Edge Hill (Liverpool) while the classical conception of Liverpool Crown St was extended to the London & Birmingham and Temple Meads Station in Bristol with its fine hammer-beam roof is as impressive an equivalent in terminal buildings as Box Tunnel and Sonning Cutting are in respect of major engineering features. Temple Meads offered a mock-Elizabethan frontage which must have seemed appropriate in close proximity to St Mary Redcliffe and surviving merchants' houses. The Tudor Gothic character was strengthened in Matthew Wyatt's rebuilding of 1865–78, with the centrepiece tower added as recently as 1935.

So Brunel's work at Bristol introduces an important variation however. The classical approach was certainly in good standing since it had been revived a century earlier by Wren and firmly established in both its Greek and Roman forms. But there was an alternative view which held that the idealism of the Victorian age could be better expressed in Gothic forms, which involved a whole series of inspirations from Norman castles to Tudor and Jacobean mansions. And on the grounds of expense pure classical styles were quickly superseded, though not before a number of charming examples had been completed, including Lytham on the Preston & Wyre Railway (1846), Monkwearmouth (1848), where a fine classical terminus building with Ionic portico was unfortunately superseded by the extension of the railway into Sunderland, and Ashby de la Zouch in 1849. The Midland Railway had used the Leicester & Swannington Railway as a springboard for a new line to Burton upon Trent and Ashby was one of the places to benefit from the new scheme. A splendid classical station was built as the company's contribution to a plan to develop the town as a spa, drawing mineral water from the nearby coalfield at Swadlincote. The railway station fitted in very well with adjacent buildings including the

11.  *Ashby de la Zouch, Leicestershire* A fine example of classical architecture intended by the Midland Railway to be part of a complex of buildings which would help to promote the town as a fashionable watering place. Since closure the station has been converted for use as business premises.

Ivanhoe Baths and Royal Hotel. The station is now closed but has been restored for use as offices and a dwelling house, and despite invasion of surrounding land by modern housing development something of the original conception can still be seen in the juxtaposition of station and hotel.

But equally there was a fine display of Italianate architecture during the 1840s and 1850s and examples can be found in such places as Alton Towers (1849) on the North Staffordshire, Gobowen (1846) on the Shrewsbury & Chester and Kenilworth (1844) on Warwick & Leamington Union Railway. It is rather anomalous that the designer of Alton Towers, A. W. N. Pugin, was a great advocate of Gothic styles and had, moreover, recently completed the estate mansion nearby in this manner. But Tudor and Jacobean architecture soon found their way into the railway world. William Hurst's design for the terminus of Stamford East (1856) was a worthy replica of the

Elizabethan mansion house of Burghley. One of the greatest anomalies must be Maldon East in Essex where a Jacobean mansion was built at the end of a minor branch line. It is believed that railway construction workers were regarded by one of the local candidates in the 1846 election as an important nucleus of support and work was therefore found to keep them in the constituency until polling day. Jacobean styling was also used by H. A. Hunt at Stoke (1850) where the North Staffordshire integrated the station into an architectural complex for the whole of Winton Square: opposite the station lay the Stafford Hotel while the other two sides of the square were taken by matching groups of railway houses. Also noteworthy is the baroque of Newmarket (1848) for the branch from Great Chesterford, the monastic gothic used at Richmond in 1847, in deference to the castle, and at Shrewsbury where T. K. Penson's original design of 1848 was substantially rebuilt in 1903.

There are cases where whole sections of railway were endowed with beautiful stations designed as a set. David Mocatta provided stations for the London & Brighton line (1841) as did Sancton Wood and Frederick Barnes for the Ipswich & Bury Railway (1846). Francis Thompson on the North Midland produced a series of masterpieces for the North Midland in 1840 including Ambergate, Clay Cross and Chesterfield, while John William Livock produced a fine set of buildings for the London & North Western Railway's Blisworth–Peterborough line of 1845, all showing subtle variations on the theme of the Elizabethan manor house. Perhaps the finest examples are those at Oundle and Wansford where stone was used: Oundle station is boarded up but Wansford's façade now graces the operations of the Nene Valley Railway (although separate ownership means that station business is actually transacted in a wooden structure which has been brought to the site and stands opposite the native building). That this was possible is a measure of the prevailing view whereby platforms were laid along the outer edges of a twin-track railway, but where all the effort went into the buildings on the side with road access: the other side would often appear rather naked, perhaps with a humble shelter underlining its status as some distant outpost. In sharp contrast to this convention is the Great Central Railway's championing of the island platform, used throughout the London Extension. This raised problems of access, usually solved by taking steps down from the centre of a road bridge.

By the time the Great Central was approaching London railway companies were developing company styles which brought the ultimate in standardisation with the desire for economy carried further by adoption of some extremely utilitarian styles. The L.N.W.R. for example made use of wood and achieved a large-scale standardisation of components, while the substantial brick-built villas on the North Eastern reflected the norms of high-class Victorian suburban development. Efforts were still made in large towns where rebuilding carried an obligation to project the railway as a positive contributor to the general urban fabric: prominent examples are the Queen Anne frontage at Market Harborough, a joint effort by the L.N.W.R. and Midland in 1885 to provide facilities in keeping with the greatly enhanced importance of the town as a junction not only between the original Rugby–Peterborough line (1851) and the Midland's Hitchin (later London) line of 1857 but additionally with the L.N.W.R. line from Northampton which led on northwards as a joint line with the Great Northern, ending at Newark in contact with the latter's main line. A flyover at the northern approach to the town was another aspect of the expansion that took place. Nearby is Leicester London Road, rebuilt in 1892, with extensive squat arcades set off by a prominent hexagonal clock tower while the Norwich Thorpe rebuild of 1886 produced a most distinctive pavilion roof.

Where the major stations lost out in sensitive details they compensated, like the Forth Bridge, in their massive proportions. Much more attention was given to roofs. Canopies over individual platforms should not be despised, for the ridged glass greenhouse roofs on the Leicester–Bedford line of the Midland Railway 1857 were supported by elegant iron work with Kettering remaining as a superb example of C. H. Driver's design. But the

12.   *Oundle, Northamptonshire* Oundle Station, now standing derelict, was one of a set designed by William Livock in the Tudor style for the London & Birmingham Railway's Blisworth–Peterborough branch.

arched iron roof made a dramatic visual impact and indicated a big increase in scale over the distinctive wooden trainsheds that Brunel built for the Great Western. Some inspiration for the late Victorian roofs has been identified in contemporary estate building, like the Chatsworth greenhouse of 1836–40 and the Palm House of Kew (1848), while the idea was carried over into market halls and shopping arcades. The North Eastern Railway spawned quite a family of arched roofs beginning with John Dobson's classical masterpiece at Newcastle Central in 1850 and including the most distinguished example of York, where a new through station by Thomas Prosser (1877) replaced the old terminus of 1842. The magnificent Gothic façade of W. H. Barlow at London St Pancras provided access to a massive covered area with vast latticed arches erected in 1874, complemented by Manchester Central six years later. Cost factors eventually forced greater interest in simple awnings but while some roofs have been removed, as at Shrewsbury, or lost through closure, others can still be appreciated.

The decline in aesthetic standards was perhaps most marked in the rural areas. Here there had never been any concerted attempt to impress, rather to reassure through familiar and homely styles. But the various rural styles usually suited their localities well, especially through the use of local building materials, as with the gritty cottages of moorland country and the employment of flint in East Anglia. Somewhat more elaborate were the *cottage orné* styles, involving embellishment of basic cottages in sympathy with the Gothic inspiration: ornate chimneys and dormer windows or elaborate bargeboarding fitted to gable ends brought a clear resemblance to lodges and were particularly appropriate at places like Fenny Stratford, Woburn Sands and Ridgmont (1846), associated with the Bedford estate. Such features had previously been used by Francis Thompson in 1840 for the North Midland stations at Wingfield and Ambergate (now demolished) which J. F. Loudoun adapted as a basis for a pattern-book *cottage orné*. Much of the detailed layout would depend on whether the station master's house was incorporated in the platform complex or provided separately. As the chief of what might be a significant number of railway employees and as one of the leading professional people in the rural community the station master would be housed in suitable style. Alton Towers is dominated by the three-storey tower that forms the station master's house. On the Great Western too, Brunel departed from the usual practice by building detached houses and as a result the station master's accommodation greatly overshadowed the modest passenger facilities.

Apart from the basic tracked and associated engineering features the Victorian ethos of the railway is best preserved in the passenger stations – and even on lines where the wayside stations have been closed it is often possible to find enough of the old stations (sometimes converted into dwelling houses, offices or warehouses) to appreciate the diversity of railway

13.   *Portrush, Co Antrim* B. D. Wise's remarkable station, built in 1892 for the Belfast & Northern Counties Railway. The railway has now retreated from these stately buildings and freed them for tourist use.

architecture. Where the stations are still used for their original purpose British Rail often find themselves caught in a dilemma between a sense of tradition and an ideal for modern functional buildings that would put the railways on a par with the airports. Some complete rebuilding, as at London Euston (1968), has however been followed in an age of 'listed buildings' by imaginative attempts to reconcile the inherited façade with modern functional requirements.

# 10

# Railway Station Locations

In addition to the architectural aspects of railway stations there are basic geographical questions which may usefully be asked. How did the stations come to occupy their chosen sites, and related to this, what factors determined the number of stations which a particular town or city came to support? Answers may appear basically obvious. A station would gravitate towards the centre of a town to attract traffic. The number of stations would tend to be a function of the size of the city (for the larger cities would have terminal stations, arising from the difficulty of building through lines) and the number of companies serving it (because rival organisations would hardly sit comfortably in the same station). However, the element of truth in these generalisations does not remove the possibility of numerous interesting variations – and indeed of blatant anomalies.

As regards position in relation to the centre it is usual to find some displacement from a perfectly central position. In towns that were small before the railway arrived it would be satisfactory to plan the line so that it simply touched the edge of the built-up area. Over the years towns have grown, with particular emphasis on the railway site, so that this original geometrical relationship is not quite so obvious. But study of the town plan of Bury St Edmunds or Ludlow will bring it out. At Cambridge the situation is particularly curious because opposition to the railway in the early years led to the decision to site the station more than a kilometre beyond the edge of the town: over the years the city has grown towards the railway and modified the anomaly, though the distance between station and centre is still remarkable. Sometimes there would be compelling topographical reasons for a considerable distance between town and station. Where a railway followed the opposite side of a river from the town the station would have to be placed in a position convenient for bridging. At Oundle the station was placed well to the north of the town because the intervention of the river Nene reduced the choice effectively to one site where the railway crossed to the town side of the river and intersected one of the principal radial roads. The river meadows were not attractive for building and there has been no tendency for the town to grow nearer the railway since 1845 when J. W. Livock built his Elizabethan masterpiece. In other cases local politics kept the railway at arm's length, as in Norwich where the Great Eastern could advance no further than Thorpe because of local authority opposition, while shipping interests at Aberdovey pushed the Cambrian Railways back from the seafront and landowner influence kept the railway out of Otley town centre.

In large towns the railway could move in towards the core by running between two radial roads where land would be relatively cheap, but this strategy would involve expensive work where the two radials met: so bridging or tunnelling was often resorted to. The Caledonian Railway had to burrow through the chemical waste to extend the railway from St Rollox to a new terminus at Buchanan Street in 1849 while in 1892 a branch from the C.L.C. at Irlam was pushed from Lower Ince (reached in 1884) to Wigan Central along a viaduct which cleared both the river Douglas and several major roads. Yet there are many cases of railways cutting right through the heart of large towns. The connection between the Caledonian and G.N.o.S. in Aberdeen was pushed through the core of the city in the same way as the G.S.W.R.–N.B.R. link in Glasgow, although while the former scheme resulted in a new joint station the latter project did not disturb the pattern of separate terminal facilities. And the Great Central progressed through the East Midlands by burrowing beneath the centre of Nottingham, while driving along the Soar Valley in the heart of Leicester by means of a three-kilometre viaduct. The new railway had to go through these cities and a tangential course would have left it too far from the centre to compete with the Midland Railway which had arrived some sixty years before. So cases must be looked at individually and only in central London can the possibility of through lines be excluded. Here, a special commission in 1846 defined a central area that was to be out of bounds to surface railways. Some breaching of the designated area was allowed in the south (where the Waterloo Extension had been sanctioned in 1845) but the northern line (Edgware Road–Euston Road) remained firm. This is brought out by the alignment of stations from King's Cross (1852) to St Pancras (1868), Euston (1837), Marylebone (1899) and Paddington (1854). To the south, terminal stations proliferated because certain companies were anxious to serve both the East End and West End. This is seen most clearly on the South Eastern & Chatham, but other companies made *ad hoc* arrangements. The Great Western and the London & South Western would not cross the centre of London so they supported the underground schemes: the G.W.R. assisted in promotion of the Metropolitan in 1863 and the L.S.W.R. promoted its own tube railway, Waterloo & City, in 1898.

Finally there are two other factors that have exerted some influence. Callington Station was a long way from the town because the railway was built originally as a mineral line and the terminus was situated with the mining operations in mind rather than passenger handling. And then

Malmesbury Station is situated in an anomalous position, with the railway overshooting the town centre at the expense of considerable engineering works because the original plan was to continue the line to Stroud.

So the position of railway stations will depend on topographical considerations assessed in the context of the alternatives of terminal facilities or through running. The number of stations is also related to this basic question: each radial may support a terminal station or alternatively all may run to a common focus where a single joint station is possible. There is no doubt that where interconnections are possible local authorities have tended to press for single stations and discourage fragmentation. But this is hardly possible unless all the railways belong to the same company or unless all the companies involved are offering broadly complementary services with competition being locally absent. At Aberdeen the two companies involved, Caledonian and G.N.o.S., had clearly defined regional interests and there was no conflict involved in handing over traffic. Yet in Banff and Moray, where the G.N.o.S. was in contact with the Highland Railway, an element of competition led to separate stations in Buckie and Elgin. In Cambridge the one remote station attracted not only Great Eastern services but Great Northern, London & North Western and Midland as well, with the latter two companies running in from the west (from Bletchley and Kettering respectively) and sweeping round the edge of the city to gain access to the station on the eastern side. But the Great Eastern was the only company which actually ran through Cambridge. For the other companies Cambridge was the limit of their operations and cooperation over the station was easier to contemplate. Goods yards were separate, however. At Birmingham, where the Great Western interest was clearly in conflict with the L.N.W.R. and Midland companies, a joint station was not practical, although the separate facilities of Snow Hill and New Street were both well placed in the centre of the city. The local authority in Sheffield was anxious that a single station should be built in the 1890s but the difficult relations between the M.S.L.R. and Midland, as the former company followed the latter's example in building a London extension, effectively ruled this out.

On the other hand significant differences in levels would tend to rule out a single station: thus L.N.W.R. and Midland companies had separate stations in Thrapston although their respective lines (Blisworth–Peterborough and Kettering–Cambridge) were in no sense competitive. A possible option was to build a station on two levels where the lines crossed and this was done by the same two companies at Tamworth, although it resulted in a greater distance from the centre of the town. On the other hand in Wigan, where the complementary L.N.W.R. and L.Y.R. services crossed on different levels in the centre of the town, the resulting pairing of stations (North Western and Wallgate) combined convenience to townspeople with ease of interchange. But it has been shown that company relations were fluid. Thus while two

Isle of Wight companies initially used the same station at Newport a dispute in 1913 led to the Freshwater Company building its own station, leaving the I.o.W. Central Railway in sole occupation of the original building. By contrast amalgamation could produce rationalisation of station facilities with the creation of a new central station as at Harrogate and Sunderland. Dualism could arise where towns were served by short branches, giving rise to stations at both the junctions and the branch termini (Llandudno and Yeovil) and where harbour interests demanded a separate station (Dover, Fishguard and Stranraer). Southampton is an interesting case in this respect because the first station served both the town and the docks. But the expansion of the central area led to the designation of a former suburban station on the Dorchester line as Southampton Central in 1935. The original Terminus Station was retained for a time but has since been closed.

To conclude this section some examples will be mentioned to show the pattern of events at certain places in more detail. First, two towns where there was a remarkable degree of cooperation over station facilities: Carlisle and Shrewsbury. At Carlisle Citadel Station, a magnificent Gothic structure, albeit somewhat incongruous in the context of surrounding buildings, accommodated the trains of three Scottish companies (Caledonian, G.S.W.R. and North British) and four English (L.N.W.R., Maryport & Carlisle, Midland and North Eastern). The station opened in 1847, contemporaneous with the completion of the main lines from Glasgow and London over Beattock and Shap respectively. A good site was found that combined ease of preparation with proximity to the town centre. It was entirely logical that the Caledonian and L.N.W.R. would cooperate over a station since their lines made an end-on junction at Carlisle, but how did the other companies come to use the same nest? The North Eastern (originally Newcastle & Carlisle) and Maryport & Carlisle operated what were essentially feeder lines and there was no competition involved. Initially each company had its own station: London Road (1836) and Bog Street (1843) respectively. But after Citadel opened it was a logical development to concentrate services on the one site, although London Road, which the Maryport & Carlisle started using in 1849, after a few years at Crown Street (1844), was also convenient for access to the centre of the town. The transfer took place in 1852. What is a little harder to appreciate is the use of Citadel by the G.S.W.R. in 1850, the North British in 1861 and finally the Midland in 1876, for although each company served its own area their services operated between cities in which the established companies had an interest (Edinburgh, Glasgow and London). But locally, relations appear to have been good and the local authority attitude was conducive to the continuance of a joint approach, although each company maintained its own goods yard.

As with Carlisle, the first years of railway building at Shrewsbury scarcely involved the town but the railway age burst in during the late 1840s and the

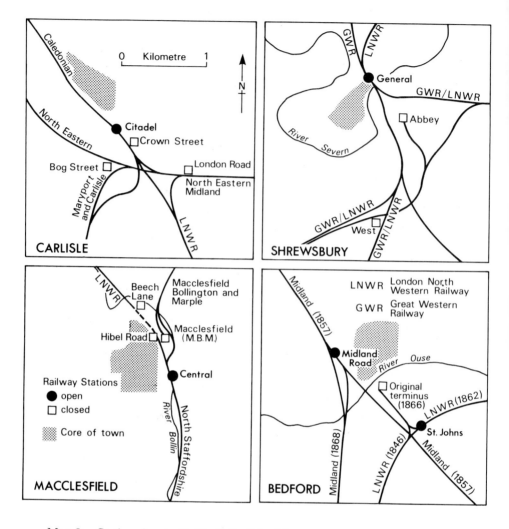

Map 8.   Station sites in Bedford, Carlisle, Macclesfield and Shrewsbury.

1860s. The Shrewsbury & Chester reached a temporary terminus north of the town in 1848. The following year saw the opening of a joint line to Wellington where the Shrewsbury & Birmingham and Shropshire Union (to Stafford) would separately take off. Naturally the two companies built a joint station which came to be shared with the S.C.R., and with the Shrewsbury & Hereford which completed its line to Ludlow in 1852 (and which ultimately led through to Newport). Subsequently further railways arrived from Crewe (1858), Welshpool (1862) and Worcester (1862). The company structure was simplified by amalgamations which reduced the joint interests of two (Great Western and L.N.W.R.) and made the use of shared facilities less remarkable. Of course, there was a clear division of regional interests which facilitated peaceful coexistence, while the difficulty of finding alternative station sites to serve a town centre enclosed within a river meander was also significant. The joint station was built across the neck of the meander and platforms eventually came to extend over the river. Happily the harmonious relations between the companies was expressed in noble architecture and T. K. Penson's Gothic masterpiece was attractively rebuilt in 1903: the station remains unchanged today apart from the removal of the all-over roof in favour of simple verandah coverings. However, there was one separate station in Shrewsbury. A project for a new main line to rival the Chester–Holyhead route was largely killed off by financial difficulties but it did lead to the opening of a branch line from Shrewsbury to Llanymynech in 1866, using a terminus station at Shrewsbury Abbey. The line was closed in 1880 but reopened as the Shropshire & Montgomeryshire between 1911 and 1933.

In contrast to the record of harmony just outlined, Bedford and Macclesfield show how strained relationships could increase the number of stations. In Bedford the first railway arrived in 1846 from Bletchley. Riverside Station was opened on the south side of the town. Connection with the town centre road system was rather difficult but the chosen site avoided the need for a bridge over the Ouse and also provided the Duke of Bedford with good prospects for the development of the surrounding land which he owned. But the continuation of the line to Cambridge in 1862 called for a new station in a suitable position on the through line. St John's Station, however, was even further from the centre than Riverside. But by this time the Midland Railway had arrived, for the Leicester–Hitchin line was ready in 1857 and this reduced the company's dependence on the L.N.W.R. which had previously taken over the Midland's London traffic at Rugby. The local authority was strongly in support of the idea of a joint station on the south bank of the Ouse but relations between the two companies were rather strained at the time and although the Hitchin line ran alongside Riverside and crossed the L.N.W.R. on the level (one of the very few instances where a railway crossroads situation exists) separate stations emerged. The Midland station was built on the northern side of the river. This has recently been replaced by a new station situated nearby on realigned tracks prepared to smooth the sharp curve which arose in 1868 when the St Pancras line was opened.

In Macclesfield the tradition of separate stations began early when the Manchester & Birmingham (later L.N.W.R.) and North Staffordshire arrived at Beech Lane (1845) and Hibel Road (1849) respectively. A link between the two companies made Hibel Road the main station for the town under an agreement in 1847 which the local authority had strongly encouraged. But the arrival of the Macclesfield, Bollington & Marple in 1869 created difficulty because although the line was complementary to the North Staffordshire it competed with the L.N.W.R. for Manchester traffic. So while the alignment of the new railway would have made a junction at Hibel Road quite feasible, the conflict between the M.B.M. and the L.N.W.R. led to a separate station adjacent. However, the North Staffordshire was anxious to make a connection and after considerable clearance of property a junction was made south of Hibel Road where a new Central Station opened in 1873. In all these examples the relations between the companies involved has been regarded as a key factor but an essential context is provided by the urban geography at the time the railways were built and the policies of the local authorities. Railway company perceptions of the scope for attractive alternative sites would be geared to such considerations and the elucidation of these circumstances in other towns could provide a useful practical exercise in local history.

# 2

# The Significance of the Railways for Economic and Social Development

# 11

# Some General Perspectives

The economic effects of the railway were not felt immediately, apart from direct effects of construction expressed in the demand for finance, labour and materials. The railways placed a great strain on the capital market and stimulated the rise of a new class of pure investor who looked for best return available on his money. Huge numbers of people were employed at the height of the mania – perhaps as many as a quarter of a million – while the demand for iron, bricks and other commodities was very great. But it soon became clear that the railway offered a more efficient means whereby an industrialist was placed in contact with his suppliers and his markets. However, it could not create potential where it did not exist. A classic case of regional industrial change concerns the rise of woollen textiles in Yorkshire and a corresponding decline in Norfolk. The delay in railway development in Norwich was certainly an issue in this competitive situation, just as the relatively poor river navigations of West Yorkshire had been an impediment in the north before the canal age gave reliable access to east and west coast ports. But the key factor in the nineteenth century was ease of access to coal (for the application of steam power). And also the relatively easy perfection of machinery for the coarser cloths, which meant a closing of the quality gap with the hand-woven Norwich products and an inevitable decline in demand and profitability that led to a change to new industries like footwear, where traditional skills could be used. The belated arrival of the railway in Norwich cheapened the price of coal and allowed the persistence of a shrunken textile industry 'when otherwise it would have been priced out of the market'. But the principal handicaps could not be offset and the cost advantage of the Yorkshire industry remained. Indeed, in general, railway services enabled the best-placed producers to invade the market areas of firms which had previously enjoyed some immunity from competition because of high transport costs. Industries now threatened in this way could either contract or find ways of improving their performance. It has been pointed out that the railways could have had disastrous consequences for the Scottish iron industry, due to the inevitable growth of competition from English and Welsh producers, had it not been for the application of the hot blast technique which cut costs so dramatically that it was the Scottish ironmasters who were able to benefit from the improvements in transport.

Market towns as well as industrial centres gained considerable nourishment from the railway. Marketing would be improved by the railway service and intensification of local road carrier services would extend the hinterland and increase the intensity of intercourse between town and country. Towns in agricultural regions became important depots for handling artificial fertilisers brought in by rail and distributed by road, while marketing of grain made the urban railheads logical centres for development of malting and flour-milling. The stronger link with the rural areas would then justify expansion of output by agricultural engineers, some of whom would find nationwide markets for particular types of machinery. The firm of Gardeners at Banbury, famous for their turnip cutters in the 1830s, gained a high reputation at a critical time. The company grew into the Britannia Iron Works and became a leading enterprise in the town. But it is also evident that, especially in Midland England, main lines passing by small towns created a powerful stimulus for industrial development in terms of relocation on spacious line-side sites of firms from congested city centres in London or Sheffield. Such sites would be relatively cheap yet have a physical connection with the railway through private sidings and could thus profit greatly from a location in the geographical heart of the country. Rugby attracted the Portland Cement Company in 1851 but engineering arrived with English Electric in 1897 and British Thompson Houston in 1900.

Indeed, it is an intriguing question how far railway promoters anticipated the selective development of towns as a result of the railways. The impression from the literature is that there was considerable uncertainty. While the railway was expected to stimulate trade and bring smaller places within range of services provided by the larger ones there was misplaced hope that this would boost the potential of the outlying centres which now lost the protection which distance from the cities had previously afforded them. Thus the Dublin & Drogheda Railway was actively promoted by Thomas Brodigan of Piltown who was anxious to find a solution to the unemployment that had resulted from the collapse of the cotton industry in Balbriggan and Drogheda. A coastal route was challenged by another group of promoters who preferred an inland route that would expedite the flow of cattle through Dublin. The result was a confrontation between town and country interests with the former anxious to boost the flagging fortunes of Drogheda while the latter sought more efficient agricultural marketing through the primate city. Yet either route would in fact extend Dublin's hinterland and ultimately destroy the independence of smaller towns. Promoters could not fail but think of this local line in the context of possible inter-city connections: the big question was whether the Dublin–Belfast line should go through Drogheda and Dundalk or further inland through Navan and Armagh.

However, the physical impact of the railway was often modest in small towns. It was usually acceptable for the railway to pass through by merely touching the town at its edge (the tangent principle). Certainly the town might grow in the direction of the railway and eventually engulf the station in urban spread. Rugby grew eastwards towards the London & Birmingham Railway and Albert Street was laid out in 1851 to connect the station with the centre. The town centre would thus retain its traditional character though the morphology of the new development might well be strongly influenced by the railway through streets being laid out in grid-iron fashion from a railway base line. In addition there might be considerable displacement of the railway station from the point closest to the town centre on account of physical obstacles. These could consist of railway engineering works (tunnels, embankments, cuttings or viaducts) or they might arise from unsatisfactory road links, as at Porthmadog, or because of a river barrier, as at Oundle. At Cambridge, however, political considerations forced the railway to pass a whole kilometre beyond the edge of the built-up area. But the town was able to grow towards the station and eventually engulf it in urban development. Unlike the situation at Fenny Stratford where the London & Birmingham Railway passed 1.5 km to the west: the new town of Bletchley grew up around the station, engineers' yard and permanent way depot and remained quite separate from the old coaching settlement. There are also cases where railways were built into town centres to form branch line terminals, as at Ayr and Helensburgh, but when extension was contemplated the new line took off short of the terminus and followed the edge of the built-up area rather than push on straight through the centre. Finally there is the not infrequent occurrence of the double tangent, sometimes affecting opposite sides of a town, as at Leicester, but sometimes coming close enough for the tangents to cross each other, usually on different levels, as at Rugby, Tamworth, Thrapston and Welling-borough. Usually the stations on each tangent are sited for best access to the town centre but at Tamworth the station is displaced to the crossing point where it is developed at two levels.

For the larger cities the railways were much more potent in influencing patterns of development. In his *Curiosities of London Life* C. M. Smith wrote of 'the deep gorge of a railway cutting which has ploughed its way right through the centre of the market gardens and, burrowing beneath the carriage road and knocking a thousand houses out of its path, pursues its circuitous route to the city'. Certain railways might pass through a city centre by tunnelling beneath it, like the Great Central at Nottingham, with the result that a 'window' for the station would be the only pressure exerted on the central area. There might be some exemplification of the tangent principle, as at Hunt's Bank in Manchester where a connecting link between the Liverpool and Leeds lines followed the edge of the city core. Victoria

Station was opened on a route which moderated damage to the city while meeting engineering requirements and simplifying land acquisition (from the two substantial proprietors, the Earl of Derby and Lord Ducie). But the railway presence was not always so subtle. Rival companies manoeuvred for the best sites, naturally taking a strategic view and safeguarding their business interests by whatever means were needed. And with privileges of corporate form and power to acquire property by compulsory purchase the railway companies would drastically alter the cores of cities, especially when allied with contractors with vested interests in redevelopment and opposed only by the 'friendly neutrality' of local authorities who were generally powerless to exert strong checks on the railway companies before the 1860s.

It is difficult to resist the view that the negative aspects of competing railway services was most clearly seen in the cities. Cities needed the railway in order to expand and to work efficiently: the railway provided transport and also acted as an agency for the remodelling of city centres to accommodate a growth of commercial activity. Yet excessive duplication of facilities could break up areas that became criss-crossed with railways while expensive developments would be reflected in poorer services, higher fares or lower dividends. Not that the railways can be entirely blamed for this situation. The limited powers of local authorities in the mid-Victorian period meant that sanitary problems (which were a local authority responsibility) were dealt with by slum clearance, with the railway as an effective agent, while the corollary of rehousing for low status families was not properly recognised because housing was largely a private sector responsibility. And private landowners tended to press railway development towards areas of low status housing by being particularly apprehensive over adverse effects to highly rated property. It is worth noting that the Great Central's first attempt to gain parliamentary approval for its London terminus was successfully opposed on the grounds of damage to property and a modified bill involved compliance with important restrictions including tunnelling and walling to conceal the railway, appropriate architectural standards for buildings, avoidance of fashionable suburbs (Marylebone and St John's Wood) and allowance for housing projects to accommodate displaced working-class families.

More generally the central business areas were expanding anyway. The growth of retailing and warehousing merely accelerated through the railway. But 'it is noticeable that districts divided and confined by the railways tended to be cast finally and irretrievably into the now familiar mould of coal and timber yards, warehousing, mixed light and heavy industrial users and fourth-rate residential housing'. Some businesses needed a physical contact with the railway through private sidings, but most required close proximity to stations and goods yards. Such concentration was logical, but it brought social problems. The great demand for casual

14. *The Great Central in Leicester* The Midland and Great Central Railways touched the city centre on the eastern and western sides respectively. But the G.C.R. had the more difficult task for it cut through a suburban district and both embankments and girder bridges were required to maintain the level above the Soar Valley.

labour led to a large resident population, yet one which had to put up with the nuisances of housing areas being physically broken up by railways and subjected to greater noise and pollution through the road and rail traffic. People also found themselves forced to live at higher densities through the loss of property to make way for railway lines, along with their stations and warehouses. Railways took up between five and ten percent of land in the central cores of cities – with still greater demands in some peripheral areas where cut-off lines were built and marshalling yards or carriage sheds built.

The threat to the cities was not immediately evident, for railway companies had limited capital resources and were anxious to complete inter-city lines as quickly as possible to start earning profits. But with the growth of traffic better terminals were needed, while working agreements and outright amalgamations raised the question of through lines. By the 1860s there were strong pressures to improve capacity at city stations and to attract further business by locating stations in the most convenient situations. Hence the rush to provide better city stations and for the railway companies 'their principal fear in the 1860s was that of being left out in the cold with inferior access and facilities at the great cities where the busiest lines terminated'. Of course, conditions varied from one city to another. While Birmingham experienced a balance of genuine competition, Manchester was the victim of extreme rivalry between companies involved in shifting alliances and sometimes building stations through tactical necessity. London was protected by a designated central area into which entry could only be gained with difficulty. Railways came over the river from the south from London Bridge (1836), Nine Elms (1838) and Waterloo (1848) to Cannon Street (1866), Charing Cross (1864), Holborn Viaduct (1874) and Blackfriars (1886), while to the north the Great Eastern advanced marginally from Bishopsgate (1841) to Liverpool Street (1874). In Glasgow, too, the provision of large central stations was long delayed, though not because of any prohibition. Although a Royal Commission in 1846 considered central stations undesirable there was no attempt made to exclude the railway and technically satisfactory projects failed largely because of the tactics of opposing railway interests. Eventually the pressures were eased by the Union project of the 1860s which led to the construction of St Enoch Station and the provision of goods yards at College (the original university site, vacated through relocation to Gilmorehill). Indeed until this project was completed, and Central Station opened nearby, Glasgow was poorly served by its railway companies.

# 12

# The Railways and Suburban Development

The railways did not initiate the development of suburbs. In Birmingham for example, Small Heath and Sparkbrook were established before the railway arrived. But there was a growth of interest in the suburban habit as railways provided services for those not affluent enough to have their private means of transport. Railways also assisted in change because they made heavy demands on space in city centres and forced thousands of people to find other accommodation: this created heavy pressure on surrounding areas which was relieved by an outwards movement in response to the 'knock-on' effect. Yet it would be wrong to suppose that there was any immediate or massive explosion – many people depended on casual employment and, quite apart from their lack of financial means to cover the cost of commuting, had to stay close to their work to take advantage of opportunities. It was the richer people who tended to move out to enjoy the better amenities – while the railwaymen with their free passes could also assume greater travel commitments. Developers in central London who provided high-class residences, for example in Bloomsbury on the Duke of Bedford's estate, certainly found difficulty attracting interest as affluent families chose to live in the suburbs. Nevertheless the railways did not affect the trend very greatly and they cannot be held wholly responsible for the miscalculation. Suburban railway services were quite modest until the 1860s.

Suburbs clustered round pre-existing villages and small towns where a nucleus of skills and services already existed. The picture of London for the 1860s and 1870s is of villages with railways rather than railway suburbs. There was growth in Croydon, Epsom, Kingston and Richmond quite independent of the provision of railway facilities to Central London. There was also the multiplier effect which boosted the impact of a small number of commuters: well-to-do families (first-class travellers up to 1860s and middle-class during the 1870s and 1880s) would have a retinue of servants who would not be regular travellers. Railways were seldom disposed to provide services to lead demand since peak hour running at concession fares was unprofitable and managers were determined not to squeeze out the more profitable trains. Trams were normally much better at running pioneer routes in anticipation of demand, due to their free wayleaves and inexpensive equipment. Yet even so the hazardous nature of transport-led suburban growth can be seen in the chequered history of the tramway project for Howth Hill on the northern side of Dublin Bay. A branch railway reached the old packet station (eclipsed by Kingstown in 1834) in 1847 and although the steamers never returned the line served a growing number of commuters later in the century. However, excessively optimistic expectations of housing developments over Howth Hill, on the road to Sutton, led to a tramway project, first proposed in 1883 but only given parliamentary sanction in 1897 and eventually opened in 1901. The modest growth of population meant only a slight growth of traffic since the richer families were now becoming car owners. Certainly there was considerable affection for the line among those Dubliners who flocked to Howth during fine weekends, but nevertheless a highly variable tourist trade could not make the line profitable and closure occurred in 1959.

Eventually parliamentary pressure induced the companies to introduce workman fares to help reduce the travel expenses of less affluent commuters. Hence the Cheap Trains Act of 1883. Although the aim was to assist those with the more poorly paid jobs it was impossible in practice to distinguish between different groups of workers and in practice the concession was available to all rush-hour travellers. In this way the railway certainly provided a social service with cheaper fares in circumstances where economic forces would normally call for higher charges – for catering for peak-hour travellers is extremely costly, introducing a capacity in terms of locomotives and rolling stock, track and station facilities which cannot be used for the rest of the day. This is to say nothing of the investment costs and rating burdens involved in building new lines for commuter services. The subsidy on travel meant that wages for commuters could be kept down, or alternatively higher rents could be charged for accommodation. Of course, neither implication was helpful to railway companies (unless they were directly involved in the suburban housing market) but such considerations did allow the suburban working class colony to become a feasible proposition provided that the right location could be found. For the prospective commuter a long journey would be too expensive, while landowners liked to keep attractive sites reserved for middle-class housing: only on ground with relatively few scenic amenities would any development be better than none. Hackney and Walthamstow acquired a working-class character and the rapid growth of these areas in north-east London was certainly assisted by the low fares offered by the Great Eastern Railway. Construction of cheap housing was also encouraged by the growth of industry in the Lea Valley.

This reminds us that industry was also on the move and that the dispersal of industry was an important factor in the growth of interest in suburban housing. In the cities whole suburbs tended to develop on the basis of industry with associated housing. In Manchester, Gorton and Longsight became in effect railway suburbs for there were locomotive depots for the L.N.W.R. and M.S.L.R., not to mention carriage sidings, freight yards and railway workshops (including works for the private locomotive builder, Beyer Peacock). 'This represented a concentration of railway plant, by the companies and manufacturers together, that was unique in England.' Housing in these areas would tend to assume a working-class character because the industrial environment would repel high status families. However, the railway did allow the possibility of a greater separation between work and home. This can be seen in the South Wales coalfield where exhaustion of reserves in one area was balanced by development on virgin sites further away: the decline of mining and associated industry on the exposed coalfield at the Heads of the Valleys was complemented by a southward spread of mining. People living on the exposed coalfield were able to commute to their new places of work using workmen's trains,

15. *Leicester's London Road Station* The fact that the Midland Railway approached Leicester from the north almost at ground level made it easy for industries occupying lineside sites to install private sidings.

provided under the Cheap Trains Act of 1883, or laid on under contract between employers and the railway company. Industrial change was therefore reconciled to a considerable extent with community stability.

The lineside sites developed by industry were not selected at random. In areas of high-class residential development land would be expensive, even if available at all, while the existence of cuttings or embankments would tend to repel businesses that required private sidings. For although many types of industry required only reasonable proximity to stations and goods yards, firms engaged in heavy industry usually required their own physical link with the railway system so that wagons could be loaded or discharged within the factory. In Leicester the Soar Valley emerged as a prominent industrial zone after improvement of the river for navigation and the building of canals in the area. This north-south industrial axis was consolidated by the unsuitability of the damp valley bottom lands for high-status housing, despite close proximity to the city centre. But the Great Central Railway thrust itself along this corridor, passed by means of embankments and viaducts that prevented any physical connection with lineside industry, while the lateness of the scheme meant that throughout the late nineteenth century heavy engineering firms desiring private sidings were obliged to locate in the north-east of the city where suitable land was available beside the Midland Railway. A similar trend can be seen in smaller Midland towns which benefited from the boom in engineering at the turn of the century. Where the railways steered well clear of town centres, as at Loughborough, Rugby and Stafford there were few impediments to the acquisition of spacious lineside sites. Further locational change in Leicester engineering followed the arrival of the Great Northern Railway at Humberstone and Belgrave Road in 1883. Although the boom in light engineering in the gas engine era at the turn of the century relaxed the necessity for private sidings and loosened the linkage with railways, the availability of cheap land along the Evington Valley, conveniently situated for both the Midland and Great Northern stations, extended the ecological contrasts within the city.

On the other hand in Birmingham a close correspondence between canal and railway routes emerged at an early stage and so locations were chosen where both services were available in close proximity. This meant an extension of the location patterns which had emerged during the canal era, up to 1850. Growth occurred along the L.N.W.R. in Ladywood and Winson Green, especially where the canal lay close by, and over the years the whole Birmingham–Wolverhampton axis with its rival railway lines (Great Western as well as L.N.W.R.) became a mixed residential-industrial zone. To the north-east of Birmingham (Aston and Witton) industry had grown up along the Fazeley Canal where the flat land of the Tame Valley provided good sites for factories. This growth continued in the railway age, taking up the land between the canal and the L.N.W.R.: a major metal plant appeared as well as a cartridge factory and the G.E.C. electrical works. The industrial zone extended along the eastern flank of the city through a railway knot at Washwood Heath and Saltley (where gas works and railway carriage works were prominent) to Adderley Park where the Wolseley car factory opened in 1895. In the south-east the Warwick Canal attracted industry, including a gun factory at Small Heath, but by the end of the century the factories of the Birmingham Small Arms Company lay in the middle of an industrial belt from Bordesley to Tyseley, endowed with rail as well as canal services. At Tyseley the transformation was astonishing. The railway itself spawned a locomotive depot and freight yards, but the factories followed and in turn came the housing, with associated shops, schools, chapels and institutes so that a rural district quickly became part of a crowded city.

However, to the south-west of Birmingham as far as Selly Oak the parallel canal and railway lines failed to attract industry, for here in Edgbaston the landowners kept a strict control over the use of land and the area acquired the cachet of a select residential district, as did Harborne and Moseley. Of course, in Birmingham the canal network was so extensive that it was almost inevitable that the close association of rail and canal would emerge, while the importance of the canal for industry in the railway age was particularly marked in the Black Country since a whole industrial system had relied on it for the supply of coal. For coal-mining companies on Cannock Chase, where new shafts were being sunk in the railway age, canal access was considered essential because of the importance of marketing to canalside factories. Canal extensions were built until the mid-nineteenth century in this area and subsequently colliery development in northern parts of Cannock Chase was linked by the Littleworth and other private railways with the Cannock Extension Canal at Old Hednesford. Certainly the railway companies provided connections as well but the canal was the key until the turn of the century when road transport, plus the decline of the iron industry and conversion of many canalside factories to the use of oil or electricity, undermined the waterway system.

# 13

# The Railway Town

Although railway workers were to be found in all towns and cities, due to the need for station staff, goods clerks, platelayers, signalmen and footplate men, it was perhaps in the towns with locomotive building and repairing facilities that identification with the railway was most noticeable. Until about 1840 private engineering firms tended to supply the needs of the railway companies for locomotives and rolling stock. Businesses which had previously built stage coaches were able to switch to railway passenger carriages, a fact which helps to account for the close resemblance between the early railway carriage and the road vehicles which they superseded. But the rapid growth in demand during the mania years obliged the larger railway companies to provide their own capacities by building new workshops or by adapting accommodation already used for repairs. This was quite a remarkable development, for the one-man business or small partnership was regarded as the normal type of industrial organisation. But the railways were great innovators in the organisation of large efficient businesses and progressive managers thought it eminently logical to do as many jobs for themselves as possible. The ultimate was reached in the late nineteenth century when the major companies not only provided their own locomotives but produced all the component parts as well. Such an industrial complex was created by F. W. Webb who was Chief Mechanical Engineer of the L.N.W.R. between 1871 and 1903 and built up Crewe Works (first opened for repairs in 1843 and for locomotive building in 1845) into a mammoth industrial enterprise during his long and distinguished term of office. This meant not only the installation of furnaces for the production of steel but the growth of a host of ancillary industries: during the 1870s signals were made at Crewe and factories opened for production of leather, soap and bricks, not to mention footwarmers for winter railway travel and artificial limbs for men injured in the company's service.

Swindon tells the same story. The Great Western Railway settled on Swindon since it was an intermediate station and junction on the line to Bristol. The directors decided in 1841 'to provide an engine establishment at Swindon, commensurate with the wants of the company, where a change of engines may be advantageously made and trains stopped for the purposes of passengers taking refreshment'. A locomotive shed opened in 1841 followed by repair shops in 1843, locomotive building in 1846 and carriage building in 1852. But the Swindon complex became increasingly important as the company expanded territorially: the locomotive building at Newton Abbot, Saltney (Chester) and Worcester was transferred to Swindon later in the nineteenth century while Caerphilly, Oswestry and Wolverhampton followed after the 1923 grouping. In 1869, further growth arose because of the concentration of coach building in Swindon. This represented a transfer from London, where there was insufficient space to enlarge the small works at Paddington, and also a rebuff from Oxford where relocation was first proposed. Swindon produced its own steel plate while at the lighter end of the scale came the central laundry and depots for clothing and kitchen equipment. The Great Western complex at Swindon became even more comprehensive than the L.N.W.R.'s at Crewe, for the amalgamations which gave rise to the latter company yielded rival installations at both Crewe (Grand Junction) and Wolverton (London and Birmingham). Wolverton emerged like Swindon as a central depot with refreshment facilities, coking plant (engines were initially not allowed to burn coal) and locomotive workshops. The latter were transferred to Crewe between 1865 and 1877 but compensation was found in carriage building for the new company.

Although the Great Eastern retained its works in London, using cheap land in the Lea Valley at Stratford, movement out of the city was a commonplace. The South Eastern gave up their shared facilities at New Cross (with the London & Brighton) in 1845 and moved to Ashford. There was some expansion there in 1901 when the working agreement between the S.E.R. and the London Chatham & Dover led to a closure of Battersea Works. The London & Brighton began the move from New Cross to Brighton in 1848, while in 1909 the L.S.W.R. carried out a relocation from London to Bishopstoke Junction near Southampton (where the Fareham and Southampton lines diverged) and the Eastleigh complex was planned as an integrated unit. As with the move by the Lancashire & Yorkshire from Newton Heath (Manchester) to Horwich in 1884 the relocation was necessitated by the need for a more spacious site and pressure from other railway uses (such as goods yards) for the land occupied by the original works. In this respect the railway company was a manufacturing industry and therefore conformed to prevailing trends over dispersal from city centre locations. The new railway settlements attracted migrants from far afield, especially from northern industrial regions. B. J. Turton has examined birthplace statistics from the 1851 census for the southern railway towns Ashford, Swindon and Wolverton. He found that on average 144 people per thousand of the population came from London (and Berkshire, Hertfordshire, Middlesex and Surrey) compared with 313 for the northern regions (57 from Staffordshire, Warwickshire and Worcestershire; 101 from

Cheshire, Lancashire and Yorkshire; 79 from Northumberland and Durham; 77 from Scotland).

This activity meant that in some towns the railway company assumed considerable responsibility for the provision of housing and for administration of the town. In Crewe the L.N.W.R. built houses in the centre in the 1840s, leaving only enough space for a Market Place. But after two decades of growth the property came to occupy sites of commercial value and so the 1870s witnessed a process of demolition, with redevelopment for shops and offices. The company also assumed responsibility for the provision of services like roads and sewage while generous contributions were made towards the erection of churches and schools. A second matter of concern was industrial diversification to provide more employment for women. In 1869 what amounts to an 'advance factory' was built at Crewe in the hope of attracting a new industry: a fustian cutter quickly took up residence. The initiative was taken by John Rigg, assistant locomotive superintendent. He was involved in another experiment – the Crewe Cheese Manufacturing Society – although this venture did not succeed. Crewe did however attract ready-made clothing industries. John Rylands set up in 1872 and Coop & Co. arrived shortly after 1887. Then C. H. Holmes came from Congleton to set up a tailoring business in 1891: a small clothing factory opened three years later. In 1896 a branch factory opened in Crewe from the Nantwich clothing firm of John Harding. A number of other businesses including shirt manufacturers opened at the beginning of the twentieth century.

But on the whole the problem of diversification was not properly grasped at Crewe before the First World War, yet it affected not only female employment but also the mechanics who were trained in larger numbers than the works could absorb. The company was concerned, but not sympathetic to industrialists when it came to allowing preferential rates for the transport of their manufactures and raw materials. Swindon is similar as regards railway company involvement in its amenities and facilities. A cluster of cottages formed a small railway town near the station and the company provided services including a private health service in 1847: the Medical Fund Society eventually became extremely comprehensive and included hospital facilities at Swindon in 1872. But at Swindon there was also considerable dependence on private companies already established in the town. Thus the Castle Foundry of 1855 produced bridges and railings for the Great Western Railway as well as milk churns and dairy appliances for the surrounding area. A brick works opened in 1871 supplied railway needs as did two clothing works which opened in 1876 and 1899. A raincoat manufacturer started business in 1912 and a tobacco factory opened in 1915.

Yet not all companies finished up with workshops in small towns at convenient points on their respective railway system. The opposite extreme is reached where a complex of railway engineering works appears in the same quarter of a city. The Springburn area of Glasgow provides a good example. The Glasgow & Garnkirk Railway ran to the northern end of the city (St Rollox) where workshops were provided. Subsequently the railway became part of the Caledonian system and the terminus was advanced to Buchanan Street, closer to the centre of Glasgow. But the workshops were retained and substantially enlarged to serve the larger company. By coincidence the Edinburgh & Glasgow Railway entered the city in the same area: a motive power depot (Eastfield) and locomotive works (Cowlairs) were built where the line began to descend down a steep bank to the Queen Street terminus. Once again the importance of the works was increased by amalgamation and Cowlairs (named after a mansion house whose grounds adjoined the railway property) became the main locomotive building plant for the North British Railway. Finally, W. M. Neilson gave up marine and general engineering in favour of railway locomotive building during the 1850s and then moved his works from a cramped site at Stobcross to a more spacious site in Springburn where the Hyde Park Works opened in 1861. Glasgow was an attractive location for locomotive building, with iron manufactured nearby in North Lanarkshire and a tradition in engineering to generate skilled labour. But concentration in one small part of the city is unusual. Only St Rollox remains at work today but the district retains some distinction because the postwar closure of the other two works freed large areas of land, with railway access, and helped to make Springburn an inner city area where urban renewal has been closely bound up with light industry.

Intermediate between these extremes come established towns like Darlington and Derby. Darlington emerged quite late as an important railway town. Despite its association with the Stockton & Darlington Railway, it was only in 1861 that the S.D.R. established their principal workshops in Darlington (previously all building was done at Shildon). Two years later Darlington's horizons broadened through the amalgamation of the S.D.R. with the North Eastern and greater role was assumed, especially after the closure of the works at York in 1906 and the transfer of staff to Darlington: by this time the works was the largest industrial unit in the town. At Derby on the other hand the railway works was established relatively early. In 1840 Derby was not just a fashionable centre for the county and an important focus of coach services but an industrial town as well, with factories associated with a mix of manufactures, predominantly textiles (silk and lace). At the end of the year the railway had made a dramatic appearance with three different companies established. Connections with the London & Birmingham Railway were available through both Hampton (near Birmingham) and Rugby while services operated northwards to Leeds. The three companies amalgamated in 1844 to form the Midland Railway and the network developed to the point where the company had its own rails between London and the Scottish border and a strategic position on the line from North East England to the West Country. It was logical enough that the company's workshops would be placed at the intersection of these arms, but why Derby? No other town better symbolised the union of three small companies since each had established a locomotive depot there prior to the amalgamation. But this factor would hardly have been crucial: more relevant was the proximity of Derby to centres of iron production (foundries already existed in the town) and lack of strong competition for male labour. Moreover, there was ample land for development: railways from the south met on the edge of the floodplain of the Derwent and with some attention to drainage this provided an adequate site for both the station and the workshops. Perception of these siting factors and the leading role that railway workshops could play in the industrial development of Derby helped to create a political outlook favourable to the Midland Railway: certainly more so than in Leicester and Nottingham.

There was a sharp increase in population in Derby as employment rose and people came in from other regions of the country, particularly from Yorkshire and the North East. Housing provided between the works and the

16.    *Derby Locomotive Works*, showing a High Speed Train (Inter City 125) under repair.

town centre created a continuous built-up area with the railway forming the eastern limit. A fairly distinct railway quarter emerged where the Midland Railway was much involved in community development: St Andrew's Church was essentially a railway church since company shareholders contributed generously to its building. The railway company established an orphanage in Derby and provided both a sports club and a cultural complex (with library, reading room and lecture hall) known as the Midland Institute. The expansion of housing stimulated the building and timber trades, while the railway gave a boost to local industry. There was an expansion of the iron foundries, like Canal Street Ironworks (1846) which made wheels for carriages and wagons, while additional female labour enabled the silk mills to expand. New industry was attracted by Derby's accessibility and by the availability of drained flood-plain land for industrial building. Derby therefore shared in a rapid growth of this industry which occurred in the Midlands in the late nineteenth century and helped to diversify the town's economy away from an unduly heavy dependence on railway employment. Rolls Royce was perhaps the most prestigious of these incoming firms. Derby remains a railway town today, for the works have survived two waves of rationalisation, under the L.M.S.R. and later under nationalisation, to emerge not only as a major centre for repairs but also as a research and design centre.

14

# The Impact of Railways on Canals

It is frequently assumed that railways killed off the canals and that because of the vigorous growth of steam locomotives the development of a valuable waterway system was nipped in the bud. Existing waterways were adversely affected by the sheer force of competition, backed up by the superior capital resources of the railway companies (which made it easy for them to buy up those canal companies that provided some threat to their prosperity). But the argument may easily be overstated to the point where it may seem surprising that any canals managed to survive at all. Yet in fact the proportion of the canal system now closed is probably considerably smaller than the comparable figure for railways. Thus the adverse effect of the railways (and later of the roads too) should be carefully examined. In the first place the superiority of rail transport, using locomotive haulage, ruled out any further construction of main line canals. The Birmingham & Liverpool Junction scheme (authorised in 1826 and opened in 1835), which provided a relatively direct connection between the Midlands and North West England, was undertaken just in time to avoid the depression in canal building as capital was diverted to the potentially more profitable railways. It represented an improvement over the much older Trent & Mersey Canal of 1777, just as the Grand Junction Canal (1805) provided a more direct route from the Midlands to London than the Oxford Canal (and associates) completed in 1790. Further improvement of the basic inter-regional system was ruled out, and equally the provision of new 'cross-country' links was prevented: for example, the Kington & Leominster Canal would have connected the Severn near Stourport with South Wales, using the railroad from Kington to Hay and Brecon to connect with the Brecon & Abergavenny.

The sudden termination of canal development was unfortunate because the existing network was manifestly incomplete but there could be no basis for effective competition with a comprehensive railway layout. Moreover the incomplete canal system was poorly organised for the struggle: ownership of canals by many separate companies and significant differences in physical capacity (especially the size of the canal locks) complicated through running. Grave difficulties arose through the archaic conditions on some of the old river navigations. Furthermore the fact that canal proprietors could only be toll-takers (being forbidden until 1845 to act as carriers on their own canals) made concerted opposition all the more difficult. On the other hand it must be said that the railway companies did not emerge from the outset as a homogeneous interest group corporately dedicated to the destruction of the canals. Much of the bulk freight which the canals handled was left in their hands as the railway companies concentrated on passenger and parcels traffic. The higher operating costs of the railways resulted in the low value, less urgent goods remaining on the canals until such time as public demand, falling charges or even business convenience overcame the cost differential. For many canal companies direct railway competition did not arise until the mania years.

Ireland provides an interesting example of the change in strategy. The Irish Railway Commission of 1838 recommended a modest railway under strong state direction. The investment made in canals (especially between Dublin and the Shannon) was to be protected by concentrating railway projects on links between Dublin and Ulster and between Dublin and the southern cities (Cork, Limerick and Waterford). Subsequent development by private enterprise frustrated this coordinated plan but the railways running west from Dublin took several years to complete, reaching Galway in 1851, Sligo in 1862 and Westport in 1866. However, the Royal Canal was taken over by the Midland & Great Western Railway as early as 1845, to provide land on which the railway could be built with no major earthworks being necessary. Railway and canal run parallel as far as Mullingar, apart from short deviations on the approaches to Dublin and Mullingar. Later, when the Liffey Branch was built, the railway followed the canal right into the docks (North Wall). Passenger services on the canal ceased with the opening of the railway but the company was obliged to keep the waterway open under the agreement made at the time of purchase and it was kept in repair until the mid-1950s. It is also worth noting that for a time the Midland & Great Western sought competition with the Great Southern & Western by purchasing the Grand Canal as well. The latter ran from Dublin to the Shannon along a more southerly course and was built to compete with the Royal Canal. Thus for a short time the two canals were brought together to facilitate rivalry in a new technical age.

As railway competition increased the canal companies were obliged to make drastic reductions in tolls, so that traffic was maintained at the cost of a catastrophic fall in income. More flexible working procedures might be adopted, while some farsighted companies went into the railway business, like the Manchester Bolton & Bury Canal Navigation, which built a railway alongside its canal in 1838. The Lancaster Canal also reacted purposefully and took a lease of the rival Lancaster & Preston Railway in 1842. But neither railway could stay outside the process of railway amalgamations and these lines eventually merged into the Lancashire & Yorkshire Railway and L.N.W.R. respectively. The dominant theme very quickly became the takeover of canals by railway companies anxious to overcome opposition to bills or to remove competition. A particularly extreme case of adverse railway influence applies to those canals which were acquired so that railways could be built over them. This happened in Scotland in three instances: the main line of the G.N.o.S. out of Aberdeen, the canal line of the G.S.W.R. at Paisley, while the Lanarkshire & Dunbartonshire Railway made use of the short Forth & Cart Canal. In other cases where the canals remained physically intact there was a diversion of trade partly by intention, partly by indifference, and the general effect was seen in increasing neglect of waterways: lack of dredging, closings for leisurely repairs, decaying warehouses and wharves, failure to provide or maintain cranes and no effort to get business. Some canal companies were in a sufficiently strong bargaining position to gain understandings that the new railway company owners would not raise canal rates as a means of eliminating any prospect of competition – and parliament belatedly intervened with legislation (1873 and 1888) which laid down safeguards governing railway control of canals. But inevitably the railways, and later the roads, were able to reduce the commercial importance of the canals (irrespective of ownership).

Vigorous canal operations became restricted to the local level. But here there are some remarkable cases of survival and even development. Because in areas where the canals gave access to industries and mines the logical step for the railway company was to exploit the system as a local distributor and aim simply at a transfer point where goods could be taken over for long-distance transport. This applied most clearly in the West Midlands where a very intricate canal system was the basis of the industrial geography, and also a means of coal supply from the Cannock coalfield to the factories of the Black Country. Hence, even after agreement between the Birmingham Canal Navigations and the London & Birmingham Railway, some improvements could be made to the waterway system including the Cannock Extension and Wyrley Bank branches. But goods remained on the water *within* the Birmingham system only for short hauls and railway basins provided links with the L.N.W.R., the Midland and the Great Western. Another special case arose over the Shropshire Union system which comprised a group of canals given permission in 1846 to amalgamate and to provide additional lines of communication by railway including the Wellington–Stafford line. Even after 1857, when a lease by the L.N.W.R. became effective, the canals continued to seek traffic because they provided a means of penetration into Cambrian and Great Western territory. And the opening of the Manchester Ship Canal gave increased importance to the Shropshire Union's foothold on the Mersey, with the result that facilities at Ellesmere Port were greatly enlarged and the railway company became a

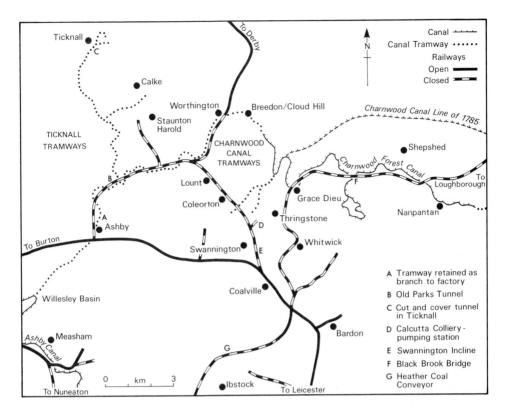

Map 9.  Railways and canals in West Leicestershire.

substantial canal carrier at the turn of the century! Finally, the Aire &
Calder system was supported by the growth of the Humberside port of
Goole during the 1830s and the close association fostered with the
Lancashire & Yorkshire Railway. The waterway prospered with significant
technical innovations like the compartment boat train system introduced in
the 1860s.

A useful example of the relationships between canal and railway
communications relates to the attempts to improve access to the coalfield of
west Leicestershire. It has already been mentioned how the opening of the
Soar for navigation as far as Leicester was linked with the construction of a
branch canal from Loughborough to Swannington and Breedon in 1794.
The railway interest derives from the use of tramways to link an isolated
section of contour canal from Nanpantan to Thringstone with the Soar at
Loughborough and quarries at Breedon. Another line extended the Ashby
Canal from Willesley to Ticknall by way of Ashby de la Zouch, a town which

17. *Ticknall Tramway* The trackbed of this early nineteenth-century railway, an accessary of the Ashby Canal, is still a conspicuous feature on the Derbyshire–Leicestershire border.

gave its name to the canal although no waterway ever reached it. Railways thus came early to Leicestershire, although these lines were strictly accessary to the canals and were never worked by locomotives. But the most curious development came in 1830 when parliamentary assent was forthcoming for a direct railway between Leicester and Swannington. This meant competition with the canal, the first such case to occur south of Manchester. The explanation for such early interest in railways lies primarily in the failure of the Charnwood Forest Canal to provide an efficient connection with the Leicester market. High operating costs certainly arose because of the failure to ensure that the trucks used on the tramways could be rolled on to the canal barges: this meant that in addition to loading at the colliery and transfer to river boats at Loughborough the coal had to be reloaded twice, at Thringstone and Nanpantan. But in addition, traffic was interrupted in 1799 by a burst in the dam of the Black Brook Reservoir which supplied the canal. Repairs were carried out and the canal reopened in 1801, but by this time the dispirited coalmasters were closing down their pits. They could have carted their coal to Leicester by road, as they had done regularly before the canals were built. But in order to compete with Erewash Valley coal (which used the Soar Navigation to reach

18.   *The main street at Ticknall in Derbyshire*, still graced by the stone bridge that gave the Ticknall Tramway access to the limestone quarries on the northern side of the village.

Leicester) the pit-head price would have been so low as to make mining unprofitable. The exact circumstances are rather obscure. There is some evidence that further structural defects caused the canal to be emptied in 1804 but repairs were not carried out and in the prevailing climate of despair users did not press the company to accept their obligations.

The possibility of a horse tramway on the canal bank, creating a railway right through from Breedon to Loughborough, was seriously considered in the early 1830s but parliamentary approval was not given and the situation was only resolved in 1845 when the Charnwood Canal was officially closed. By this time the Leicester & Swannington Railway had opened (1833). The coalmasters (especially William Stenson of Whitwick Colliery) were aware of the success of the Stockton & Darlington Railway and were able to attract the attention of George Stephenson through the intervention of a progressive farmer, John Ellis of Beaumont Leys. Ellis had agricultural contacts with central Lancashire, where George Stephenson was at work with the Liverpool & Manchester project. The scheme was approved by the canal company, anxious only to ensure that parliamentary assent would release them from any obligation to put the canal in order! However, if the coal owners were ready to support a railway more than twenty years after the canal's inefficiency had been demonstrated it is hard to imagine that all the pits had closed down. Some contraction may well have taken place in the early years of the century but it is possible that during the Napoleonic Wars, when there was a considerable growth of industry in Leicester, there was some carting of coal into the town (at least from the pits in closest proximity) and that it was only in the more difficult economic conditions of the 1820s that the hopelessness of the situation became clear. The railway was certainly the success that the canal had never been. The improved economic potential of the coalfield led George Stephenson himself to invest in mineral rights, at Snibston. This proved a profitable speculation once the coal had been found beneath a bed of granite. The whole section of railway between Desford and Snibston (eventually fused with adjacent mining settlements to form the town of Coalville) developed into a mining axis with pits at Desford and Coalville as well as Bagworth, Ellistown and South Leicester. After takeover by the Midland Railway and extension westwards through Moira to Burton in 1849 further sections of the coalfield were opened up.

This railway affected the Ashby Canal because the Ticknall Tramways were 'captured' by the M.R. at Ashby (leading to the closure of the section between Ashby and Willesley Basin). But the canal itself remained active. Indeed, there is a curious contrast between the early appearance of the railway as a replacement for the Charnwood Forest Canal and the late duplication of the Ashby Canal. Although the section between Nuneaton and Ashby had featured in some main line proposals of the mania years (proposals reminiscent of canal schemes involving extension from Moira to

19. *Railway revival at Shackerstone* The Ashby & Nuneaton Joint Railway built its stations in a distinctive architectural style. Shackerstone was once the junction where the Coalville and Moira lines diverged and is now the headquarters of a preserved railway.

20.  *Railway reopening with a difference* Part of the Ashby & Nuneaton Joint Railway has been used to install a coal conveyor to connect the Heather opencast project with the railhead at South Leicestershire Colliery near Coalville.

the Trent) no major strategic interest emerged and the Midland claim to control (through its ownership of the canal in 1845) was not seriously questioned until the 1860s. To oppose the L.N.W.R. proposal for a coalfield railway at this time the Midland reactivated railway legislation of 1846, but their shortage of capital prompted the idea of a joint railway which the L.N.W.R. accepted. The Ashby & Nuneaton Joint Railway opened in 1873, exactly forty years after the Leicester & Swannington. It linked up with both companies at Nuneaton (Midland at Abbey Street Station and L.N.W.R. at Trent Valley) and ran to Shackerstone, where lines to Coalville and Moira diverged: at both points there were junctions with the Midland Railway's Leicester–Burton line, but a connection with the L.N.W.R. at Hinckley was never used. The L.N.W.R. used their access to Coalville as a launching pad to reach Loughborough (in 1883) by a line along the flanks of Charnwood Forest which, incidentally, intersected at several points with the meandering course of the old contour canal. Although worked as a minor branch line up to its final closure in 1963 there was a possibility that the speculations of the mania years might be rekindled by a connection with the Great Central at Loughborough, proposed in 1899 and again in 1905. It did not succeed, possibly because the L.N.W.R. was not prepared to countenance Great Central access to Birmingham as a reciprocal concession for its own penetration of Nottingham. The entire joint line is now closed, apart from the Moira–Measham section which is worked as a branch of the Leicester–Burton freight line. The activity on the old Swannington line (as modernised by the Midland Railway) compared with the closure of the joint railway, is balanced by a reverse situation over canals. The Ashby Canal remains open (south of Measham) for cruising (and even the last surviving section of the Ticknall Tramway, from Old Parks to Ticknall, remained open until the First World War) while the Charnwood Canal continues to lie derelict. The local contrast with origins in the late eighteenth century thus lives on today and shows how the railway adapted to the varied legacy of the canal age.

# 15

# Railways and the Ports

While the railway had a generally adverse effect on the canals of the British Isles, the consequences for shipping were considerably more varied. Coastal shipping, even between points which enjoyed competing railway services, was able to flourish since costs were relatively low and the scale of operations could be increased much more easily than on canals where the entire waterway needed enlargement if bigger boats were to operate. Railways on the banks of the Clyde and Thames were unable to divert traffic decisively from the steamers, which adjusted capacity to fluctuating demand more precisely than the railways and refused to become simply railway feeders. Indeed, the competition from coastal shipping was effective in trimming railway rates. Thus ironmasters with inland locations tended to pay higher charges than colleagues who had the option of using shipping services. Such discrimination has been considered a relevant factor in the decline of iron production in the Black Country once the local ores were exhausted. But although the coastal shipping trade survived through the late nineteenth century with its lower costs, competition from the railways stiffened from the 1890s with an increase in the number of exceptional rates, many of them quite uneconomic from a railway point of view. The diversion of traffic, coupled with the decline of the coal trade through the decline in mining during the war years, had a devastating effect by the 1920s. There was little potential for recovery and most of the business was concentrated in the hands of the Coast Lines syndicate formed in 1917.

Except for cattle and perishable goods, coastal shipping remained profitable: and all the railway companies could do was to operate their own ships in competition. Even in sparsely populated rural areas like Sutherland, links with Burghead in Moray, first established by sailing boat in 1809 when the new harbour opened there, continued by steamers from the 1850s to the First World War despite the presence of the Highland Railway. Indeed, for a short period the G.N.o.S. entered the steamer trade to try and draw traffic from the Highland line.

But that is not to say that the geography of ports and harbours in north Scotland remained unchanged during the railway age. In some cases the extension of railway services across the mainland made it feasible to open new steamer terminals on island routes and lengthy voyages, which had previously been necessary because of the poor state of overland roads, could be shortened. So the growth of railways in the Highlands led to the rise of Oban, Mallaig and Strome Ferry (later Kyle of Lochalsh) as terminals for sailings to the Hebrides. Services from Glasgow were retained, but were increasingly restricted to cargo handling. However, there can be no simple rule about such trends because on the east coast of Scotland the North Isles services continued to operate from Leith and Aberdeen: Orkney, however, could also be approached through Scrabster in Caithness. But travel time was important and whereas on the east coast the steamers could follow a direct course to Orkney and Shetland (while the railway meandered through the northern counties) on the west coast most steamers faced a long detour round the Mull of Kintyre, due to the small capacity of the Crinan Canal.

Normally it seems that the selective improvement of harbours led to considerable polarisation of trade. But the decision to expand facilities at a particular port would depend in part on the timing of railway connection. Falmouth has a long history as a packet station by virtue of its fine natural harbour and its westerly position, which meant that ocean shipping could not be seriously molested by enemy action in the Channel. In the age of sail these operational factors led to Falmouth's growth during the eighteenth century despite the rigours of the overland journey, with twin hazards of bad roads and highway robbery. However, while the road journey was greatly eased by through coach services in the early nineteenth century (with Falmouth experiencing a rapid rise in population) the early arrival of the railway at Southampton at a time when the steamship was coming into service created a stimulus to provide services for the steam packets at Southampton and create a new transport layout in which Falmouth had only a modest place. As steam power became general in world shipping there was less need for a special class of swift packet boat: the shipping companies based their operations at ports with the best services and the best situation. It was believed that a railway to Falmouth would allow the Cornish port to regain its glory, but the enlargement of the port, associated with the arrival of the railway in 1863, could do no more than attract calls by some New York steamers: although Falmouth attracted some cargo traffic and ship repair business it never again became a major terminal. Weymouth, on the other hand, had a positional advantage in relation to the Channel Islands trade and was able to regain this traffic when the railway arrived in 1857. The grip was strengthened when the conversion of the broad gauge opened up more direct links with northern England. It is not really surprising, looking back, to observe that the ports with the best hinterlands were the ones which expanded quickly and offered good facilities to attract the shipping companies. But arguably the disadvantages of some peripheral ports were accentuated by the delayed arrival of the railway. With the railway available they could belatedly expand, but only in relation to the established port hierarchy. Falmouth could, therefore, expect to prosper as a secondary harbour for its modest hinterland and also as a centre of tourism, just as the West Highland ports provided for island services and the fishing industry. The competitive spirit tended to generate frustration when basic central place principles were overlooked.

There was certainly a close link between the growth of a port and the quality of its railway service. The support of a railway company was very important for a port. This can be seen at Newhaven, where the arrival of the Brighton company in 1847 improved the hinterland of a small port previously associated only with the Ouse Navigation. A new authority was established for the harbour in 1847 when it was clear that the port had a bright future and major improvements were made which assured its position in the cross-channel trade as traffic built up after the 1878 Paris Exhibition. The railway company's shipping interests were based at Newhaven in preference to Shoreham. On the other hand, a railway might adopt a more ambivalent attitude towards a particular harbour and this can be seen at Hull, since the North Eastern quoted equal rates between west Yorkshire and east coast ports, thereby preventing Hull from taking full advantage of its relative proximity to Leeds and Bradford. The situation was particularly galling because across the estuary at Grimsby was a port which enjoyed the single-minded support of the Manchester Sheffield & Lincolnshire Railway. The result was the formation of a new company, the Hull & Barnsley, whose railway ran into the city from a junction with the Midland Railway at Cudworth. Within Hull a tentacle swung round the north-eastern flank of the city to Alexandra Dock, paralleling the N.E.R. connection with Victoria Dock (in much the same way as the Caledonian and North British each cut through the northern suburbs of Glasgow to reach the docks at Stobcross and Clydebank). The H.B.R. also made a tactical entry into the steamship business in order to improve Hull's position. Relations became cordial enough for a joint interest to be staked in the King George V Dock opened in 1914. It is arguable whether or not this 'outstanding campaign of civil action against a railway company' was well-conceived, since gentle persuasion might have stimulated the North Eastern to invest in the docks. On the other hand the H.B.R. made a bold gesture in penetrating a territorial monopoly and injecting an element of competition which assured Hull of substantial growth as the coal production from the south Yorkshire field increased at the turn of the century.

Irrespective of the degree of railway company backing it was a logical development in port cities for rail connections to link docks with the main stations. This can be seen emerging in the Irish cities of Dublin and Cork, even though population decline in nineteenth-century Ireland tended to depress railway development. In Dublin the railway system consisted

initially of four main lines each running from its own terminus and having
no connection with other railways or with the docks. The first lines were
opened by the Dublin & Kingstown (later Dublin & South Eastern) from
Westland Row to Kingstown (Dun Laoghaire) in 1834 (and eventually
extended to Wexford in 1872), the Great Northern (originally Dublin &
Drogheda) opened from Amiens Street to Drogheda in 1846 (and Belfast in
1855) and the Dublin & Cork (later Great Southern & Western) opened
from Kingsbridge as far as Kildare also in 1846. It was the last main line to
be built out of Dublin, the Midland & Great Western from Broadstone to
Mullingar (1848) and Galway (1851), which made the first move for the
docks in 1864 when the Liffey Branch was built along the line of the Royal
Canal from Cabra to North Wall. By purchasing the canal the company had
already gained easy access to land on which to build its railways westwards
and the main line to Mullingar ran at the side of the canal. The same
procedure was now applied within Dublin. A similar link from the docks to
the Great Southern & Western at Kingsbridge, using the Grand Canal
route, failed on two occasions but access was eventually gained by tunnelling
under Phoenix Park to join the Liffey Branch in 1877. A completely
independent route subsequently emerged through the Drumcondra Link
(1901) running into North Wall, parallel with the Liffey Branch. Although
providing an easier alignment through Amiens Street, the duplication was
essentially a product of company politics. Further integration was provided
by the City of Dublin Junction Railway in crossing the Liffey between
Amiens Street and Westland Row in 1891 (with an intermediate station at
Tara Street) and connecting with the Liffey Branch. These connections and
Drumcondra Link were opened in 1892 and 1906 respectively and were
valuable in linking the various companies with the docks and so avoiding the
need to drive cattle through the streets, and they were also useful in allowing
through running by boat trains from Queenstown (Cobh, on Cork Harbour)
to Kingstown (Dun Laoghaire) and by the Belfast–Dublin–Cork 'Enterprise' expresses. (See Map 17 on page 196.)

   At Cork the Great Southern & Western arrived at Kilbarry on the
northern edge of the city in 1849 and did not tunnel its way through to
Glanmire Road until 1855. By this time there were two other railways
operating from the city centre: the narrow gauge Cork Blackrock & Passage
which opened in 1850 was analogous to the Dublin & Kingstown because,
prior to the growth of Queenstown, Passage was a busy place for the
unloading of vessels too large to get higher up into the river Lee at Cork: the
railway increased its importance by making it the terminal for water
connections with various places situated around Cork Harbour. Its
terminus in Cork was south of the Lee at Albert Street very close to Albert
Quay, where the Cork & Bandon Railway began operations in 1851. Three
other developments followed: the Cork & Youghal Railway from Tivoli on

the east end of the city in 1859, the Cork & Macroom from Albert Quay in 1866 (later Capwell 1879) and the Cork & Muskerry opened from Western Road to Blarney in 1887. Integration then occurred in two stages. First, the Cork & Youghal advanced into the city at Summerhill (1861) and after opening a branch to Queenstown in 1862, sought a physical connection with G.S.W.R. This was made in 1868 and was given further emphasis in 1893 when both companies began to use a new Glanmire Road station. Second, the Cork City Railway reconnected the Bandon and Macroom lines and brought them both over the Lee into Glanmire Road in 1914. A branch to Victoria Quay was also provided. The narrow gauge Muskerry and Passage railways remained isolated but the others were gradually brought together and enjoyed common access to the docks. Queenstown, which became the leading packet station on Cork Harbour, was also made accessible for boat trains from Dublin. It is an indication of the continued importance of the ports in these two cities that despite considerable recent contraction of railways the harbour links are still retained.

The case of Bristol is also useful in bringing out the essential functional relationship between port development and associated land transport. Bristol's first port emerged at the lowest bridging point on the Avon in the context of trade between Viking settlements in England and Ireland and later through the medieval wine trade which was dominated by the Bristol–Bordeaux axis. With a high tidal range involved in the Severn estuary ships had to spend low tide standing on the stony bed to Avon and it was to provide a softer pad that the main anchorage was moved to a specially straightened course of the Frome. However, to overcome the problem more effectively William Jessop's proposal for a 'New Cut' for the Avon was accepted and work began in 1802. The original river course was then locked against the new channel to form a 'Floating Harbour' with a stable water level to which entry could be gained at high tide. This was an attempt by Bristol merchants to make up ground lost in relation to Liverpool, Glasgow and other rivals. Completion of the scheme in 1809 did not bring the desired results because the high harbour dues (necessary to recoup on the costly investment) and the more difficult approach to Bristol compared with west coast rivals. The city docks continued to function and slowly gained railway connections. In the early 1860s the only connection with the docks in Bristol was through a small dock (upstream of Bristol Bridge) adjacent to Temple Meads goods shed. Temple Meads remained the railway centre with a rebuilt station (opened 1878) to which road access from Clifton was improved by the contemporaneous building of Victoria Street. The city docks gained access by the Harbour Junction Railway of 1872.

Railways became fundamental to the provision of docks lower down the Avon in the nineteenth century. A harbour at Sea Mills opened in 1716 was not successful because the merchants wanted close contact with the city.

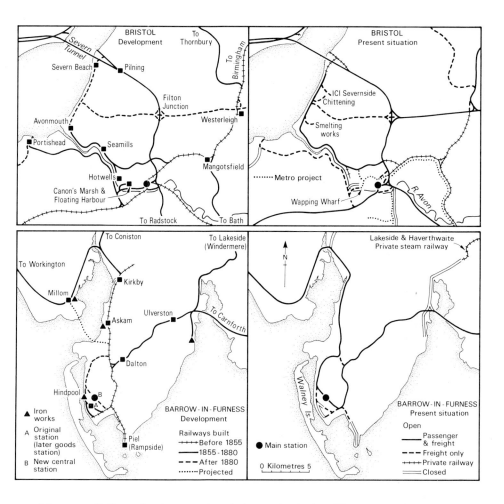

Map 10.  Railway development in relation to the docks of Barrow-in-Furness and Bristol. Lines in Bristol shown as private railways should be read as 'closed'.

The dock was disused by 1766. The wreck of the *Demarara* in 1851, caught by a strongly ebbing tide, increased interest in docks lower down the Avon. Yet the authorities in Bristol refused to countenance the building of a dock at the mouth of the river, with connection with the city by railway. Some leading townsmen therefore took the matter up. The Bristol Port Railway & Pier Company was formed in 1862. The scheme involved a nine kilometre railway from Hotwells, close to the Clifton suspension bridge, to Avonmouth through Sea Mills and Shirehampton. The line opened in 1865 and provided access to the pier (for passengers, livestock and merchandise) which was first used in the same year. The pier soon silted up but docks were built and the railway retained its commercial rôle. Indeed, the Avonmouth branch (with its terminus now advanced into the docks) was connected through Clifton Down Tunnel with Temple Meads in 1876 in good time for the opening of the dock three years later. Furthermore, there was a recreational function, for a hotel concert hall and pleasure centre was opened as part of the B.P.R. scheme.

Competition arose between Avonmouth and Portishead, which enjoyed a modest coasting trade and was also a destination for day trippers sailing down the Avon from Hotwells Spa. From the late 1840s various proposals were made to extend either the leisure facilities or the shipping trade (through a pier or dock). But neither option was feasible as long as transport links were poor. The necessary improvement came in 1862 when the opponents of the B.P.R. formed a rival Bristol & Portishead Pier & Railway Company. Their line was opened in 1867, with the pier completed in 1870. A dock was ready in 1879, the result of support by the Corporation (as important landowners) balancing the interest shown by the Midland and Great Western companies in Avonmouth. However, Avonmouth was the more successful port and after Bristol Corporation took over both the outports in 1884 it was at Avonmouth where further investments were made – with the opening of the King Edward Dock in 1908 (extended in 1928). The railway to Avonmouth was connected with the main line in Bristol (Hotwells terminus closed in 1922) and a further link was forged with the Great Western at Pilning near Severn Tunnel. The Midland and Great Western jointly took over the B.P.R. in 1890 and the coordination of railway services therefore paralleled the belated merger of harbour authorities. These developments meanwhile left Portishead with the option of promoting tourism and although overshadowed by Clevedon and Weston it re-established itself as a resort by the turn of the century. The railway link has now been lost.

The link between a railway company and dockland development is particularly close in the case of the Furness Railway and the expansion of Barrow. A railway was built in 1846 to connect mineral workings at Lindal (iron ore) and Kirkby (slate) with shipping points at Barrow and Piel. This was much more efficient than the old system of carting. Steamers had previously operated out of Ulverston but in 1847 a Fleetwood service started from Piel Pier which continued to be used until 1882. At the time Barrow was a very small settlement, but a railway colony was established by the end of the decade and during the 1850s an ambitious plan was drawn up to provide for the growth of Barrow as a major industrial town. There is little doubt that Middlesbrough provided an inspiration but Barrow's development was specifically controlled by the railway which acted as a regional development agency for Furness. The author of the town plan of 1856 was John Ramsden, engineer of the Furness Railway (and subsequently general manager) and the economic foundation was provided by a dramatic re-appraisal of the industrial potential. The iron ore of Furness was becoming extremely valuable because Coal Measure ironstone was becoming scarcer in traditional areas of iron manufacture while the introduction of steel making made the local haematite ore particularly acceptable. Output rose from 0.4 m.t. in 1841 to 1.19 m.t. in 1881. It could be shipped out from Barrow but the connection with the west coast main line at Carnforth in 1857 provided the option of export by rail. More important however, this line, along with the Stockton & Darlington line to Tebay, coming over Stainmore (1861) from the Durham coalfield, made it possible to envisage iron and steel production in Furness with the coking coal brought in from the North East. In fact, the first furnaces were built on the Hindpool estate (purchased in 1854) in 1859 with subsequent addition of Bessemer steel making (1865).

The Haematite Steel Company became one of the great institutions on which Barrow's late Victorian prosperity was based. Horizons were widening still further with a link between steel making and ship building and an expansion of the harbour which would integrate with the shipyard and also provide the infrastructure for imports of raw material to provide for textile industries to employ the women. Devonshire Dock (1867) was followed by Buccleuch Dock (1873) and Ramsden Dock (1879). The shipyard and the jute mill also opened. This growth meant a logical progression from the railway and the iron and steel industry to shipping and heavy engineering, with light industry for the women. A link with the Midland Railway was made through Wennington in 1867 and this led to the transfer of the Midland's Belfast steamer service to Barrow. Other companies were encouraged to base their operations in Barrow and place orders for ships in the local yard.

But the plan to establish a diversified industrial community in Barrow with a port that was very much at the centre of world trade was not a success. By 1886 there was a distinct prospect that the whole edifice would collapse. Development under boom conditions meant costly overheads during depression. The railway company gradually unloaded its industrial interests. The shipyard which passed to Vickers in 1897 was a financial failure for the Furness Railway, though the industry is retained in Barrow today thanks to the demand for naval armaments. Was the railway policy a misguided one? A clear answer is impossible. There was a solid potential for industry in Furness and this would surely have been realised irrespective of railway company policy. It is worth considering the rôle of the seventh Duke of Devonshire, a quiet scholarly man who found himself caught up in the growth of the region. From modernisation of the Kirkby Ireleth quarries, connected by the inclined plane with the Furness Railway, he went on to play an active role in railway management and in the development of industries in Barrow, including powerful financial support in some sectors in hard times in order to keep the whole structure afloat. Such was 'the powerful effect of an environment encouraging and applauding commercial activity and money making that it is hard to regard the enterprise as intrinsically unique'.

The support of the Furness Railway for industrial development, encouraging enterprises to set up in Barrow and providing sites, houses and financial loans, was progressive and enlightened, as was its decision in 1865 to absorb the Whitehaven & Furness Junction Railway to prevent the company building a direct line across the Duddon estuary to Ulverston which would have bypassed Barrow (the Furness Railway themselves proposed a Duddon Viaduct but it was permanently postponed in the depression of 1867–9). The integrated plan which catered for the needs of the docks, railways and industries (and which could be implemented without effective opposition because of the Furness Railway's position as landowner and administrator) reflects the ideal of the planned community which Scottish improving landlords struggled to achieve in the eighteenth century. But Barrow was hardly a model town, for neither housing nor services were good and belatedly the Furness Railway had to adopt a social policy for the rapidly growing town which attracted not only rural dwellers from the vicinity but labourers from Ireland and industrial workers from Scotland. And a company with a wide range of interests ran the risk of overreaching itself with excessive capital outlays and shortages of management skills in the different industries. There was always the danger of being caught out during a period of depression. Certainly no such integrated approach would have been taken had the L.N.W.R. or the Midland Railway provided the services in Furness and it is doubtful if other enterprises would have put together the same complex of industries that the Furness Railway was able to induce. But whether or not a more fragmented business structure would have brought better results for Barrow in the long term is a matter for speculation. Either way, Barrow stands as an excellent example of the impact of the railway on port development.

# 16

# Railways for the Slate Quarries of North Wales

Although the Welsh slate industry does not have the same historic significance before the nineteenth century as the coal mining and the working of metalliferous ore it became a monument of the railway age and one which is perpetuated today by the tremendous popularity of some of the quarry lines which form the bulk of the 'great little trains' of Wales. The main area of slate working lies in Gwynedd (the old counties of Caernarfon and Merioneth). Until the eighteenth century the quarries were shallow workings serving local needs. The first serious attempt to put the quarries on an efficient commercial footing was made by Richard Pennant, who took over the Penrhyn estate in 1785: he was aware of the potential for slate in distant urban markets (having previously been M.P. for Liverpool) if better transport was provided. So work went ahead with a tramway, suitable for horse traction, to the coast at Port Penrhyn (Abercegin), near Bangor, where a harbour was developed. The gauge was 0.57 m or 1 ft 10¾ in. and the line was ready in 1801. Later on in 1876 it was rebuilt for locomotive operation, but without any change of gauge. Caernarfon also saw development after a quay was provided in 1803 (extended in 1821). Traffic came from the Nantlle quarries (which had previously exported through Voryd) and a horse railway was built at 1.1 m or 3 ft 6 in. gauge in 1828 (converted to standard gauge in 1865).

At much the same time as railway building began at Penrhyn another quarry development was taking place through Thomas Assheton Smith's enterprise at Dinorwic near Llanberis. The quarries here became particularly impressive in landscape terms through open terrace working on the hillside of Elidir Fawr up to an altitude of 600 m. Quarrying was arranged in steps or galleries (called *ponciau* by the quarrymen) of some twenty metres in both height and breadth. Efficient transport was naturally a precondition for expansion of the business to its massive late nineteenth-century proportions, when some 3000 men were employed. Road transport from the head of Llyn Padarn was not satisfactory because only carts with broad wheels could use the turnpike roads at special rates and the smallholders who acted as part-time carriers could not afford to modify their equipment. The quarry company improved roads in 1809 but rising output made a railway inevitable. A tramway was built to connect the quarry with Port Dinorwic (Velinheli) between Bangor and Caernarfon. The gauge was 0.57 m for 1 ft 10¾ in. and there were two inclines along the route. When the line opened in 1824 the gauge was the same as the one used at Penrhyn, but by 1848 the line was rebuilt to facilitate the use of locomotives. A new alignment resulted in only one incline, at the Port Dinorwic end, and the gauge was increased to 1.2 m or four feet.

Further south, development was more restrained and although Ffestiniog slate was finding outlets in Ireland the greater distance to the coast made the road journey down to Maentwrog difficult and expensive. Moreover, quays on Traeth Bach suffered from limited depth of water and barges had to take the slate out to larger vessels. However, the Ffestiniog area had huge reserves of slate and perception of this great potential at a time of rising demand (and relaxation of wartime taxes levied on coastwise movements of slate in 1831) brought about a belated improvement in transport facilities in this district as well. A start was made by another entrepreneur with a parliamentary background: W. A. Madocks undertook a major development scheme for Traeth Mawr involving construction of an embankment, with which drainage work would be associated, and the foundation of a new town at Tremadog. The embankment was completed in 1811 and the diverted river course resulted in such considerable deepening at the western side of the estuary as to suggest the development of a port without great additional expense. So Ynyscyngar became Porthmadog (opened in 1821) and complemented the inland planned village which lay at the heart of Madocks' scheme. As events turned out Tremadog failed to prosper, for the road on which it was situated did not become the main access route to an Irish Sea packet station (Holyhead was preferred to Porthdynllaen). On the other hand Porthmadog flourished as a harbour town and the difference in status was underlined when the Cambrian Railways chose to take their line through the port. However, long before this development occurred Porthmadog gained importance in connection with the slate industry. Madocks obviously had his eye on the slate traffic because he proposed a railway in 1815 to run from Moelwyn Mawr to Porthmadog along a route later followed very closely by the Croesor Tramway. But the first important traffic came from the quarries of Blaenau Ffestiniog. Barges from Traeth Bach which had previously handed over their cargoes of slate to coasting vessels standing offshore now put into the new port to make the transfer. And inevitably the efficiency of a direct rail route from Ffestiniog to Porthmadog was recognised, so that in 1836 the third major quarry railway in the North Wales slate province opened. Place-names present something of a problem. The 'madog' element in Porthmadog and Tremadog has been related to a celtic Prince Madog

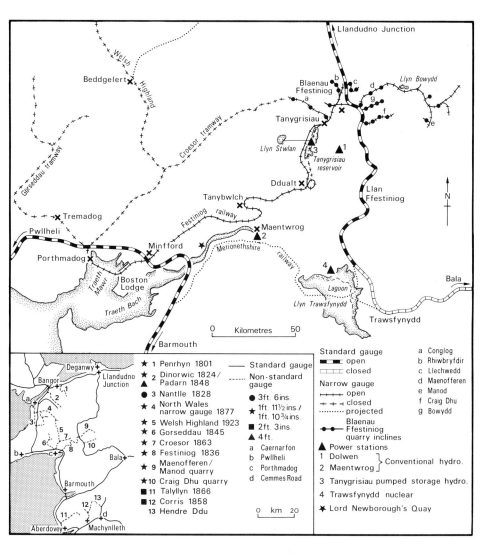

Map 11. Railways and slate quarries in North Wales, with particular reference to the Porthmadog–Blaenau Ffestiniog area.

who sailed from Gwynedd to discover America. But the anglicised version (Portmadoc/Tremadoc) has an obvious correspondence with Madocks the landowner. However, in the case of the Festiniog Railway workshops at the western end of the cob there is no doubt about the link with Madocks since the name Boston Lodge clearly relates to his parliamentary constituency in Lincolnshire.

The Festiniog Railway (using a different spelling of Ffestiniog) was sanctioned in 1831, after earlier proposals of 1824 and 1825 had failed. The line was built to 0.60 m or 1 ft $11\frac{1}{2}$ in. gauge and opened in 1836. Apart from the embankment (cob) which provided an easy means of crossing the estuary the line was carefully engineered so that a steady gradient was maintained all the way down: loaded wagons could therefore descend by gravity, leaving horses to pull trains across the cob and return empties to the quarries. This explains why the railway has a length of twenty kilometres compared with the straight line distance of fifteen. One inclined plane was included in the scheme at the outset but the growth of traffic led to realignment in 1844 including the boring of Moelwyn Tunnel. This transport system proved adequate to allow a rapid growth of traffic through the middle decades of the century. There was great activity in Porthmadog with sailing ships arriving in ballast to take slate to the Mersey, while at Ffestiniog a complex pattern of quarry development was under way. Railways to serve the quarries date back to 1825 at Bowydd, where Lord Newborough made important improvements, but it seems that although he built a wharf (Lord Newborough's Wharf) on Traeth Bach a railway to the coast was only seriously contemplated after his lease had expired. The Festiniog Railway was built with two terminals: one at Dinas to give access to Rhiwbryfdir quarries and the other at Diffwys to connect with Bowydd. Tremendous differences in level resulted in inclines being installed on a grand scale, the first at Rhiwbryfdir in 1839. A major increase in output followed from the incline at Llechwedd opened in *c.* 1855: this was the main link with the Festiniog Railway and in turn provided access to different parts of the Llechwedd complex by various other inclines which connected the various 'floors' of the quarry. F.R. wagons were supplied to the various quarry companies, each of whom was responsible for the movement of the wagons over their own systems. The most extensive system was the one from Diffwys which involved three inclines to pass through Maenofferen Quarry and reach a level at 470 m (245 m above Diffwys). The line continued for 3.75 km past the reservoirs to reach the smaller quarries of Cwt y Bugail, Blaen y Cwm and Rhiwbach and finally to end at Manod. All except Cwt y Bugail had inclines to connect with the 'main line'. Inclines could be worked simply by gravity with loaded wagons going downhill pulling up empties. Alternatively, loads could be taken uphill by employing power (steam or electricity) or using a water tank to balance the load.

It should be pointed out that the Festiniog was not the only slate-carrying railway to arrive at Porthmadog. The Gorseddau Tramway was opened in 1845 and during the 1860s the Croesor Tramway was built to draw slate from a string of quarries (Park, Fron Boeth, Croesor and Rhosydd) lying over the mountain from Tanygrisiau. The Gorseddau line eventually adopted locomotives and a vertical-boilered engine remained in service until

21. *A Fairlie on the Festiniog* Thanks to the double-boilered Fairlie locomotive it was possible to modernise the initially gravity-worked Festiniog Railway without changing the gauge or alignment.

the line closed in 1894, but horses remained the mainstay of the Croesor line throughout its working life. The lower section of the Croesor Tramway was used for the first stage of the Welsh Highland Railway which advanced from Porthmadog to Beddgelert, South Snowdon and, by re-use of the trackbed of the defunct North Wales Narrow Gauge line of 1877, Dinas Junction. But the times were not prosperous: the Croesor branch closed around 1930 and the whole Welsh Highland was derelict by the Second World War.

Important changes occurred with the arrival of the standard gauge railways. The L.N.W.R. were building southwards from Llandudno Junction and began to tap the slate quarries when Betws-y-Coed was reached in 1868. This provided a fillip to slate working at Dolwyddelan and Penmachno. At the same time the Cambrian Railways had plans to build along the Merioneth coast and the Great Western were advancing from Wrexham through Bala to Dolgellau. The Ffestiniog quarries stood out like a beacon in the minds of railway developers, all the more so as slate output was increasing. The Festiniog Railway continued to cope and made remarkable efforts to increase capacity on its system by introducing steam locomotives in 1863. The narrow gauge had been considered too restrictive for locomotives of adequate power to be developed, but the emergence of suitable designs (especially the Fairlie double-boilered locomotive) brought the railway more closely into line with modern technology. This development represents one further achievement for the Spooner family, whose activities span virtually all the major railway engineering works of the nineteenth century. James Spooner was involved in the building of the Festiniog Railway (and indeed envisaged such a railway as early as 1821). He became manager of the railway and the responsibility passed to his son Charles Easton on his death in 1859. The new manager approached a London engineering firm about locomotives and the first machines performed well enough to allow passenger services to be started in 1865. The first Fairlie engine, *Little Wonder*, made its debut in 1869 and trials held in the following year drew a considerable crowd including representatives of Continental railways. Shortly afterwards steam locomotives were introduced on the private quarry systems, beginning with the Welsh Slate Company at Rhiwbryfdir Lower.

The standard gauge companies saw a strong case for diverting some of the Festiniog's expanding traffic. The Festiniog Railway acknowledged the inevitable and agreed to a connection with the L.N.W.R. who would then have running powers into Diffwys. The extension from Betws-y-Coed took four years to complete because of the need to bore a 3.5 km tunnel and in the meantime it was decided to use standard rather than narrow gauge. The competition was severe, for not only did the L.N.W.R. take slate to markets directly by rail but the company also shipped out slate through a dock opened at Deganwy, near Llandudno: narrow gauge trucks were supplied for loading in the quarries and for conveyance to the dockside at Deganwy mounted on standard gauge 'host wagons'. Coal was imported and supplied to the quarries as a return cargo.

Meanwhile further progress was being made to connect Blaenau Ffestiniog with the national railway. In 1868 a narrow gauge line was opened between Llan Ffestiniog and Blaenau (the Ffestiniog & Blaenau Railway) and three years later a project was advanced by the Merionethshire Railway to join Llan Ffestiniog with the Cambrian Railways Barmouth–Pwllheli line (opened in 1867) at Talsarnau where slate traffic could be exchanged. This plan was forestalled by the Festiniog's decision to build an exchange siding where its own line met the Cambrian, at Minffordd, in 1872. But there was still a possibility that the Ffestiniog & Blaenau could become part of a link with the Great Western at Bala. The connection was made in 1882 and the following year the F.B.R. was converted to standard gauge (though with a third rail provided so as to preserve the physical link between some quarries and the Festiniog Railway at Diffwys). With so much competition it might seem surprising that the Festiniog survived but it did have excellent links with the quarries (without transfer problems) and it connected 'downstream' with a good port which was easy to approach from the south. The port became less important by the end of the century since the larger steamships could not be accommodated, but the Festiniog also linked up with a standard gauge railway system (the Cambrian) with which close relations were maintained, to the point of jointly offering competitive tariffs to the L.N.W.R. This rivalry was perpetuated into the inter-war period as the Great Western inherited the Cambrian position at Minffordd while the L.N.W.R. became part of the London Midland & Scottish Railway.

In contrast to these various quarry lines which provided connections with the harbours stands the Talyllyn Railway. From the beginning this line was integrated with a standard gauge railway, namely the Cambrian Railways at Tywyn. Since the Talyllyn terminated at Tywyn Wharf it might appear that it was associated with a harbour but this was not the case. The commercial development of the Bryneglwys quarries (by Lancashire capitalists seeking new investment outlets during the cotton famine of the 1860s) did involve a plan for railway building to a port but the only suitable harbour was Aberdovey. It was the only harbour accessible to sea-going vessels and as such has an extensive hinterland. When the quarries above Corris at Aberllefenni were developed the narrow gauge Corris, Machynlleth and River Dovey Tramway of 1859 took slate to the edge of the Dovey estuary for conveyance in small boats to Aberdovey. The first slate from Bryneglwys (opened in 1847 by the owner of the Hendre Estate) had been carried there by packhorse. But the railway route to Aberdovey (proposed in 1865) was difficult and it was providential that the impending arrival of the Cambrian Railways allowed a narrow gauge line of 0.63 m or 2 ft 3 in. to be built instead down to Tywyn through Abergynolwyn and Dolgoch in the Afon Fathew Valley. There were steep slopes immediately below the quarry and three inclines were needed (Hendre Wallog, Cantrybedd and Alltwyllt) to plunge the slate wagons down into the Gwernol ravine from where a conventional railway could operate to Tywyn. The line opened in 1866 and may be compared with the standard gauge Mawddwy Railway which led from Dinas Mawddwy to the Cambrian Railways at Cemmes Road in 1867. However, the most colourful aspect of the evolution of transport systems to serve the slate arises through the capture of the narrow gauge lines by the expanding networks of the major companies. There is no better example than that of the Festiniog Railway.

# 17

# Railways for the Iron Industry

Another case of mineral working with which the railway has been closely associated is afforded by iron ore and the related manufacturing activity in large metallurgical plants. When railways were first built on a large scale the iron industry was closely associated with the coalfields, for not only were large amounts of coke needed in the blast furnaces (in place of charcoal which had been used until the eighteenth century) but the most prolific ironstone deposits were found in the Coal Measures. It is therefore difficult to disentangle the railways associated with the iron industry from those connected with coal mining. The coal and iron industries together generated railway schemes near Glasgow in the 1820s and 1830s and it was the web of railways in this district of Monklands, initially tributary to the canals but later competitive with them, which provided the core around which the Caledonian Railway's main lines developed. The railways in turn stimulated the ironmasters through the demand for metal which the railways unleashed while they exerted a locational influence in support of the Coatbridge area where a massive concentration of heavy industry emerged. Coatbridge had its raw material advantages of course: a devastatingly potent combination of splint coal and blackband ore linked together by the technology of the hot blast demonstrated by J. B. Neilson. The reduced fuel consumption meant production costs which enabled Scottish pig to undercut the English product. Ironmasters south of the border were no longer protected by high transport charges, for the railway now made it possible for the cheapest manufacturer to dominate the national market.

The first use of coke in Scotland had been at Carron on the Forth and by the turn of the eighteenth century furnace developments had given rise to a dispersed location pattern extending from Balgonie (Markinch) in Fife to Muirkirk (Cumnock & Doon Valley). But the industry was not very competitive, yet despite high production costs, using clayband ore and indifferent coking coal, the poor transport system provided a degree of protection against iron from other regions. Many of these early locations were retained despite the rise of Coatbridge, but for a time the Monklands attracted virtually all the new investment. The railway (and coastal shipping) sustained growth in this 'least cost' location by providing access to a market large enough to make full use of the capacity. Coatbridge is therefore a good example of the railway's influence on economic activity through permitting a greater scale of production in the best locations. Once the vigour of Coatbridge was underlined by dwindling iron ore reserves the railway provided a means of salvation by enabling raw material to be brought in from further afield. But equally there was a logic in setting up plant on the alternative orefields, for the cost of installing plant in a new location (usually higher than providing extra capacity at an existing works) would be balanced against savings in transport of iron ore. Hence the dispersal of the industry in Ayrshire in mid-century, a trend which was all the stronger because several local firms which had failed to prosper were available for takeover by Coatbridge firms, especially Bairds of Gartsherrie.

Today the pattern is a very simple one because there has been a complete abandonment of domestic ores in Scotland in favour of foreign ore imported through the Clyde and this situation, plus the economics of concentrating investment in very large integrated iron and steel plant, means that Scotland has now only one blast furnace location: Ravenscraig near Motherwell. This represents a post-war expansion of the Dalzell site, first developed for a malleable iron works by David Colville in 1872. The railway inevitably influenced the location decision because a lineside site was essential: the main line of Caledonian Railway, closely linked with both pig iron suppliers, engineering works and shipyards, ran through extensive tracts of undeveloped land which at this time formed a logical new frontier for the booming heavy industry of Clydeside. For social reasons it has retained its importance although the new iron ore terminal of Hunterston on the Clyde estuary may provide a basis for relocation at some future date. This further discussion provides a second lesson in the significance of the railway as a location factor: industries which make sufficient use of the railway as to require private sidings will select lineside sites (within the preferred region) beside railways which provide the best services, provided of course that sites are sufficiently large, level and stable. In the case of the Caledonian Railway in the Motherwell area the potential was created by the opening of the direct line along the Clyde Valley in 1849 and it became more attractive as links with the shipyards were made and as the capacity of Coatbridge was exhausted.

For a further elucidation of the links between railways and the iron industry it is worth considering one particular ironworks in Scotland. Dalmellington in the Doon Valley of Ayrshire witnessed a development of coal mining in the early nineteenth century and this was followed up by ironstone working in the 1840s when the Houldsworths, who owned blast furnaces at Coltness in Lanarkshire, decided to stake a claim to additional raw materials. Their furnace at Waterside, between Dalmellington and Patna, was opened in 1848. It stands as part of the process of locational diversification which took place as Lanarkshire ironmasters moved into Ayrshire to safeguard their position as some of the older iron ore fields approached exhaustion. At the time, however, there was no railway beyond Ayr and all the plant had to be taken in by road. However, the works opened in full anticipation of a railway being built and the line was duly provided in 1856. What is particularly interesting about Dalmellington, however, is the internal use of railways to convey coal and ore to the furnaces. Mining took place on the high ground to the north and iron mines at Corbie Craigs and Drumgrange were reached by private railways, including inclined planes. By 1875 a more efficient system had developed. The internal system and the public railway (Glasgow & South Western) were segregated so that local minerals could go directly to the furnace bank while all activities on the plateau, which extended from Bowhill through Burnfoothill and Lethanhill to Benwhat (Corbie Craigs) were integrated by a single steam railway (previously horses had been used), extending from the top of Drumgrange Incline. Exhaustion of the ore led to dependence on Spanish imports, but even before the closure of iron mines on the plateau there had been difficulties arising from the unsuitability of blackband ore for steel making. Postwar rationalisation led to closure of the furnaces in 1921, leaving Dalmellington to concentrate on coal mining, at Craigmark (Chalmerston and Minnivey) and at Pennyvenie, until the 1960s. Drumgrange Incline survived until 1933 when access to the plateau was restricted to narrow gauge inclines linked to the Pennyvenie Branch. Thus a rapidly changing local railway system becomes an important frame for the study of a vigorous local industry.

Similar developments can be traced in other parts of the country. There is a colourful story to be told in Cleveland where ironstone quarries and related ironworks created a stimulus for construction of mineral railways. Activity at Glaisdale and Grosmont followed the opening of the Esk Valley line to Whitby, but workings at Rosedale in the 1860s and 1870s required construction of a purely mineral railway which ran from Battersby, reaching the plateau by means of the Ingleby Incline and then contouring round the hillsides to Blakey and Rosedale. However, detailed study will concentrate on the East Midlands of England, where iron ores which had apparently been used to a modest extent in Roman times at Colsterworth and Hunsbury Hill. There may have been ironworks in Edward the Confessor's time at Corby and Gretton. The low grade ores were then in effect rediscovered in the mid-nineteenth century, the interest arising from the exhaustion of Coal Measure ores which led the ironmasters of Derbyshire and Staffordshire to seek out alternative supplies. But another factor was the exposure of ironstone beds as the main line railways were cut through the scarps. For example the Midland Railway line from Leicester to Hitchin in 1857 provided useful evidence of the extent of the iron ore through the cutting at

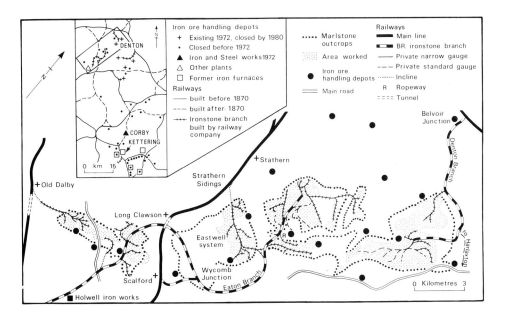

Map 12. Railways and ironstone quarrying in the East Midlands, with particular reference to the Belvoir area of Leicestershire. The inset shows the East Midland ironstone field and the location of the Stathern–Denton area.

Glendon, while the same company in building their direct line to Nottingham cut into the ironstone beds at Holwell near Melton Mowbray where the new line swung away from the Syston–Peterborough line. Indeed, at Holwell it was Richard Dalgleish, surveyor of the new railway, who noticed the geological characteristics and eventually set up the Holwell Iron Company: the first ore was sent to Derbyshire in 1876 but five years later blast furnaces were lit at Asfordby Hill where the Holwell Branch joined the Midland Railway's main line.

However, it was back in 1851 that the first consignments of Jurassic ore were sent to Staffordshire and it was in 1853 that a local industrialist set up a small furnace at Wellingborough and developed smelting techniques which helped to overcome prejudice against a new type of raw material. For the Jurassic ore had distinctive chemical characteristics which needed research before the material could be assimilated by the industry. There was rapid expansion of output during the 1860s and 1870s when the ores of Marlstone and Northampton Sands became established as a basic element in the national supply pattern. A crucial factor at this time was introduction of basic refractory linings in steel converters (the Gilchrist-Thomas method) which made the phosphoric ores of the Jurassic Belt acceptable for steelmaking. Hence the flow of Northampton Sand ironstone to Scunthorpe for blending with the low-phosphorous Frodingham ironstone. But because the material was of relatively low grade (20–25 percent) and was therefore bulky in relation to value, it was important that any workings should be situated close to a railway and should also allow quarry working with minimum depths of overburden. Private railways could be built to link up with the main lines but unless very large amounts of ore were being forwarded such lines would have to be as short as possible. Thus in areas with suitable geological conditions the geography of ironstone working shows development taking off from the principal railways. Working in the quarries was done entirely by hand until the introduction of the steam navvy at the turn of the century. The result was that a relatively large number of working faces were needed to meet a particular level of demand, relative to twentieth-century situation when individual quarries could be worked more intensively. Hence the late nineteenth-century geography involved a large number of quarries, each with a relatively modest output, and therefore elaborate railway building was not economically feasible.

There were further hazards arising from the variable quality of the ore: ambitious plans were made for quarrying at Nevill Holt near Medbourne in Leicestershire in the 1860s and they included proposals for blast furnaces, puddling works and rolling mills. But the local raw material was unsatisfactory and the quarries were quickly abandoned. Hence in addition to their short length the early ironstone railways were almost invariably narrow gauge as well, while the substantial differences in altitude between hillside quarries and a scarpfoot railway were overcome by inclines. At Nevill Holt the tubs were lowered down to the Rugby–Peterborough railway which followed the floodplain of the Welland Valley. The inconvenience of transferring ore to standard gauge wagons could be minimised by using the break of gauge point as the site for calcining ore (roasting it in banks to increase the iron content). It could also contribute to a decision to establish blast furnaces on the orefield at points where local quarry systems linked up with the main lines. The Holt project failed but after the experiment at Wellingborough furnaces followed at Heyford (1855), Finedon and Stowe (1866), Irthlingborough (1867), Hunsbury Hill and Islip (1873), Cransley (1875) and Kettering (1877). Although there was no coal available in these localities fuel could be railed in at reasonable cost as a return load for wagons taking iron ore to traditional centres of metallurgy.

The 1880s saw the opening of a further plant at Holwell (1881) and modernisation at Irthlingborough (1884), Wellingborough (1885) and Cransley/Kettering (1889–90). Hunsbury Hill and Islip were the only others still open at this time. The idea was to concentrate investment in places where there were ample local ironstone reserves. The ultimate stage in this trend was reached at Corby where the first furnaces opened in 1908. The relatively great depth of overburden delayed the commencement of quarrying until long after the opening of the Kettering–Nottingham line in 1879. The steam navvy eventually became available and was first introduced by Lloyds at Corby in 1895. Huge resources were available in the area especially as draglines of larger capacity allowed overburden of up to thirty metres to be tackled in the post-war period compared with only twenty before. There was enough iron ore accessible to justify building an integrated iron and steel plant. This was closed in 1980 not because of exhaustion of raw material but because of falling demand and the lower production costs from giant complexes on the coast which draw high grade imported raw material shipped in by large ore carriers. The smaller ironworks surviving from the late nineteenth century had, meantime, all closed down by 1960.

It is notable that in the Wellingborough–Kettering–Thrapston triangle, where the railways were conveniently aligned for the quarry companies, there was an intensive development of quarrying and also a cluster of ironworks. Further north the lines were more widely spaced, certainly before the developments of the 1870s when the new Midland link between Kettering and Nottingham and the L.N.W.R.–G.N.R. joint line between Market Harborough and Newark were put through, with ironstone trade as a probable factor in their calculations.Ironstone had been revealed through a geological survey of Belvoir for the Duke of Rutland by I. A. Knipe, but distance from the railway was a problem and discouraged such trials as were carried out at Croxton Kerrial and elsewhere. In the 1890s the Midland & Great Northern Joint Railway made a contribution and opened up the Market Overton area. Further stimulus from the main railway companies came through the building of short branches specially for the benefit of the ironstone traffic. The Midland built lines to Cottesmore (1882) and Cransley (1877) while the Great Northern served Denton (1885) and Stainby (1917); both companies reached out to Eaton – the Great Northern in 1884 while the Midland Railway which had provided a branch as far as Holwell in 1876 continued to Wycomb Junction in 1887. These lines reduced the length of private railways and accelerated the development of quarries. However, although there are considerable reserves in the Eaton–Denton area, especially north-east of Scalford, some beds have been left because they are too thin and too lean (only fifteen percent iron). This is particularly true of the limey marlstone which has been valued in the past largely because of its rôle as a flux when mixed with Northampton Sands ore. Nevertheless there was a considerable growth of small private railways in the Belvoir area of north-east Leicester. Apart from the lines from Wartnaby to Old Dalby (1878) and from Eastwell to Harby & Stathern (1880), both using inclines to negotiate the scarp face, all the quarry lines linked up with the branches built by the major railway companies. These private lines continued to be narrow gauge at first but from the beginning of

22.   *Railways in the service of the iron industry* Diesel locomotives outside the British Steel Corporation's shed at Corby in Northamptonshire. This ironstone quarry railway system was the last one in Britain to close and survived until 1980.

the twentieth century the convenience of direct shipment usually led to standard gauge and this trend reached its climax with the avoidance of inclines in favour of zig-zags across the scarp face (as at Harlaxton, built during the Second World War as a branch from the Denton line) and conversion of older narrow gauge lines, although Eastwell with its incline and narrow gauge remained unchanged up to closure in 1962. Internal lines within iron and steel works were also standard gauge, as at Corby where the private system reaches out towards Gretton, Harringworth and Stanion.

The recent rundown has been rapid. The reorganisation of iron ore depots in 1972 has been overtaken by a further contraction of demand which left Corby as the only remaining centre of activity in the late 1970s. And Corby itself closed in 1980. After generating considerable areas of derelict land through the dumping of spoil in a 'hill and dale' formation appropriate only for rough pasture and forestry, an Ironstone Restoration Fund has operated since 1951 to ensure a complete conversion back to agriculture. Lack of sufficient infill results in the persistence of some gulleys, discreetly hidden by tree planting, which became haunts of anglers and ornithologists. Railways too have largely reverted to farmland, though the branches built by the major railway companies and passed into British Rail ownership do not come under the restoration scheme and remain derelict. The

23. *Preservation at the ironstone quarries* The Ironstone Railway Preservation Society, now established at Cottesmore in Leicestershire, is seen exercising one of its preserved engines at Market Overton, the initial base of operations.

Saltby–Stainby line has been mentioned as a possible means of transporting coal from Saltby should the Belvoir coalmining project gain approval, though a new line direct to Saxby may well be preferred by British Rail. But an Ironstone Railway Preservation Society is making good use of the Cottesmore Branch having transferred their operations from a less satisfactory base at Market Overton.

So today the ironstone railways are often difficult to trace. But to the discerning eye there are many subtle features in the landscape and anyone armed with details of these industrial layouts can see that today's countryside is not completely secretive. Yet the railways can also be enjoyed as a chapter of history with their development slotting into the local geology but with the mainline railways, the estate structure and the technology (both of quarrying and iron production) as essential contexts.

# 18

# Railways and Distilleries in North Scotland

A particularly colourful linkage between railways and industry may be traced in Scotland in respect of the tradition of whisky distilling. The early history of this industry is obscure, and this provides some scope for speculation and a contribution to the mystique of the Scotch whisky romance. Popular belief in close links with the Highlands, originating in a Dark Age celtic migration from Ireland and perpetuated assiduously by medieval monastic communities who practised the art in remote northern outposts, is difficult to reconcile with the fact that the bulk of the production has always been from the Central Belt as long as reliable statistics have been available (since the late eighteenth century). However, there is no doubt that the industry was prominent in parts of the Highlands by the end of the eighteenth century. It was expanding because grain which was not required for subsistence but was too poor to stand the cost of transport to markets in the south could be converted into a more saleable product. And it is not surprising to hear of whisky distillation in those remote areas with grain surpluses or in places well situated to collect grain from a surrounding catchment. The product would be consumed locally and in the West Highlands where relatively little cereal growing took place, while some export to the south by pack ponies would pay for the import of textiles and metal goods.

An essential ingredient in the complex saga of economic history is the attempt by government to create a uniform system of excise duties and controls. In the Central Belt where distillers were prominent industrialists there was no way that the new impositions could be evaded but in the Highlands unacceptable regulations led to a large illicit sector: freedom from controls resulted in better whisky which was acceptable in the south in preference to the local product and with bitter resentment against 'English' excise laws, so fully acknowledged in the novels of Sir Walter Scott, the Highland product stood to gain in prestige from its illegality alone. A further factor derives from the switch from French to British spirits, partly through a revulsion association with the Napoleonic Wars and partly through increased vigilance against smuggling. It is impossinle to measure the importance of these considerations in an industry which depends so heavily on prevailing fashions but it is a fact that Highland whisky first attracted significant outside demand in a context of changing relationships with France and a Westminster government feeling its way towards a new excise regime. A reputation was established which was crucial to survival after 1822, when sufficient concessions were made by government to bring the bulk of the Highland industry on to a legal basis. The Highland malt whisky had its own specific characteristics arising from the secondary constituents of the local water supplies and from damp yet mild maturation climate, but its history provided some further protection against the stiff competition from the Central Belt distillers who were closer to the urban markets and gained economies from a relatively large scale of production.

The transition in the Highlands from illicit to licensed production can be seen with greatest continuity in Glenlivet, a Speyside district notorious for its illicit stills at the turn of the eighteenth century. As long as there was no basis for a legal distillery (because quite apart from rates of duty the regulations over whisky strength and still size were inappropriate to the district) the landowner was obliged to condone lawlessness: without illicit stills his tenants could not afford to pay their rents and what was at the time an expanding population would become destitute. But a licensed distillery would be far preferable to the landowner if the terms were right: activity could be located in a more central place and the modernisation of the estate could go ahead on a more rational and profitable basis. The owner of Glenlivet (and also of extensive adjacent areas) was the Duke of Richmond and Gordon who strongly supported the legislation passed in 1822. The following year George Smith took a licence for his bothy business at Upper Drumin and gradually increased his production, most of which was shipped through the Moray ports of Burghead and Garmouth. The demand for barley was satisfied mainly from the nearby farms which Smith leased and improved. After a fire at Drumin he relocated his distillery at Minmore, which was more convenient for the farms that supplied his barley and for the road to the coast. It is at Minmore where the much-enlarged Glenlivet Distillery stands today. But the continuity is not always quite so clear. Although a distillery integrated very well with agriculture based on cropping and cattle rearing (with a local barley supply guaranteed as well as a market for all the spent grains or draff) the need for large financial resources and adequate managerial skills to cover such a diversified business could not always be met.

In a highly competitive situation it was those Highland malt whiskies with the most attractive character and bouquet which secured their position in the market. Although there are broad categories of whisky it is well known that in the malt sector each distillery has a unique product, arising from its water supply and distinctive distillery utensils. As some of the large Lowland distillers started to use a patent still and produced grain whisky (with very little malt) by a continuous process, the Highland malt distiller was excluded from the popular end of the market and had to take his chance in a limited market where the higher qualities were appreciated. A further twist in a complicated story is contributed by the rise of the blending firms which grew out of small licensed groceries, as it was found that there was a vast market for whisky mixtures where a combination of malt whiskies 'covered' a proportion (initially fifty percent, but usually more today) of grain spirit. Hence the crucial factor lay in the preferences of the blenders who eventually purchased their own distilleries in order to control the whiskies most important for their blends. It so happened that the Highland malts from Speyside, with their moderately peaty flavours, achieved the greatest popularity and the increased demand for malt whisky which the blending boom inevitably triggered off at the end of the nineteenth century was felt most strongly in this area.

After a long preamble, unavoidable if the complexities of the industry are to be exposed, the railway theme can be introduced. Compared with the pack ponies used by the illicit distillers and the coastal shipping services patronised by the first generation of whisky lairds, the railway provided vastly improved connection with the Central Belt. Highland malt whisky could compete more effectively but the advantage varied according to proximity of the railway from each distillery. Distilleries in the small towns such as Forres, Keith and Inverness were close to the station but for Glenlivet the station at Ballindalloch still involved considerable carting although it was a shorter haul for the Clydesdales than the journey to the Moray coast.

However, although the quality of the railway access varied from one distillery to another it would not be expected that distilleries would prosper simply in accordance with the transport service available to them. For each whisky established its own reputation and modest differentials in transport costs would not have the same rationalising impact as with a more homogeneous product. On the other hand if new distilleries were being planned then locations would be sought where acceptable water supplies could be combined with rail access. This comes out very clearly in Speyside where many new distilleries were built or rebuilt in the late nineteenth century. The expansions seem to have begun with Cragganmore (Ballindalloch) in 1869 and its success was attributed to the services of a Dundee merchant who had first marketed the product and, at the time of distillery journalist Alfred Barnard's visit in 1887, was taking all the production. The older distilleries which had been planned without any conception of rail transport happened in some cases to be very close to a railway: at Belmenach and Dailuaine for example branches were built

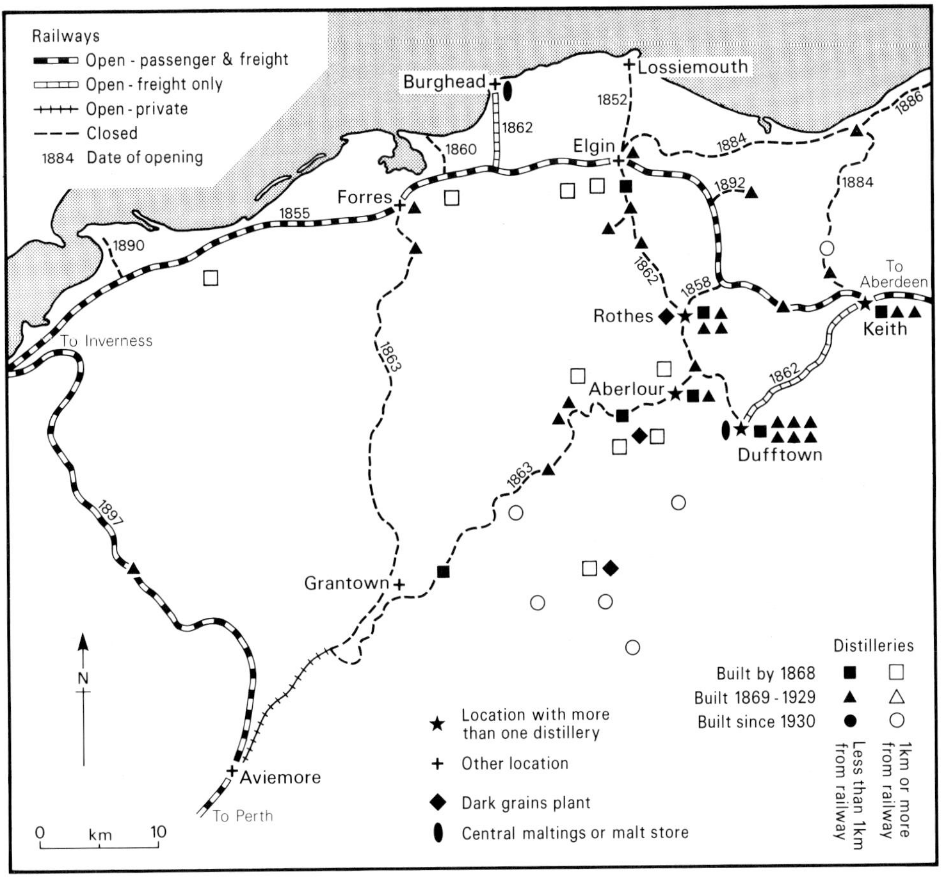

Railways
Open - passenger & freight
Open - freight only
Open - private
Closed
1884 Date of opening
Burghead
Lossiemouth
1852
1862
1860
Elgin
1884
1886
Forres
1855
1892
1884
1890
1862
1858
To Aberdeen
Rothes
Keith
To Inverness
1863
Aberlour
1862
Dufftown
1863
1897
Grantown
N
Distilleries
Built by 1868
Built 1869 - 1929
Built since 1930
Location with more than one distillery
Other location
Dark grains plant
Central maltings or malt store
Less than 1km from railway
1km or more from railway
Aviemore
To Perth
0 km 10


Map 13. Railways and whisky distilleries on Speyside.

into the distilleries. But Cragganmore was situated alongside the Craigellachie–Boat of Garten Railway and all subsequent distillery developments up to the First World War show a very close relationship with local railways: Knockando and Tamdhu are right on the railway while the older Cardow distillery is higher up the hill and Craigellachie, while not physically connected to the railway, is nevertheless much more conveniently situated for the station than Macallan on the opposite side of the valley. Considerable clusters emerged at Elgin, Rothes and above all Dufftown, where the town's 'seven stills' (six of them dating to the railway age) were considered analagous to the 'seven hills' of Rome!

The distillery traffic, complemented along the coast by the growth of fishing in the settlements between Banff and Buckie, helps to account for a

24. *Distillery landscape* Standing beside the now–abandoned Elgin–Dufftown–Keith railway is one of the several distilleries which opened in Rothes during the railway age.

curious concentration of railway lines in the Lower Spey area. Although partly induced by the rivalry between the Highland Railway and the G.N.o.S., whose systems touched at this point, only the Highland Railway's Keith–Buckie line and the parallelism of the Buckie–Elgin and Fochabers–Elgin lines are plainly anomalous cases of duplication to increase competition. The railways did not significantly affect the decision to locate distilleries in the Moray district because this was determined primarily by the demand for the local whisky characterised by the secondary constituents of the water draining off peaty moors developed on granites and granulites (with limestone bands having a pronounced effect on the water supplies around Keith). But the siting of the new distilleries shows an obvious functional connection. In other parts of the Highlands there was little demand for additional distilleries and so the building of railways was not generally associated with new industrial development although in the few cases available, Ben Wyvis (Dingwall), Glenglassaugh (Portsoy) and Glenugie (Peterhead) the siting shows the usual awareness of the railway. Probably the most dramatic expansion outside of Moray has taken place in Islay, which is dependent on shipping services. The Islay malts have heavy peaty flavours which make a contribution to most blended whiskies.

Location decision-making is dominated by considerations of quality and the anomalous Islay case provides a decisive rebuttal of any supposition that the railways were a direct cause of distillery expansion.

After the boom of the late nineteenth century, the whisky trade went through a very difficult period. Wartime shortages of cereals forced a drastic cut-back during the First World War while the temperance movement (reflected most dramatically by prohibition in the U.S.A.) greatly upset market demand. On the other hand, depression created opportunities for the blending companies to strengthen their grip on the industry and most malt distilleries are now owned by vertically integrated companies. The Distillers Company provides the best example, with ownership of nearly half the grain whisky capacity and forty percent of the malt (1973) as well as several major blending and bottling establishments. But smaller organisations, some British like William Grant and some foreign like Hiram Walker & Sons and Long John International, follow the same pattern. In each case the prime concern with blended whisky ensures a continuing role for the Highland distilleries: the former animosity between the grain and malt distillers has been overcome and straight grain whisky is now hardly ever seen on the market. This business structure underpins the postwar

25.  *Station overhaul at Tamdhu* The station on the Speyside Railway (Aviemore to Craigellachie) has been taken over by the adjacent distillery and used as a visitor reception centre. The railway trackbed is now used for recreational purposes in connection with the 'Speyside Way'.

boom in whisky sales which is once again leading to larger and larger stocks being laid down for maturation. The industry must inevitably speculate because there is a minimum maturation period of three years, laid down by law, and many malt whiskies remain in the warehouses much longer. History is repeating itself as regards the popularity of the Speyside malts but today the transport pattern is again different. The use of road transport means that there is no necessity to build near to railways and it is evident that the most modern distilleries stand aside from even those few railways which remain open. Some building has taken place in remote parts of Glenlivet, once the stronghold of the illicit operators. However, the railway is used to transport cereals to the central maltings (at Burghead and Keith) which have led to the closure of malting floors at individual distilleries. But apart from use of the railway to take malt to a store, as at Dufftown, distribution is done by road.

So the railway connection is now rather tenuous in the Highland distillery trade. The Craigellachie–Boat of Garten line which provided a lifeline for so many distilleries in its time closed in 1968. But the line has not disappeared completely because a walkway has now been provided. The Speyside Way will eventually run from Spey Bay on the coast to Glenmore at the foot of the Cairngorms and use will be made of old railways, with visitor facilities at Aberlour. Specific links with distilling come out at Tamdhu (Knockando) where the local distillery has taken over the station as a reception centre for visitors (Tamdhu being one of several distilleries on a highly popular 'whisky trail'). Again, between Aviemore and Boat of Garten a private steam railway has opened, with ambitions to extend as far as Grantown. The locomotive stock includes *Balmenach* and *Dailuaine*, which are both o–4–o tank engines formerly used for shunting in distillery sidings and given to the Strathspey Railway Company by Scottish Malt Distillers. Less authentic is the 'Glenfiddich' label attached to one of the restored coaches on the railway: it ties in with the Glenfiddich distillery of William Grant, one of the first in the district to cater for large numbers of visitors and so becomes a key element in the local tourist trade.

# 19

# Railways and Farming

Even during the construction phase the railway could make a strong impact on a rural district, through the need for lodgings for labourers and the demand for sand, timber and other commodities from local estates. But much more important was the long term benefit for agriculture through the easier movement of livestock and crops, as well as manure and machinery. All this made it easier for farmers to specialise in whatever production for which their land was physically suitable. And for traditional products there was a wider choice of markets as food could be sent to places where the highest prices were obtainable. In the West Country for example, through rail services to London allowed farmers to gain access to more lucrative markets. Meat and fish were diverted to London and this led to local difficulties since farmers had previously supplied Cornwall at relatively low prices. Products like potatoes and broccoli increased in importance: before the railway only small quantities had been shipped from Hayle to Bristol. Flower growing also flourished. In the 1935 centenary of the Great Western Railway the company claimed that it had played an essential part in the growth of the flower-growing industry of the Scilly Isles, since 'thousands of tons' of cut flowers were being annually transported in ventilated vans by fast trains to Covent Garden and the principal provincial markets.

The dairying industry was greatly affected by the railway. While many farmers produced milk there was not usually any great local demand for liquid milk and so most of the production went for butter and cheese. Demand for fresh milk in the cities was met by cow keepers operating within the built-up area, or working on farms close to the suburbs. Thus, in the late eighteenth century the pastures of Islington were renowned and milk was taken into London by milkmaids (often the wives of immigrant Welsh and Irish labourers). But by the mid-nineteenth century the size of London was such that cows had to be kept within the city and fed on spent grains from breweries. Many of these dairy businesses were situated in the eastern suburbs where rural families with a knowledge of dairy farming (including many from Cardiganshire) had settled. Standards of hygiene were not good and serious cattle diseases broke out (rinderpest in 1865). During the 1870s health regulations were enforced and insistence on better conditions reduced profit margins and gave greater opportunity to the country dairy farmers to market liquid milk. The railways were of course well established but it needed a willingness on the part of the companies to cope with the special requirements of trade in terms of equipment and operation and to stimulate traffic by attractive rates. An adequate wholesale organisation was also required. So although it is claimed that the first farmer to send milk to London by express train did so in 1864 it was not until the 1870s that the traffic assumed significant proportions.

London's milkshed extended outwards from Berkshire and Wiltshire in the 1870s to Somerset in the 1880s and right through the West Country by the end of the century. Milk trains were worked from Penzance, Wellington, Weymouth and Wootton Bassett – also from the Whitland/Carmarthen area of South Wales. In the old days milk trains consisted entirely of vans loaded with ten-gallon churns. But the pattern has changed considerably with the introduction of glass-lined tank wagons: also with the appearance of the Milk Marketing Board which collects milk from farms and pasteurises it before transporting it to rail-loading centres. Initially the milk train was a significant influence in connecting town and country. Thomas Hardy writes in *Tess of the D'Urbervilles* how 'modern life stretched out its steam feeler' to the country dairy 'three or four times a day, touched the native existences and quickly withdrew its feeler again as if what it touched had been uncongenial'. Milk churns were loaded into trucks and locals reflected on the destination of the milk in London where it would be drunk by 'noble men and noble women, ambassadors and centurions, ladies and trades-women, and babies who had never seen a cow'.

Agriculture in the Fenlands of East Anglia was considerably intensified by the railways. In the Wisbech area there was a particularly powerful contribution since the main line services were complemented by a branch line which ran along the side of the public highway as far as Upwell. Normally carts or lorries were required to connect the farms with the railheads but at Wisbech many farmers had the railway at their gates. Railway services in the Fens started in the 1840s. The line from March through Wisbech to King's Lynn was open in 1848 and it presented the possibility of extending the production of fruit and vegetables, given the greater ease of distribution, for the soil and climate were admirably suited to horticulture and market gardening. Over the years smallholdings multiplied in numbers and cottages became strung out along the roads in the Wisbech area, anticipating the ribbon development which was to become so common after the First World War. Some food processing was carried on locally and the canning industry remains very important locally, but there was also distribution of vegetables and soft fruit over considerable areas: hence the 'strawberry specials' which delivered Fenland produce to the East Midlands. Such was the intensity of production round Wisbech that in addition to the main lines of the Great Eastern and Midland & Great Northern Joint companies a tramway was built from Wisbech along the road from Wisbech to Outwell (1883) and on to the next village of Upwell the following year. In addition to the places mentioned there were depots at Elm, Boyces Bridge and Outwell Basin. Timber and coal (some of it for supply by water to Fenland pumping stations) was taken into the country while the fruit was brought out. Although roadside tramways were once quite numerous this one is remarkable for its late appearance and also for its retention by British Rail until 1966 (though the passenger service was ousted by road competition in 1927). And until 1962, when diesel locomotives took over, motive power was provided by tram engines: steam locomotives were boxed in, with cowcatchers and side places, to minimise risk of injury to road users. The railway was also important in stimulating market gardening in the Vale of Evesham where the river terraces were accessible to both the Great Western and Midland Railway by 1868: the presence of two companies, as in the Fens, meant good facilities and attractive preferential rates.

Hill farming also benefited from the improvement in communications. Before the railways were built livestock were normally driven 'on the hoof' from the upland rearing areas to the markets, especially London. Because of the loss of condition brought about by arduous journeys along the 'drove roads' it was essential for animals to be fattened only when they neared their final destination. Even on the comparatively short journey into London from fattening pastures animals might lose several pounds in weight. The remote rearing areas had inevitably to concentrate on production of store animals. However, the railway system greatly eased the movement of cattle, with special trucks being provided, and farmers in remote rural areas now had the option of fattening if they so desired. The decision would rest on such considerations as the availability of feeding stuffs on the farm and the supply of store cattle. The north-east of Scotland was able to intensify its livestock industry quite remarkably in the late nineteenth century and Aberdeen became a great beef factory consigning both live and dead meat south. The railway assisted through provision of branches to railheads on the margins of the uplands as well as by main line links with southern markets. Some store cattle came from crofts newly broken on the moorland edge while other animals were brought in from Ireland: regular steamship services were of great value in this connection. Specialisation was reinforced by the greater ease with which food could be imported so that the subsistence function of upland farms was eroded to some extent.

The railways also facilitated the transfer of young Highland sheep to mild wintering grounds on the Moray Firth coastlands, or in the case of the Argyll and Perth districts, to Lothian and Tayside. To W. Ackworth, writing in 1890, it seemed a suitable response by Highland farmers to the

26.   *Hill farming in the Grampians* More land was reclaimed for smallholdings on the flanks of the Grampians when the availability of railway services stimulated farmers and crofters to rear more store cattle for the fattening farms on the lower ground.

lead given by the then Prince of Wales in sending his hunting horses from Sandringham to Windsor each spring for a change of air! But it was also a logical answer to the problem faced by west Highland farms in having little sheltered low ground for wintering stock, when on the east coast there were suitable pastures and a plentiful supply of fodder to go with them. There was a widespread belief that young sheep wintered in the east subsequently performed better as breeding ewes on the Highland hills and the practice has continued to the present although road transport is now universal.

Of course, it does not follow that farmers automatically took advantage of every opportunity the railway may have afforded them. Some interesting discussion has taken place over the situation in Wales. Here the railway offered possibilities of supplying dairy products to a wider market and giving greater emphasis to cattle fattening rather than rearing. But farms were small and tenants were reluctant to invest in buildings or equipment, so closely was efficiency related to minimum capital outlays. Any improvement, whether by individual or by cooperative initiative, was seen as a lever which landowners could use to raise rents. In the livestock sector the railways put an end to the cattle droving which had previously flourished on a countrywide scale and also taken place locally, between the Vale of Glamorgan and the Heads of the Valleys. And although some fairs were retained, as a convenient form of periodic marketing in rearing areas with a sparse and scattered population, there was a switch to regular auction markets at railway centres for dealing in fatstock. But a pronounced switch to fatstock was ruled out by inadequate investment in shelter on the small farms. It could be argued that the increasing mobility of labour (again related to the railway) reduced interest in orthodox pastoral farming in favour of dairying, which could pay well and make only modest labour demands. But although some liquid milk found its way into the cities (including Liverpool) and coastal resorts, there was a strong traditional emphasis through continuation of butter and cheese production which was suited to the local taste (especially on the coalfield) but not attractive in more distant markets. Welsh butter marketed in the Black Country was generally found to be too salty while native cheese (including Caerphilly, which Welsh miners appreciated because it didn't crumble) lost ground to foreign competition, even within the Principality. Cooperatives could have provided a basis for improving quality, with due attention to branding and packaging, but the prevailing peasant mentality prevented full advantage being taken of the admittedly modest opportunities which the railway offered.

# 20

# Railways for Recreation

The railway was certainly very important for the growth of interest in tourism, and especially seaside holidays, in the nineteenth century. For example, the tramways of the Isle of Man have been considered 'at once the product and the means of the tourist industry's growth'. There is no doubt that the great increase in the number and the size of watering places dates from the railway age. However, the initial growth of the seaside resorts lies in medical benefits which were seriously advocated in the late eighteenth century. After the Napoleonic Wars removed the insecurity of living on the coast the tourist traffic could develop and more and more coastal settlements gained a new function: one which Bath had known since Roman times and which inland spas like Cheltenham, Harrogate and Tunbridge had found more recently. Some coastal resorts were able to exploit mineral waters, notably Scarborough, but it was mainly the interest in sea bathing that stimulated development. Sometimes old harbours and fishing ports were developed (Brighton, Margate, Weymouth) but in some other cases virgin sites were involved.

Southport is a good example of the latter type of development. In response to the growing popularity of bathing carnivals in the area a local hotelier built a hostelry among the dunes of South Howes, as Southport was then known. This initiative of 1792 grew into a bolder speculation, the South Port Hotel, which can still be seen, standing at the junction of Lord Street and Duke Street. During the early nineteenth century Georgian terraces developed along a natural axis running from the seaside hamlet to the older settlement of Churchtown. Landlords played a positive rôle in selling off land for development while laying down onerous standards and preventing any penetration by factory industry. But an important element in the picture is provided by the Leeds & Liverpool Canal which provided a means of access as far as Scarisbrick Bridge, where visitors were met by hotel carriages. So Southport was already established as a fashionable watering place before the railway arrived from Liverpool in 1848. But the railways exerted a strong influence through the conveyance of larger numbers of holidaymakers and through the possibilities that were made available for the more affluent families to live in Southport, while the breadwinner commuted to work in Liverpool or Manchester. The town grew rapidly, with its baths, promenade, marine lakes, opera house and winter gardens, yet retained its fashionable air and excellent public health image: landowners continued to give close attention to planning matters and in the Birkdale suburb the Weld-Blundell family encouraged the building of large residences. The railways were part of a successful process of urban development – a point brought out dramatically in the rebuilding of Lord Street with the erection of Marine Villas, various exclusive fashion establishments and Lord Street Station.

There was a massive increase in tourism in Cornwall associated with the railway. Although Falmouth failed to regain its packet it did succeed in attracting tourists. A drive around Pendennis, constructed in 1860, was much appreciated and the juxtaposition of the tourist route with the old castle of Pendennis, built by Henry VIII in 1544 to defend the harbour (also St Mawes 1539) points dramatically to the change in function. Railway interest in expanding the tourist trade can be seen in advertising. Although in part this preoccupation with publicity reflected a concern over the threat of competition from road transport in its various forms there was also an awareness of the greater income that could result from popularisation of the holiday habit. The Great Western had good possibilities through its position in South Wales and the West Country and its publications encouraging 'Pleasure Parties' in the 1870s developed into a more substantial 'Programme of Excursion Arrangements' twenty years later. In 1906 came the first edition of *Holiday Haunts* and it cannot have been a coincidence that this was the year that marked the completion of a long series of railway improvements affecting the West Country. The main line through Cornwall had needed substantial improvement in order to make it satisfactory for handling heavier passenger traffic associated with the tourist trade during a period of rapid growth in the 1890s. Track was doubled after the abolition of the broad gauge in 1892 and the work spread over a decade. Some realignment took place simultaneously, notably between St Germans and Saltash, where a new line through Shillingham Tunnel opened in 1908. Such improvements, plus the provision of a direct line between Reading and Taunton, meant an acceleration of through trains like the 'Cornish Riviera' Express introduced in 1905. The 'Cornish Riviera' label was carefully fostered by the company (including analogies with its Italian counterpart) and it was fundamental to the concept of the G.W.R. as 'The Holiday Line', a rewarding publicity coup which made its first appearance in *Holiday Haunts* in 1908. Renewed growth of tourism brought another round of railway improvements and Penzance Station was much enlarged in 1937.

Encouragement of tourism was very much in the railway interest. It is interesting to consider the Furness Railway which was suffering from a trade depression in 1895 when a new secretary was appointed. Mr Alfred

Aslett, who came from the Cambrian Railways, which relied heavily on passenger traffic, naturally looked to this area of business as a means of increasing receipts. The potential of Furness for tourism was appreciated and a 'Six Lakes Tour' was advertised – a combined rail, coach and steamer excursion taking in Windermere, Ullswater, Derwentwater, Thirlmere, Grasmere and Rydal Water. As a result of this and other promotions there was a considerable increase in the number of passengers. Efforts were also made to reinforce Barrow's position on the route to the Isle of Man and Ireland. Although Heysham Harbour opened in 1904 the Midland agreed to maintain its services through Barrow for a period while arrangements were made for the North Eastern to run a daily service from Newcastle to Barrow in connection with the sailing to Douglas. There was also the excursion traffic to Fleetwood.

Direct railway interest in resort development can be seen at Whitby, with its strong associations with George Hudson, and at Silloth where the North British Railway gained access in 1856 by building over the Carlisle Canal (with a short extension) and went on to provide a harbour and tourist facilities. Docks were opened in 1859 and 1885, attracting considerable trade (despite competition from Maryport) including cargo boats and passenger steamers, while the company's provision of public baths helped to encourage the recreational function. Not that the railway always contributed directly to the growth of facilities. On the Lincolnshire coast the resorts of Mablethorpe, Skegness and Sutton certainly owe their origins to the presence of the railway network. A great arc of railway swung through the county from Boston to Grimsby and Gainsborough by 1849. A branch was taken off to the market town of Wainfleet in 1871 and extended to the coast at Skegness two years later, while separate branches to Mablethorpe (1877) and Sutton (1886) were connected together along the coast in 1888 to complete a loop. But in all three cases however the railway company, the Great Northern, did not actively invest in the facilities. This was different from the experience further north at Cleethorpes, where the Manchester Sheffield & Lincolnshire were directly involved in a dockland development. The same combination of tourism and docks might have been promoted at Sutton had the Lancashire Derbyshire & East Coast Railway succeeded in building a new east-west railway from Warrington to Chesterfield, Lincoln and Sutton, as envisaged in an act of 1891, but only the central section was ever built.

Even in the Scottish Highlands the growth of tourism seems to have opened up new horizons in the planning of railways and provided a spur to a new explosion of rivalry after some relatively tranquil years. W. Ackworth, writing on the railways of Scotland in 1890, described the tourist traffic as 'splendidly profitable'. Holidays could be afforded by more and more people and 'if the working classes, who are steadily cutting down the drink bill, only come to expending half their economies in railway fares, this alone would suffice to pay handsome dividends on a whole series of Forth Bridges'. Such sentiments may well have provided some impetus for new railway schemes to Inverness. First the Great North of Scotland planned a line in 1882 from Dundee to Ballater, Boat of Garten and Inverness. This was blocked by the Highland Railway on the grounds that it was itself building a direct line from Aviemore to Inverness with which the G.N.o.S. might make contact at Carr Bridge. The same tactic was used to counter further G.N.o.S. pressure for a second line from Elgin to Inverness, but the construction of the West Highland Railway to Fort William led to an acceleration of the work on the direct line since it would have been comparatively easy for a competing branch line to be built along the Great Glen into Inverness. The direct line was ready in 1898 and was certainly effective in preventing a line from Fort William being approved: only a short line from Spean Bridge to Fort Augustus was ever built. So the Aviemore–Inverness was not built in the expectation of profit but simply as a defensive measure to prevent loss of traffic to rival companies, spurred on to some extent by the considerable potential for tourism associated with Highland deer forests, grouse moors and spas.

Some final examples of direct railway company involvement in the tourist industry may be associated with the Northern Counties Railway in Ulster. The scenic attractions of the Antrim coast offered an obvious potential. Initially this was linked with a pattern of country living with daily commuting to work by train. Villa tickets were issued to provide concessionary travel for families building substantial houses close to railway stations, but in 1860 a particularly attractive package was offered whereby a free first-class ticket (valid for ten years) was given to anyone building a villa within a mile of any station between Belfast and Castlerock. This concession stimulated development at Whiteabbey and Greenisland, and subsequently, as the scheme was extended through to Larne, at Whitehead. A thriving settlement emerged during the late nineteenth century on an attractive coastal site hard up against the basaltic cliffs of Islandmagee. Growth was managed in many respects by the railway company which acted as a local authority. The transition at Whitehead from fashionable suburb to tourist resort was underpinned by the construction of a promenade and landing stage in 1902 (rebuilt in concrete in 1911) while a beach was artificially created by dumping loads of sand (brought from Portrush) and stabilising the material with groynes. A golf course was provided in 1904. Whitehead became a base for touring Islandmagee and jaunting cars were made available. The increasing number of day trippers were accommodated in a special excursion siding. Railway hotels were proposed in the 1930s for Whitehead and Castlerock but finance was not available.

In contrast to these conventional facilities stands the coastal path built in

1892 which gave access to the foot of the cliffs below the Black Head Lighthouse and by means of tunnels and footbridges allowed some virtually inaccessible places to be reached. Still more elaborate was the Gobbins Path which started near Ballycarry Station (north of Whitehead) and was intended to open up a particularly impressive five kilometre section of the Islandmagee cliffs running north to Heddle's Port. This remarkable undertaking called for tunnelling and bridge building on a grand scale which eventually proved incapable of fulfilment. The scheme owes a great deal to Berkeley Wise who joined the company in 1888 and deployed his engineering and architectural skills on a very broad front up to his retirement in 1906. The first section of the path opened in 1902 but six years later scarcely more than half the programme was complete (though this included a 75 m suspension bridge at a group of caves known as the Seven Sisters). And sadly the accumulated damage of winter storms made it impossible to retain even this beginning: arrears of maintenance resulted in closure between 1940 and 1951 and then serious landslips led to a further closure in 1961 which continues to the present.

Other possibilities existed on the Antrim coast but exploitation was difficult because there was no railway beyond Larne. Several narrow gauge lines were built on to the plateau from Ballymena but only at Portrush was there a standard gauge connection, opened in 1855. The Earl of Antrim was anxious to develop the resort and in support of this plan railway hotels (Laharna, Midland Station and Northern Counties) were provided to accommodate affluent tourists heading for local beaches and for Giant's Causeway (the latter reached by an electric tramway built to Bushmills in 1883 and Giant's Causeway in 1887). Facilities at Portrush were augmented by the Royal Portrush Golf Club (in which the railway company had an interest) in 1888 and a fine new station building with mock Tudor facade in 1893. But meanwhile, the narrow gauge lines built to expedite mining and quarrying on the plateau were facing difficult times. Because of its tourist potential the Northern Counties took over the Parkmore branch in 1884 and improved it to the point where it became suitable for passenger traffic. At an altitude of 300 m Parkmore was the highest railway station in the whole of Ireland. Very steep gradients to the coast ruled out any railway extension to Cushendall, although after the purchase of the Belfast & Northern Counties by the Midland in 1903 the matter was briefly reconsidered. But travellers arriving by rail at Parkmore in 1888 (when passenger services began) could continue down to the sea by road. A particular attraction was Glenariff Glen, an impressive defile lying below the Cushendall road. It was leased by the railway company who developed the glen in 1891 by providing footpaths, rustic bridges, and a teahouse.

Hence the road journey between Parkmore and Cushendall was made particularly attractive, and through effective publicity Glenariff became

27. *The Antrim coast* At Whitehead, a small town greatly influenced by the development policies of the railway company, a cliff walk was laid out for Victorian tourists.

widely known throughout the British Isles. Unlike the Gobbins Path the facilities remain open today. They were purchased outright by the railway company in 1930, for although passenger services to Parkmore ceased in that year the glen still featured in excursion itineraries along the coast road from the railhead at Larne. The property passed through the Ulster Transport Authority to the Northern Ireland Ministry of Agriculture in 1969 and are now part of a parkland complex managed by the Forestry Service, which began planting the peatlands around Parkmore in the 1950s. The walk has been rebuilt and the fog house at Ess-na-Larach waterfall restored. It is also worth noting that the Glenariff estate embraces part of the land traversed by the Red Bay mineral railway of 1873–6 and a 'zig-zag' section is preserved in the footpath system. So exploration of this beauty spot involved railway associations in two senses. The Northern Counties also took over the Ballycastle Railway which had opened in 1881 and encouraged tourists, many of whom took advantage of the coach service to Giant's Causeway.

# 3

# The Contemporary Scene

# 21

# A Changing Railway Industry

During the present century the emphasis has been placed on the contraction of the railway rather than its further expansion. Long before the First World War railway company profits began to dwindle, the result of diminishing returns: working expenses accounted for 62 percent of receipts in 1910 compared with only 47 percent half a century earlier. The problem arose inevitably from the expansion of the network (37.7 thousand kilometres of route in Britain in 1910 compared with 28.8 in 1880) into less profitable areas. Yet the percentage increase in both passenger and freight traffic was greater than the increase in route length, thanks to the growth in traffic density on the principal routes. Unfortunately the financial benefits were reduced by the prominence of cheap fares and freight rates, and also by a very slow improvement in labour productivity. Arguably the railway companies should not have placed so much emphasis on building new lines: instead of expanding their empires territorially, railway managers might perhaps have concentrated most heavily on more efficient operating procedures. Yet while rail transport held a virtual monopoly, pressures to provide new services or improve existing ones could not be rejected. Acceleration of passenger services on main lines involved additional tracks and the construction of new locomotives and rolling stock: large expenditures were required to cater for what at the outset was just a small increase in traffic. And it is noteworthy that in order to expedite rail construction in rural areas government passed a Light Railways Act in 1896 and sponsored special measures for remote areas of Ireland and Scotland.

At the same time as extensions to the rail system were being made in some of the remoter parts of the country the electric tram made its appearance in towns and cities. In London the severity of the challenge was increased by the construction of new underground railways. Change came to the countryside too as the internal combustion engine provided the option of rural transport services by means of motor buses rather than railways and the number of buses on the roads increased sharply after the First World War. Perhaps because of the introduction of these new forms of transport (soon to multiply through the start of inter-city air services) government finally overcame its long-standing objection to regional railway monopolies.

The Railways Act of 1921 (effective in 1923) reduced the number of companies from 120 to four. Although each of the old companies was treated as an indivisible unit it was possible to combine the principle of a regional monopoly (including unified control of coalfields) with retention of competition on a number of profitable inter-city routes. Since the railways had been placed under state control in 1914 and a unified system of rates and charges imposed, it was difficult to envisage any return to the old order, artificially perpetuated for many years by sensitivities over the monopoly question. On the other hand, until the potential of other forms of transport had been properly assessed there could hardly be a consensus in favour of nationalisation. Many people remained 'railway-minded' and even in the 1920s the governors of Lord Wandsworth College near Odiham (Hampshire) seriously contemplated a railway to the London (Waterloo)–Salisbury line at Winchfield to expedite the delivery of coal. Only the difficulty in acquiring land brought a change of plan in favour of road improvements. Hence the political compromise favoured the 'big four' with territories not fundamentally different from those of the six original regions of British Rail: the principal anomaly was Scotland, which did not enjoy its own company in 1923 because of the lack of a core of really profitable railways and the administrative division that would occur in respect of the various main lines across the border. The latter consideration argued against a separate railway company for the London area while separate eastern and north-eastern groupings were ruled out by complementary traffics: unrewarding rural routes in East Anglia and profitable coal traffic in Durham, Northumberland and Yorkshire.

How were the new railway companies to cope with the problems facing them? The administrative problems were dealt with by varying levels of centralisation, with the ultimate reached by the L.M.S.R. under J. C. Stamp, who was Chairman and later President of the company from 1926 to 1941. He reorganised management on modern lines and created an executive of vice-presidents, each responsible for a particular type of activity throughout the system. Stamp had few illusions about road competition which he described as 'the menace to our industry' in a circular letter to company staff in 1928. Yet when bus and lorry services could offer both greater flexibility and lower cost there was no real answer. Unfair competition could be dealt with by strict licensing procedures for road vehicles (through the Road and Rail Traffic Act of 1933) while the railway companies themselves could acquire road vehicles and deny some feeder traffic to their rivals. Indeed, bus services were introduced by some railway companies before the First World War as an alternative to further branch line construction (by the Great Western between Helston and the Lizard in Cornwall for example). More bus operations might have been sponsored by the railway companies but the immediate post-war situation was very favourable to the small private operator as ex-army vehicles were sold cheaply. Yet the long-term benefit of such a policy would appear unpromising since it must ultimately make economic sense to accept the superiority of the road vehicle where this is established, no matter whether the operating company is basically a road or a rail concern. After 1928 railway companies acquired interests in bus and road haulage companies but this had no significant bearing on the erosion of rail traffic which resulted in a spate of closures in the depression years of the early 1930s. Likewise, the railway companies gained air transport powers in 1929 and these were used shortly after when rival air services on the main railway routes were contemplated: the first experimental railway air service was opened by the Great Western between Cardiff and Plymouth in 1933 and the following year the big four joined forces to set up 'Railway Air Services'. With railway company involvement the competition between rail and air on certain routes could be made as harmless as possible, but this could not overcome the fact that air services would cream traffic from the railways. On the other hand while the railway companies were in retreat before the road and air operators they were successful in taking traffic from the coastal shipping trade, thanks to the availability of 'exceptional rates' which accounted for almost seventy percent of all freight receipts by 1935.

The emerging theme of the inter-war period was one of erosion of traffic on secondary routes complemented by growth on the main lines. To stimulate such traffic against a background of air competition and duplicate railway routes the big four invested heavily. The results were clearly seen in 1937 with the 'Coronation Scot' of the L.M.S.R. scheduled to travel the 645 km between London (Euston) and Glasgow (Central) in six and a half hours and the 'Coronation' of the L.N.E.R. booked to reach Edinburgh (Waverley) in just six hours from London (King's Cross), a distance of 632 km. Such a confrontation had built up over the previous decade with both companies settling for a 'big engine' policy and extending the distance for non-stop running. But while such spirited activity captured the public's imagination and helped to fend off competition from air services it meant a widening gulf between the main line and other routes. There was a determined policy of locomotive standardisation on the L.M.S.R. but this still meant the retention of large numbers of old inherited engines which cascaded down the system and made it hard to justify any concerted programme of dieselisation which might have reduced operating costs on branch lines. The cross-subsidy principle encouraged a casual attitude not possible for some small companies in Ireland, whose entire system consisted of rural branches. It was therefore companies like the County Donegal Railways that paid the most sustained attention to the use of petrol and later diesel railcars. The Great Western introduced diesel railcars on a limited basis from 1933 and the L.M.S.R. subsequently decided to concentrate on diesel locomotives for shunting duties. While the steam locomotive was still capable of improved efficiency and while good locomotive coal was available there was no compelling case to break with tradition, given the problems that this would entail in developing suitable diesel designs and in re-profiling locomotive building and repair shops. So there was no significant dilution of steam-based traction policy, except on the Southern Railway where the great importance of commuter services in south London made a large-scale programme of electrification appropriate. The Southern wanted to increase speed (and simultaneously increase capacity) to meet rising demand and discourage the extension of trams and underground railways. Their project was assisted by the provision of large government credits in 1935 to promote modernisation. Most of the new construction in the inter-war period fitted into this picture of expanding suburban services for Chessington, Lewisham and Wimbledon. Otherwise new building was restricted to a few cut-offs (Frome and Westbury) and some rationalisation links (Pontypridd and Ramsgate).

The Second World War created a new situation. Overall, coordination of railways resulted in many more links between the systems of formerly separate railway systems. Connections were forged between the G.W.R. and S.R. lines in the Plymouth area while the L.M.S.R. line from Oxford to Cambridge sent off spurs to join the various main lines out of London which it crossed. In addition to unified working, which established a precedent for peacetime, there was the problem of staggering arrears in maintenance which meant a government liability at the end of the war so great as to make it virtually impossible for the private companies to regain control. Nationalisation came about not as part of some politically-inspired punitive action against private capitalism (for the railway companies had carried on their business in a socially-responsible way with keen competition, moderate profits and an exposure to public scrutiny), but through the loss of the railway's monopoly in British transport and the need for a larger scale of organisation to project a united front to major competitors. The war made nationalisation that much more inevitable and guaranteed the necessary consensus. But it was some time before the nationalised company, British Railways, was able to prepare itself for battle. Regional administrations were established and, as previously noted, these were based on territories closely resembling those of the 'big four' lines. However, Scotland was recognised as a region and the remaining L.N.E.R. territory was initially divided into Eastern and Northeastern regions until 1967, reflecting the marked differences in the nature of traffic handled in these two areas. Yet regional identity was discouraged and many key employees were moved round, thereby making it more difficult for the railways to compete effectively at the local level. In the absence of a coordinated transport plan it was particularly important for the railway management to be as innovative as possible, but

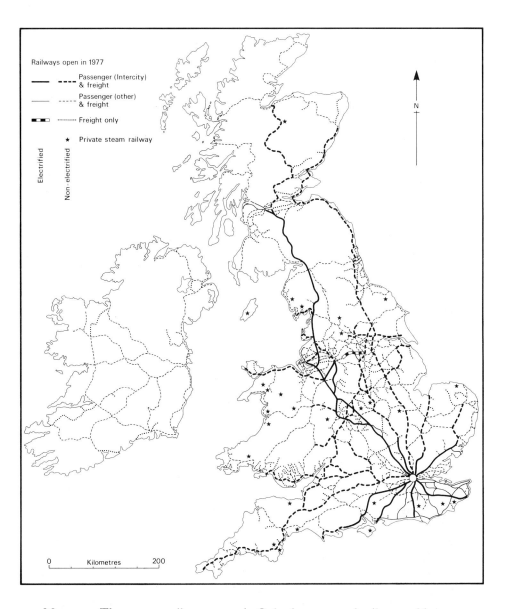

Railways open in 1977

Passenger (Intercity)
& freight

Passenger (other)
& freight

Freight only

★ Private steam railway

Electrified

Non-electrified

N

0      Kilometres      200

Map 14.   The present railway network. Only the preserved railways with more
than four kilometres of track are shown.

arguably the administrative procedures, combined with a conservative policy over recruitment, discouraged an aggressive approach to marketing to retain traffic. The situation was not encouraging, with little finance available for modernisation and a perception of the railway by members of the public which emphasised wartime austerity rather than the streamlined efficiency of the late 1930s. British Railways continued to shoulder 'common carrier' obligations even at a time when total traffic was falling, thanks to the increase in private cars and in express bus services and the decline of industries which had been traditionally served by the railways.

Looking back on the early post-war years it is clear that at a time when capital was very limited a programme of development for the main line services was delayed by uncertainty over the best form of traction: steam, diesel or electric. Electrification had obvious benefits in cleanliness and efficiency but conversion was very costly and only slow progress could be expected. So which lines should be electrified first (and at what voltage – a technical problem discussed later in Chapter 23)? And on lines where electrification could not be envisaged in the short term should there be a persistence with steam traction or should dieselisation be introduced as an interim measure? Here a cruel dilemma appeared as the case for steam, based on tradition backed up by low initial cost, was delicately balanced by

28. *Crossing the border* Dieselisation on British Rail, exemplified by this Class 40 locomotive pausing at Berwick upon Tweed with a Newcastle–Edinburgh train.

the diesel locomotive's promise of economical running and maintenance despite higher building costs and the need for experiment with suitable designs. The decision-making was then complicated by the preference for steam by the Railway Executive as against the inclination towards diesel traction by the British Transport Commission. The former sanctioned the building of several classes of standard B.R. locomotives but, after the B.T.C. assumed direct control over railway motive power in 1953 (when the Railway Executive was abolished) a modernisation plan involving diesel-isation was introduced. With strong government support capital was provided for a new generation of locomotives to improve performance on the inter-city lines and attract greater patronage. But excessive haste in developing diesel locomotives (quite apart from difficult technical choices, between electric and hydraulic transmission) complicated the transition period and committed a gross extravagance through the premature withdrawal of steam locomotives.

After much soul-searching British Rail (the official title adopted in the late 1960s) has succeeded in modernising the inter-city routes yet again. A generation after the record-breaking runs of the 1930s diesel and electric locomotives have maintained even more competitive schedules but only after considerable resistance to their introduction and capital shortages (the result of war and its aftermath) which delayed the improvements in track and signalling, as well as station facilities and rolling stock, which complement locomotive performance in providing an attractive service. The fastest diesel-hauled trains are now the 'High Speed Trains' which can maintain speeds of some 200 km (125 miles) per hour. These reversible train sets introduced in 1978 were backed not only by previous experience with the 'Midland Pullman' but by years of effort to improve track and signalling to allow fast running. As recently as 1967 only 124 of the 632 km between King's Cross and Edinburgh was suitable for running at 160 km (100 miles) per hour. Over the next ten years the figure increased to 418. Realignment of track has been needed at several places such as Offord, where a river diversion was needed, and Peterborough, where a longstanding restriction of 32 km per hour was overcome. Risk of mining subsidence has resulted in a minor shift at Monktonhall (Lothian) but a more expensive diversion will be needed between Temple Hirst and Colton (25.1 km) to allow for the development of the Selby Coalfield. Semaphore signals have given way to multiple-aspect colour lights and centralisation of control has drastically reduced the number of signal boxes. All these changes have resulted in a significantly different railway landscape on Britain's principal routes. It remains to be seen what has happened on other parts of the system.

22

# The Run-down of Cross-country
# Services

Most of the railways built during the 1830s and 1840s were intended to provide transport links between cities. There was very strong pressure for services in purely rural areas too, but railway projects serving more sparsely populated areas had to make economies in construction to moderate the financial burdens. There was in fact a sharp reaction to the extravagant years of the 'Railway Mania' through a greater concern for profitability. Cheaper railways required simpler land acquisition procedures (depending on greater landowner involvement) and lower standards of construction to cater for light traffic moving at low speeds. Local initiative was shown in promoting railways which one of the major companies might eventually operate (and perhaps absorb). For example, the branch from Leuchars through Guard Bridge to St Andrews (Fife) was opened in 1852 but absorbed by the North British in 1877. Inevitably, costs rose where lines had to be built for heavier traffic but there was to be no return to the financial abandon of the mid-1840s. During the 1870s the success of the Ballymena & Larne Railway (Co. Antrim) in handling passenger services with a 0.91 m (3 ft) gauge opened the way forward for narrow gauge railways and the achievement of the Festiniog Railway in introducing locomotives on a line with only 0.58 m (1 ft 11 in.) gauge was a further pointer to economy. In the event, most railway developments in the late nineteenth century made use of the standard gauge, with the advantage of through running and flexibility in deployment of locomotives and rolling stock, but the three foot gauge was quite widely adopted in Ireland. Finally, the Light Railways Act of 1896 allowed some compromise with normal building and operating procedures which stimulated some additional branch line construction like the Sheppey Railway (1901), Wick & Lybster (1903) and Leek & Manifold (1904).

The scope of railway services for rural services therefore continued to increase until the First World War. Long-distance road traffic was destroyed, but there was a growth of local feeder services, for the village carriers increased their services in terms of both routes and frequencies until the late nineteenth century. However, the introduction of the internal combustion engine has restored to road transport much of the importance it lost in the nineteenth century. Some projected railways (in the Scottish Highlands for example) were never built because buses and lorries appeared as cheaper alternatives. In 1903 a bus service ran along the Devon coast from Blackmoor in connection with trains on the Lynton & Barnstaple Railway which had only opened five years earlier. In the same year the Great Western provided a bus between Helston and Lizard while the London & South Western started a bus service from Exeter to Chagford in 1904. In another rural area, the Grampian region of Scotland (and some adjacent parts of the Highlands), the Great North of Scotland Railway began to operate bus services from 1904 (Ballater to Braemar) and by 1922 a route length of 160 km for bus services compared not too unfavourably with the 530 km of railway. But, from a position of ancillaries to existing railway services, buses quickly moved into a position where they were directly competitive.

The 1963 report on the reshaping of British Railways anticipated a rapid contraction of network even though some compensation would be found in the development of certain main lines. Many of the closures envisaged were carried out and they added to the many cases of service withdrawals between

29. *Railways and road transport* The railways may have undermined the long-distance road haulage business, but for local distribution there was plenty of scope for carriers and the railway companies themselves introduced some connecting services for passengers.

1950 and 1962. But before Dr Beeching's proposals were announced the progress in railway closures had been leisurely. There was much opposition from the Transport Users' Consultative Council, at both local and national levels, and this may have inhibited a large number of applications. It is also worth noting that the lack of provision for local authority involvement in support of economically unrewarding but socially necessary services placed a heavy responsibility on railway management steeped in the tradition of cross-subsidy. The 'loss leader' argument was persuasive, especially when unsatisfactory accounting methods made it difficult to reveal just how much money was being lost on particular routes. Yet, whatever the reason, it is clear that massive closures were ruled out as a viable option and instead emphasis was placed on the constructive approach of modernisation through the 1955 plan. The early post-war period therefore continued a restrained policy of closure of services in case of over-provision which had been inherited from the 1930s, and in the case of some suburban services which encountered stiff competition from electric trams from the early years of the century.

It should not, however, be overlooked that withdrawals of passenger services had occurred in the nineteenth century. Several early closures resulted from obvious lack of support, like Chesterford to Six Mile Bottom in 1850 and Stratford to Shipston in 1859. But in other cases special circumstances applied. Some railways were technically unsuitable for passenger services, as in the case of the Cromford & High Peak Railway where an inefficient service was closed in 1877. Construction of new station facilities allowed the conversion of old passenger stations to goods depots: thus in 1844 the construction of a new station in Manchester at Hunt's Bank (known as Victoria) led to the closure of two of the Liverpool Road and Oldham Road terminals. Changes in the commercial relationships between companies had some important implications for passenger routes, as in the celebrated Lancashire case of the service between Patricroft and Clifton Junction on the western approaches to Manchester. The London & North Western Railway wanted to provide an alternative service to Bury in competition with the Liverpool & Bury Railway which used a direct line between these two places. The L.N.W.R. wanted to approach Bury by means of the Manchester Bury & Rossendale's line which was joined at Clifton Junction. However, the amalgamations that created the Lancashire & Yorkshire Railway brought the Liverpol & Bury and Manchester Bury & Rossendale together, so there was no way the latter could now cooperate with the L.N.W.R. The service from Patricroft to Molyneux Junction lasted only three months.

Despite a long history of rail closures and the presence of an efficient alternative means of transport the withdrawal of railway services has been a highly controversial issue. Some railway managers competed tenaciously, notably Colonel H. F. Stephens, who managed a number of light railways in the early twentieth century. And whole communities have stoutly defended their railways even when they were not heavily used. Therefore the Beeching proposals were strongly resisted in many cases. Although British Rail deficits had to be reduced it was unreasonably provocative for many town and village communities to be told that railway services would no longer be provided. An uncompromisingly economic approach, backed up by some questionable accounting procedures, appeared to fly in the face of established policies to maintain an active and prosperous rural economy in Britain. Basic social services to rural areas have normally been provided as a matter of course, often with an element of subsidy to moderate costs to the consumer, but public transport did not fit easily into this philosophy until 1968. For many years government avoided the difficult problem of financing services that were socially necessary but economically unprofitable. It is unfortunate therefore that British Rail were forced to take a more strictly economic approach during the Beeching Era, in advance of sensible policies

30. *The most northerly railway route in Britain* The Highland lines in Scotland have never been very profitable, but supported by local authority subsidies a basic service is maintained between Inverness and Wick, while Alness Station (shown here) has been reopened to serve an expanding community.

over social transport. But British Rail (and their predecessors) cannot be exempt from criticism, because for many years a conservative policy over rail closures was not supported by vigorous efforts to reduce costs. Experiments in the 1930s like the L.M.S.R. 'Ro-Railer' (a vehicle with two sets of wheels allowing use on both rail and road) were highly restrained and in the 1950s the British Rail policy of introducing four-wheel diesel railbuses (following favourable results with such vehicles in Germany) was not complemented by efforts to simplify signalling and station facilities. Pressure to take drastic cost-cutting measures came only slowly through ministerial refusal to sanction certain railway closures. On the East Suffolk line there was a united front against closure: a less-expensive railway, involving some job losses, was then found to be the best solution. In another East Anglian case, involving the withdrawal of staff from Newmarket Station on the Cambridge–Ipswich line, a thoughtful dialogue with the local authority produced a mutually-acceptable solution where a subsidy was forthcoming to cover the cost of the service that B.R. could not continue to provide. In other parts of the country British Rail provided modest services with losses within the limits of local authority ability to subsidise. Complete closure of the Cambrian Coast line in Wales was mooted in 1971 but averted through support from Gwynedd and Powys County Councils, which is crucial for the operation of winter services. Some replacement bus services have been planned to connect very closely with trains and an instance of this is the 'Rail Line' service from Kettering to Corby, Oundle and Peter-borough. But a recent survey of the effects of rail closures shows that on the whole few people take to a bus replacement, irrespective of whether or not the family has access to a private car. Old people tend to become less mobile with closure of railways, perhaps because there is no adequate replacement for station facilities.

In some cases bus services are patently unsatisfactory in view of the deviousness of the local roads. Since there is no satisfactory road in the fork between the Tamar and Tavy valleys, trains from Plymouth still work along the Callington Branch as far as Gunnislake. Economies have been made by singling track and eliminating all signalling beyond St Budeaux through one train working. Again, journey times by bus over long distances in hilly country like the Yorkshire Dales can be considerable and so a novel experiment has been carried out on the Leeds–Carlisle line. After British Rail proposed to remove the platforms at the disused wayside stations in 1974 the Yorkshire Dales National Park authorities decided to charter trains to run between Leeds and Appleby at weekends. By means of bus connections people could then reach a range of destinations. Between 1975 and 1980 the 'Dales Rail' scheme developed to include a second service from Leeds to Carlisle (allowing the Dales people a chance of getting into Leeds for the day) while connections were introduced at Hellified from Preston,

Blackburn and Clitheroe. A number of local authorities now support the scheme as well as the National Park and some excursions have been run to resorts outside the Dales themselves. Other opportunities to reopen wayside stations may well arise in future and there are pressures to restore services on lines that have been completely closed. Given the rise in fuel costs and the cost of road improvements that may become necessary in the near future the 'Waverley Route' from Edinburgh to Carlisle through the Scottish Borders might be reopened, while the growth in traffic to the Stranraer ferry terminal (arising in part from the silting of Heysham) suggests that there may be some future for the Dumfries–Stranraer railway closed in 1965.

The various proposals to develop new centres for winter sports have implications for some derelict railways in Scotland. The plan for Aonach Mor, near Fort William, includes partial reopening of the British Aluminium Company's line which once threaded its way from a pier in Loch Linnhe to the edge of Loch Treig. Further north, the Ben Wyvis project involves the provision of a rail link with Strathpeffer. The line would descend down the mountain to the Inverness–Kyle of Lochalsh line at

31. *Scotland's mountain railway?* High in the hills above Glen Spean in Lochaber is the trackbed of the British Aluminium Company's railway to the Loch Treig reservoir. Part of the line could be reopened to give access to the ski slopes of Aonach Mor, near Fort William.

32. *Stopping train at Selby* A train of diesel multiple units leaves Selby. Much of the d.m.u. fleet will require replacement in the years immediately ahead.

Raven Rock and run alongside the railway to Achterneed. From there a link would be made across the valley with the trackbed of the Strathpeffer branch and the old terminus station could be reopened. The branch opened in 1885, but the station lay derelict from 1951 (when the service was withdrawn) until its recent restoration as a tourist facility. Incidentally, Achterneed – still served by trains running between Inverness and Kyle – was named Strathpeffer from 1870 to 1885 for it was then the nearest station to the small resort after the proposed alignment for the railway (which would have taken it through the centre of the village) was altered in the face of strong opposition from the owner of Coul House, who wanted the line to be fully landscaped where it crossed his estate.

The landscape of cross-country railways has therefore changed quite drastically through the reduction in the system, the closure of stations and simplification of signalling. Traction policy favours the diesel multiple unit, but many of the sets presently in service are approaching the end of their design life and replacements will soon be needed. Current thinking is to replace the d.m.u. on lightly-used lines with a simpler vehicle more closely resembling a bus. In fact, a 'Leyland Experimental Vehicle' (LEV) is already being tested: it is an ordinary Leyland bus adapted for running on rails. It has performed well on trials and demonstrated export potential in the United States. But British Rail face a quandary: whether to stick to a simple vehicle which can be operated cheaply on lightly used lines or whether to include remote control equipment that would allow units to be coupled together to cope with heavier traffic, but at considerably greater cost. An understandable desire to provide comfortable accommodation for all passengers inevitably conflicts with the need to minimise investment and therefore provide services at reasonable cost. Arguably, the future of many cross-country services will depend on how this issue is resolved.

# 23

# Selective Development of Railways

The substantial contraction of the railway system since the First World War should not lead to the assumption that there has been no development. In different areas of Britain rationalisation has required some short lengths of new railway. Thus the Great Western provided a link between the inherited Barry and Taff Vale systems at Pontypridd while the Southern Railway, after taking over two routes between Margate and Ramsgate, installed a short link line that allowed the closure of one branch line and two stations. British Rail have also built some new lines to facilitate rationalisation. In Edinburgh the trains from Carstairs and Carlisle that once used Princes Street Station can now be routed into Waverley because of a short connection made at Haymarket. Important freight customers may attract special arrangements when railway closures are planned. Thus the withdrawal of services from the former Great Central main line led to retention of a short length of track from Ruddington in Nottinghamshire to Loughborough in Leicestershire, where a new spur gave access to the old Midland Railway line which remains open. Moreover, in Leicester, access to coal yards on the southern approach to the city was retained by means of a new spur from the mineral line connecting Leicester and Burton upon Trent. And through running from north to south in Manchester may soon be possible thanks to the projected 0.7 km Windsor Link line between the approaches to Piccadilly and Victoria stations. Also, in Norfolk the need for a link to a manufacturer of reinforced concrete structural products justified retention of a section of the former Midland & Great Northern Railway from Lenwade northwards to Themelthorpe, where a new spur gave access to the former Great Eastern Wroxham–County School branch which provides an outlet through Norwich. This is to say nothing of the many private lines that have been built to serve new coal mines like Cotgrave in Nottinghamshire, or iron ore quarries like Exton in Leicestershire (now closed).

The greatest amount of activity in providing new connections occurred during the Second World War. In the London area the danger of railways being put out of action by bombing made it desirable to have some additional routes available to transfer traffic from one system to another.

Two new links at Gospel Oak in 1940 allowed traffic from the L.N.E.R. to reach the Great Western or Southern. There was also an L.N.E.R./L.M.S. link at Romford and a Great Western–Southern connection at Staines, both in 1940. Work was also done to expedite the movement of north-south freight through Reading: a Great Western/Southern connection was opened there in 1941 but in the previous year a spur at Sandy allowed freight from the L.N.E.R. to pass on to the L.M.S.R. Cambridge–Oxford line and a further spur in Oxford allowed transfer to the Great Western's line to Didcot and Reading. The same cross-country route of the L.M.S.R. linked up with the L.N.E.R. at Calvert. Outside the London area there was a connection between the Great Western and Southern at Plymouth and quadrupling of track between Gloucester and Cheltenham (handling Lend-Lease traffic from Bristol Channel ports) and on the remaining sections of double track between York and Northallerton where coal traffic was being delayed. Four tracks were provided on the northern side of Carlisle, over the Eden towards the junction of the former Caledonian and G.S.W.R. lines, and new branches were built in Scotland to reach the ports of Cairnryan near Stranraer and Faslane on the Gareloch. There were extensions to the Longmoor Military Railway with a second link with the Southern Railway

33.   *A special freight service for the Trawsfynydd nuclear power station* justifies the retention of the northern part of the Bala–Blaenau Ffestiniog branch. Traffic operates through Blaenau Ffestiniog to the main line at Llandudno Junction, on the North Wales coast.

(at Liss in 1942) and the completion of the Hollywater Loop (1942) to give servicemen training in continuous running.

The most conspicuous form of development has come through railway electrification. The first schemes came well before the First World War. Two short lines in Ireland were powered at 240 v d.c. from hydro-electric stations: Giant's Causeway (1883) and Bessbrook & Newry (1885). Five years later the first underground electric railway in the world opened in London, using power from a thermal station at Stockwell supplied at 500 v d.c., and the London Underground system has gradually extended through the twentieth century as the original electrified section became part of the Northern Line (London Transport). Several developments took place in Liverpool from 1903, when the independent Mersey Railway (opened in 1886) was electrified. In 1904 the Lancashire & Yorkshire Railway electrified the Liverpool–Southport route, followed by the Aintree and Ormskirk lines in 1906 and 1913 respectively. Also in 1904 came the conversion of the Newcastle Harbour branch of the North Eastern Railway. The branch is a steeply-graded line running partly in a tunnel which was extremely difficult to operate with steam locomotives. This project was part of a suburban electrification scheme for Newcastle, which developed out of the close contacts forged between the N.E.R. general manager, George Gibb, and the consulting engineers, Merz & McLellan. With the lesson of the London underground before them, other companies began to see electrification as a means of countering the competition of the electric trams: the Midland converted the Morecambe–Heysham line in 1909. The London suburbs were served by schemes of the L.B.S.C. in 1909 and by both the L.N.W.R. and L.S.W.R. in 1915. Manchester attracted the attention of the Lancashire & Yorkshire in 1916.

At this time there was general agreement that electrification at 600 v d.c. was technically feasible and that electrification allowed rapid travel between stations closely-spaced. Not that the consensus was total because the Great Eastern Railway believed that steam locomotives could match the performance of electrics and proved this by their experimental engine, *Decapod*: this locomotive did not enter regular service but nevertheless the G.E.R. maintained an efficient commuter service with steam through the famous 'jazz' trains from Liverpool Street. In contrast to the G.E.R. (and also the Great Western Railway which refused to countenance any prospect of electrification) the North Eastern Railway (especially the Chief Mechanical Engineer, Vincent Raven) was strongly attracted to electrification and saw it as a solution to their special operating problems. The mineral traffic from Shildon (Co. Durham) to Newport (24 km) was handled by electric locomotives in 1915 and the whole main line between Newcastle and York was slated for conversion (extra capacity from electrification being seen as cheaper than quadrupling track). However, although one main line locomotive was introduced in 1922 the ambitious plan was overtaken by the grouping and the L.N.E.R. perceived the contracting regional economy of the north-east as a grave discouragement. Even the Shildon line reverted to steam traction in 1935 and the Tyneside lines were dieselised by 1967.

The difficult conditions between the wars made electrification a doubtful speculation. On the L.M.S.R. lines in London there was an extension of the work started by the L.N.W.R. with electrification to Watford (1922) and extended to Rickmansworth (1927). The L.N.E.R. contemplated electrification of Great Eastern lines in London (especially Shenfield) in the late 1930s but it was the Southern Railway which maintained the greatest interest in the London area: Brighton was reached in 1933 and Portsmouth in 1937. Outside London the L.M.S.R. and L.N.E.R. cooperated over the Manchester South Junction & Altrincham Railway in 1931. The former extended work in Liverpool (New Brighton and West Kirby) in 1938 while the latter completed the North Eastern's work in Newcastle with the South Shields line in the same year. The Manchester–Sheffield–Wath line was also slated for conversion – the first main line project to be implemented outside the Southern Railway. The older systems of course stuck to their low voltages, though with marginal increases on the Southern Railway to 790 v d.c. But in 1931 the Weir Committee (appointed by the Minister of Transport to look at the prospects for main line electrification) recommended the use of 1500 v d.c. This was adopted for the Altrincham line and subsequent schemes. With higher voltages now commended for the longer routes to reduce power losses, overhead wires became necessary, partly for safety reasons and partly to overcome the problem of leakages to earth which became serious with the conductor rail system. But overhead wires are more expensive to install (though less affected by severe winter weather) and are also unsightly. However, interest has since turned to very high voltages, usually 25 kv a.c. (a.c. being easier than d.c. for voltage change).

Such voltages permit more powerful locomotives and use power at industrial frequency. This means still smaller losses and lighter overhead equipment, though more generous bridge clearances, against the need for rectifiers on locomotives to convert alternating current to direct current (for it has not yet been technically feasible to produce a variable speed a.c. motor). However, the decision by British Railways to adopt the high voltage meant expensive alteration on the Great Eastern lines which were operating satisfactorily at 1500 v d.c. and resulted in priority in the B.T.C. electrification programme of 1958 for the west coast main line over the east coast conversion of which much preparatory work had been done. Electrification from Euston reached Manchester and Liverpool in 1967 and Glasgow in 1974. The system in fact involves mixed voltage with 6.25 kv a.c. over sections with limited clearances including the London suburban lines and also track in the Glasgow area electrified in 1960 to provide the 'Blue

Train' service. Standardisation at the high voltage is being introduced. However, rapidly rising costs for the west coast electrification were embarrassing and 'inevitably the Beeching regime was soured against electrification as an extravagant way of running a railway'. High speed diesel trains became the principal objective for a time. But now once again much discussion is taking place at present on major extensions to the electrified railways. Yet for the time being the landscape shows clearly the piecemeal progress with uneven development in different parts of the country and various electrification systems in force. Standardisation and further development may create a picture of greater regularity, although the Southern Region lines (which included Dover in 1959 and Bournemouth in 1967) are too extensive for any change from the 750 v d.c. system to be contemplated.

In Ireland there have been close parallels with the situation in Britain. A grouping after the First World War was organised on political lines with the Great Southern Railways formed in 1925 in the Irish Free State (now the Irish Republic) and a Northern Counties Committee (linked with the L.M.S.R.) in Northern Ireland. The Great Northern system extended into both parts of the island with numerous border crossings and it preserved a separate identity until the system was so simplified by heavy closures in 1957 that the remaining sections could be added to what were now nationalised transport undertakings in the north (Ulster Transport Authority – UTA) and south (Coras Iompair Eireann – CIE). The late 1950s were years of drastic railway closures, although the policy of Dr Andrews of CIE was to retain some form of public transport. Closures of narrow gauge lines were particularly heavy: after some withdrawals in the 1930s and further casualties during the fuel crisis of 1946–7 the remaining survivors were liquidated: Cavan & Leitrim and Tralee & Dingle in 1959, County Donegal Railways in 1960 and the West Clare in 1961. Even the main lines were in danger, but in 1964 the Irish government accepted the case for retention of a basic network through subsidies. A similar view has been taken in Northern Ireland. Hence the future is now more hopeful with some modernisation already achieved, such as dieselisation and efficient freight handling by block train working and promise of further rationalisation through a new central station in Belfast to handle traffic on the Dublin and Londonderry routes as well as suburban trains to Bangor and Larne.

Even in respect of system development Ireland provides an interesting and varied range of examples. On the Northern Counties system there were several major developments which were partially implemented to provide employment. There was a doubling of the Belfast–Larne line between Carrickfergus and Whitehead, completed in 1929, and five years later the Greenisland Loop was ready, providing a direct path out of Belfast for trains on the Ballymena route which had previously reversed at Greenisland. But the most pressing work after the First World War was the replacement of the bridge over the Bann at Coleraine. The original bridge of 1860, which carried a link line between the Ballymena and Portrush line of 1855 and the Londonderry & Coleraine of 1853, was a wooden structure that was becoming unsafe. In building a new bridge, opened in 1924, the opportunity was taken to use a new alignment that would ease the sharp curves that had characterised the original link and also eliminate troublesome level crossings.

Further south, in what soon became the Irish Free State, the decision was taken in 1918, during the period of wartime government control of the railways of Ireland, to make three new extensions to reach the coalfields of Arigna (C. Leitrim), Castlecomer (Co. Kilkenny) and Wolfhill (Co. Laois). The Wolfhill line opened in 1918, followed by Castlecomer in 1919 and Arigna in 1920. The latter railway, much delayed by an influenza epidemic and bad weather, amounted to a 6.8 km extension of the Cavan & Leitrim Railway. The original line had reached Mount Allen Cross Roads in 1888 and drew coal from several mines in the district, particularly Aughabehy. This part of County Leitrim was quite rich in minerals and a charcoal iron industry had once flourished. Coal was later used as an alternative fuel but neither the Arigna works, which started in 1788, nor the Creevelea project of the 1850s were successful. Transport was a problem and although a short canal connected the Shannon with Lough Allen in 1817 there was never an extension of the waterway through to Sligo. However, the Arigna Works did have satisfactory local transport through a tramway from the Aughabehy coal mines some four kilometres away and this operated from 1832 until the ironworks finally closed in 1838: Creevelea by contrast was in a far more difficult situation with Altagowlan coal sixteen kilometres away by road. Modern mining has been restricted to coal, demand for which was boosted by the building of the railway. Yet curiously, although the Cavan & Leitrim drew their coal from Aughabehy, the fuel had to be carted to the head of the branch. A line from Arigna to Sligo was proposed in 1907–8 but failed to gain adequate support. Only in 1920 was a physical rail connection to the Cavan & Leitrim completed: the extension climbed 54.7 m along the Arigna Valley to meet an incline pitching down the hillside from the colliery, very close to the tramway of 1832. The colliery line was finished by 1930 due to a railway amalgamation which brought an end to the local coal contract but the first section of the extension, to Arigna Village (Derveenavoggy) survived up to the closure of the whole Cavan & Leitrim system in 1959. More recently it may be noted that some lines have been reopened to handle mineral traffic from a number of new mines and quarries, but in the case of Silvermines near Limerick the shipment of ore through Foynes on the Shannon estuary involved construction of a short branch from the Nenagh–Birdhill line in 1966.

# 24

# The Resurgence of Suburban Railways

Some of the more interesting cases of recent railway development relate to suburban projects in Britain's major conurbations. After several years of planning urban transport with the private car firmly in mind the recent renewal of interest in public transport has meant a new lease of life for some lines that had drifted into obsolescence or else been closed down altogether. Review of these recent improvements should, however, be prefaced by an outline of the railway's contribution to the growth of late nineteenth-century cities when urban transport was revolutionised. At the opening of the Victorian era travel on foot was usual in London and other cities. Hackney carriages had been available for hire in London since the seventeenth century but they did not operate regular schedules and fears of excessive congestion on city streets delayed the introduction of competing omnibus services. However, substantial street improvements after the Napoleonic Wars (including new bridges over the Thames) did allow short-stage horse bus services to start in London in 1832, while horse-drawn trams were successfully introduced in 1870. The latter cost little more to operate than the omnibuses but carried many more passengers since the use of rails allowed a more efficient use of horse power. In turn however, the horse-drawn trams were no match for the steam locomotive over substantial distances and hence the development of the suburbs owed much to the railway in the second half of the nineteenth century.

For example, the north-eastern suburbs of London were extensively developed by 1900, almost exclusively peopled by workmen, artisans and clerks. This trend was much encouraged by the Great Eastern Railway, which provided branch line access as early as 1849 when the Enfield route reached settlements on the higher ground above the Lea Valley. The line was extended to Chingford in 1870 and two years later came a direct line to Edmonton from Hackney Downs in the Lea Valley. Frequent services on these lines stimulated a mass migration out of London, with some movement also from inner suburbs like Hackney Downs and Stoke Newington. By the First World War the Great Eastern had built a steam suburban railway service unrivalled anywhere for its intensity and capacity, so that the growth of housing was particularly rapid in this north-eastern sector and in reaching to Enfield and Walthamstow extended further out than in any other part of London.

Farther west, the Great Northern built branch lines from its main line at Finsbury Park to Edgware (1867) and High Barnet (1872). These rural districts were now opened up to London commuters. The activities of railway companies and speculative builders were strongly resented by those who deplored the advance of the city. J. Thorne, in his book on the *Environs of London* (published in 1876, soon after the Barnet line opened), described Barnet as 'one of those new half-finished railway villages which we have come to look on almost as a necessary adjunct to every station within a moderate distance of London'. But the railways provided irresistible opportunities and there were good profits to be made from housing development, especially where physically attractive sites could attract wealthy families. Edgware became a high-status residential area thanks to the undulating terrain on the 'Northern Heights' and the relatively high fares to the branch line terminus. It is noticeable how Edgware residents subsequently opposed further transport improvements out of fear that cheaper fares into London would stimulate lower-status development. Of course, movement to the suburbs later became economically feasible for a range of social groups, especially where cheap fares were offered, but the opportunities for the lower classes came relatively late. Yet it was the poorer people who bore the brunt of the disturbance caused by the railway when it entered city centres and eliminated large areas of slum housing to provide space for tracks, stations, depots and warehouses. Further displacement of working people occurred through dock schemes and street improvements. Removal of bad housing was desirable but it was only a social blessing to the inhabitants if new accommodation was provided immediately at low rents and in situations convenient for employment. In practice neither condition was realised. There was a long time lag which meant that the displaced persons themselves did not benefit – and if the response had been more immediate there would still have been difficulties because the higher rents charged for new accommodation would exclude the poorer families. Although Lord Shaftesbury campaigned strongly in the 1850s for effective measures of rehousing it was only after 1885 that rules over compulsory rehousing were strictly enforced. Hence the effect of railway development was to force displaced families into the surrounding areas which were already overcrowded: thus people who had lived on the Marylebone Station site moved into the Lisson Grove area. They could not afford to move very far from their employment because of a dependence on casual work. Drastic overcrowding did not always arise (as is clear from studies of North Lambeth) though it was a frequent enough occurrence.

The rôle of the railway in late nineteenth-century suburban development can be examined in other cities. In Glasgow the Blane Valley & Kelvin

Railway did not induce the Glasgow merchant community to move to the north of the city, but the Clyde coast was more attractive and services to ferry points like Craigendoran, Gourock and Greenock multiplied, with all the major companies involved. In Edinburgh the Trinity area was opened up by the Edinburgh Leith & Newhaven Railway but a more ambitious scheme for Barnton Policies which induced the Caledonian Railway to build a branch from their Granton line in 1894, to be used by affluent families wishing to live close to their favourite golf course, was not successful. Not surprisingly the railway frequently preferred to lag behind the speculative builder rather than play a leading rôle. Where suburban services could be accommodated on the principal lines out of a city centre there was a chance of a useful increase in traffic and the G.N.o.S. ran a highly successful service in Aberdeen between Culter and Dyce, which were intermediate stations on the Ballater and Elgin lines respectively. But in highly compact cities it was hazardous for the railway to play a leading rôle in suburban development by building lines specially for the commuter.

Another approach taken by the railway in Edinburgh was a southern loop by the Edinburgh Suburban & Southside Junction Railway authorised in 1880, but this made more a circuitous journey and the opening of direct electric tram routes led to devastating competition and many closures in the early twentieth century. On the larger scale of London the same process was evident. Railways were hampered in any case by the delimitation of a central area into which the companies could not penetrate. The electric trams, and more especially the underground railways which provided Britain's first rapid transit system, gave fast and frequent journeys into the heart of London. Although the first tubes in London integrated with the railways and provided useful passenger links between main line stations, the expansion of the system led to stiff competition. The tubes were particularly successful where they provided direct access to the centre of London for areas which were served only by branches from main railway lines, which inevitably meant an indirect journey into the centre (and probably a change to buses at the main line stations as well). The extension of the Northern Line from Golders Green (reached in 1907) to Edgware in 1924 forced the closure of the Edgware branch line fifteen years later, although the line from Finchley to Barnet was conveniently enough aligned to be taken over by the underground in 1939 as an extension to a direct line built under Camden and Archway.

After a period of frustration, when railways experienced great difficulty in competing with trams and buses in tightly packed cities, not to mention the private car, which introduced the fashion for the Inner Ring Road advocated by C. Buchanan, the position is now somewhat improved. Fuel costs and environmental pressures have put the railway in a better light and in the big cities there are already many signs of a come-back. Some

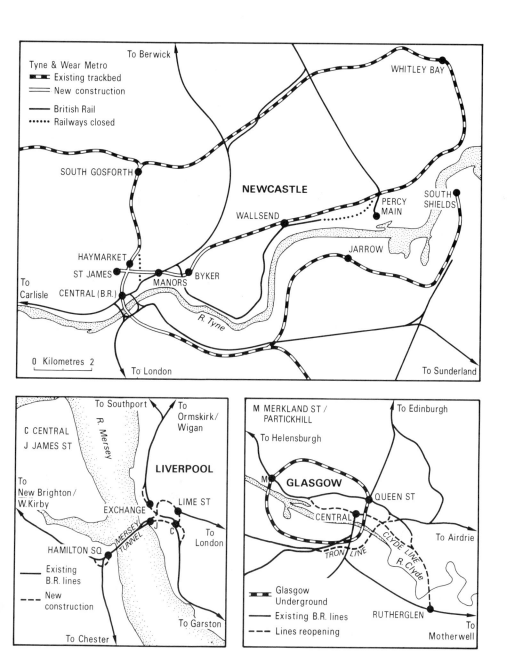

## Tyne & Wear Metro
- ▬ Existing trackbed
- ═ New construction
- — British Rail
- ••••• Railways closed

To Berwick

WHITLEY BAY

SOUTH GOSFORTH

**NEWCASTLE**

PERCY MAIN

SOUTH SHIELDS

WALLSEND

JARROW

HAYMARKET

ST JAMES

BYKER

MANORS

CENTRAL (B.R.)

To Carlisle

*R. Tyne*

0 Kilometres 2

To London

To Sunderland

---

To Southport

To Ormskirk/ Wigan

C CENTRAL
J JAMES ST

*R. Mersey*

**LIVERPOOL**

To New Brighton/ W.Kirby

LIME ST

EXCHANGE

*MERSEY TUNNEL*

To London

HAMILTON SQ

## Existing B.R. lines
- — Existing B.R. lines
- --- New construction

To Chester

To Garston

---

M MERKLAND ST / PARTICKHILL

To Edinburgh

To Helensburgh

M

**GLASGOW**

QUEEN ST

CENTRAL

To Airdrie

*CLYDE LINE*

*TRON LINE*

*R. Clyde*

RUTHERGLEN

To Motherwell

## Glasgow Underground
- ▬ Glasgow Underground
- — Existing B.R. lines
- --- Lines reopening

---

Map 15. Suburban railway development in Glasgow, Liverpool and Newcastle.
Note: In Glasgow, Clyde Line should be read as Argyle Line.

development is envisaged to integrate inter-city services more effectively: hence the project for twin tunnels through the heart of London to connect West Hampstead and Clapham Junction. Advanced Passenger Trains could use this route and improve access from cities on the northern side of London with the Channel Tunnel. However, the railway is becoming more prominent for intra-urban transport as conurbations have expanded and the largest cities in Britain are now trying to develop their own rapid transport systems.

The Tyneside 'Supertram' system was conceived in the late 1960s when Passenger Transport Executives had come into being and rapid transit was a talking point in major cities across the world. Being burdened with financial responsibility for the heavy loss (some £0.7 million) made by railway commuter services, there was a powerful incentive to evolve a more efficient system. Hence the proposal to convert the unremunerative lines into a rapid transit operation. Unfortunately, the railways that were to be taken over needed a new link through the heart of Newcastle to avoid the congested knot of railways focusing on Newcastle Central Station. Tram-size tunnels have been built under the city centre and a new bridge will carry

34. *Tyneside's new Metro* A train from Tynemouth is seen entering Jesmond Station. At this point new railway construction, burrowing beneath the centre of Newcastle and making an independent crossing of the Tyne, leaves the original railway which once led through Manors to the main station in the heart of the city.

trains over the Tyne. Trains can be coupled in rush hour, still with one-man operation, and they will call at various unstaffed halts, some of which will be served by connecting bus services. An integrated transport system for the conurbation will result, with advantages of economy over both the initial systems of trains and buses and a hypothetical solution converting railway rights of way into busways. The scheme has run into difficulties through an ambivalent (and sometimes hostile) attitude from British Rail and rapidly rising costs. But the visionaries have persevered in their aim of providing a modern transport system which could become a basis for the regeneration of the area. In addition to tunnelling under Newcastle and Gateshead, on either side of the new Tyne Bridge, a cut-and-cover tunnel has been built through Byker, where an abandoned motorway route has been used: to ensure that the new railway will not separate the commercial and residential sections of Byker the track will be concealed below ground and land above it made available for commercial development or landscaping.

Tyneside is becoming one of an increasing number of major cities with a rapid transit system – an urban transport system which operates over its own exclusive right of way. If large cities are to succeed they must offer their inhabitants a reasonable chance of personal mobility at a reasonable cost. At Liverpool an important development has been based on the Mersey Railway which ran from Birkenhead (Rock Ferry) under the Mersey to James Street and Central Low Level. The line was electrified in 1903, as were the related New Brighton and West Kirby lines in 1938. But now the line from James Street is being looped for some three kilometres under the city by a single tube to connect with Moorfields and Lime Street, as well as Liverpool Central. This will provide a link with inter-city trains at Lime Street, but it will also provide interchanges at Central and Moorfields with a new link between Central and Exchange stations which will allow trains from Southport (linking with Ormskirk and Wigan services at Sandhills) to run through to Garston. In addition to the linkage of railway terminals, first considered back in the 1850s, the new layout provides access to the office zone (James Street and Moorfields), shopping area (Central) and the National Bus Company's services (Lime Street). And finally a new layout at Birkenhead will allow an increase in the number of rush-hour trains reaching the various Wirral destinations.

The imaginative programme reverses a strategy of piecemeal railway closure which shut down Liverpool Central in 1967 (leaving the Mersey Railway stranded at the Low Level station), and previously removed the Liverpool Overhead Railway (opened in 1894 and closed in 1956) which ran through the dockland and connected with the Southport and Ormskirk lines. The present reorganisation follows from the establishing of the Merseyside Passenger Transport Executive which has coordinated the local railway system since 1973. In fact with the opening of the new lines in 1977

Merseyside became the first conurbation to benefit from rapid transit railways constructed and opened to traffic by a P.T.E. The plan is not yet complete, for a new link is to run from Central to Edge Hill to open up a route to St Helens, while the electrification of the lines to Chester, Warrington and Wigan, along with the re-opening of lines from Bootle to Aintree and Hunt's Cross, will give a total system of almost 200 kilometres. And this is quite separate from the 25 kv a.c. electrified inter-city lines from Lime Street to Crewe (for London) and, projected, to Earlestown (for Glasgow). As in Newcastle, the bus-rail interchange will become prominent as well as station car parks.

In Glasgow the underground railway of 1896 is being modernised and eleven of the fifteen stations will form interchange points with cars or buses. On the western side of the loop at Merkland Street there will be an interchange with British Rail electric services. The latter comprise the Airdrie–Balloch trains (electrified in 1960) running through Queen Street Low Level supplemented by services to Rutherglen which use the 'Argyle Line' (4.7 m) re-opened through Anderston (linking with a major bus station), Central Low Level and Dalmarnock. In future an additional 'Tron Line' will cross the Clyde and allow further integration of the once quite separate electrified networks on the two sides of the river. The scheme follows from the appointment of the Greater Glasgow P.T.E. in 1974 but the 'Clyderail' concept was already evolving through liaison between British Rail and local authorities responsible for the Greater Glasgow Transportation Study. Yet in general it must be said that the future of rapid transit schemes is rather uncertain at the present time. Since many people have the option of private car travel, the economics of modern public transport projects tends to be unstable and a period of high inflation followed by the need for restraint in local authority spending has consigned some promising ideas to oblivion. Instead, there has been piecemeal modernisation in Manchester, notably the overhaul of the Altrincham line (and its conversion from 1500 v d.c. to 25 kv a.c. in 1971) and the establishment of a successful rail-bus interchange at Altrincham in 1976: it is situated beside the shopping centre and the scheme therefore includes the main town bus station and garage.

# 25

# Irish Narrow Gauge
# with particular reference to the
# Peat Workings

Narrow gauge railways in Ireland have had a long and colourful history with a remarkable variety of systems in terms of origin, length, gauge, motive power and function. The map attempts to summarise all the systems built with gauges of less than 1.60 m (5 ft 3 in.), the standard gauge in Ireland, but the vast majority are also narrower than the British standard of 1.43 m. Apart from eighteenth-century tramways like the Ballycastle Harbour Tramway of 1740 and the Coalisland Colliery Tramway of 1754, the record does not open until 1873 with the opening of a mineral railway by the Glenariff Iron Ore Company. It ran for some 6.4 km from White Arch on the Antrim coast, near Cushendall, to mines on the flanks on the plateau. The company soon failed (c. 1876) and the stock was disposed of in 1885, but the trackbed can be seen, including a remarkable zig-zag which is part of the pathway system in Glenariff Forest Park. Further development in Antrim proved to be rather more permanent. The Ballymena Cushendall & Red Bay Railway opened in 1875, the first Irish narrow gauge railway to be authorised by parliament. The aim once again was to tap the Antrim ironstone deposits but this time from an inland point on the standard gauge railway system rather than from the coast. The line climbed to 320 m to Parkmore, high above Glenariff, and terminated at Retreat: despite the company's name the link with the Antrim coast was made only by tourist charabancs and jaunting cars, as mentioned in Chapter 20. At several points along the line (Knockanally, Cargan and Parkmore) branches led off to the iron mines. They were steeply graded and the line from Cargan to the Crommelin Mine included a rope-worked incline at 1 in 11.

Related to this line is another Antrim 'first', for the Ballymena & Larne Railway was the first 0.91 m (3 ft) gauge railway in Ireland to carry passengers: it was opened in 1877 and three years later made a physical connection with the Red Bay Railway so that ores could be taken through to Larne Harbour without trans-shipment at Ballymena. As it happened, the most persistent iron mining took place at Ballylig and Clonetrace where good quality ore was available in thick beds and where rising adits simplified drainage. But no railway was built to serve this area north-east of Broughshane after the failure of several new projects in the late 1870s. The ore was carted into Ballymena, using light traction engines. The iron ore boom subsided in the 1880s, but bauxite (known to exist in association with the iron ore) was subsequently worked on the Antrim Plateau to supply the smelters which were built in the Scottish Highlands at Foyers and Kinlochleven. The British Aluminium Company built a processing plant at Larne to convert the bauxite into alumina and in 1900 an industrial railway was provided, running between the Ballymena & Larne Railway, the factory and the quayside. The installations are now closed but there is an ample legacy of the two mineral booms on the plateau where old quarries and branch lines can be found. It is not clear just how many of the old iron mines were reopened but Cargan was certainly an important centre and part of the Dungonnel mineral railway was used.

The narrow-gauge builders had plans to enlarge the system: not only was a line from Broughshane (near Ballymena) to the Antrim coast at Glenarm mooted but extension from the other side of Ballymena to Dungiven and Londonderry was proposed. However, apart from the Ballycastle Railway of 1880 and the electrically-powered Giant's Causeway line of 1883, it fell to other parts of Ireland to continue the momentum built up by the 0.91 m gauge. The first stage of the Cork & Muskerry was ready in 1877. The oldest part of the County Donegal narrow gauge system dates back to 1882 when the standard gauge line from Strabane to Stranorlar (later converted to narrow gauge in 1894) was extended to Donegal Town. The same situation occurred on the Londonderry & Lough Swilly where narrow-gauge building to Letterkenny in 1883 led to the conversion in 1885 of original standard gauge line from Londonderry to Farland Point, which had opened in 1863. Both systems were extended with government encouragement: the Donegal reached Glenties in 1895 while the Lough Swilly's Burtonport Extension (including the famous Owencarrow Viaduct where a train was blown off the rails by strong winds in 1925) was finished in 1903. Finally, there are four other systems of significant length that require mention. The Clogher Valley (Tynan-Maguiresbridge), Cavan & Leitrim and West Clare were all opened in 1887 (though the latter's extension from Milltown Malbay to Kilrush did not come until 1892), while the Tralee & Dingle opened in 1891.

The majority of Irish narrow gauge railways are too short to be shown on a small-scale map in any other than a symbolic manner. Some of these were public railways like the urban tramways (using horse or electric traction) and curiosities such as the locomotive-operated monorail from Listowel to Ballybunion and the electric tramway from Newry to Bessbrook which, like the Giant's Causeway line, drew power from its own hydro station. But

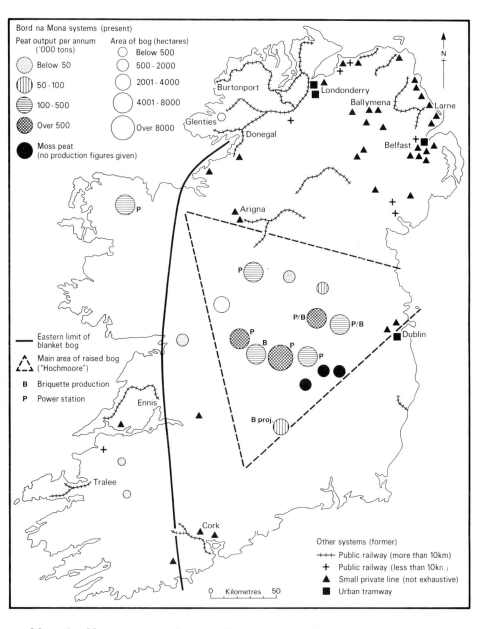

## Legend

**Bord na Mona systems (present)**

Peat output per annum ('000 tons)
- Below 50
- 50 - 100
- 100 - 500
- Over 500

Moss peat (no production figures given)

Area of bog (hectares)
- Below 500
- 500 - 2000
- 2001 - 4000
- 4001 - 8000
- Over 8000

— Eastern limit of blanket bog

▲▲ Main area of raised bog ("Hochmoore")

**B** Briquette production

**P** Power station

**Other systems (former)**
- +++ Public railway (more than 10km)
- + Public railway (less than 10km)
- ▲ Small private line (not exhaustive)
- ■ Urban tramway

Map labels: Burtonport, Londonderry, Ballymena, Larne, Glenties, Donegal, Belfast, Arigna, Ennis, Tralee, Cork, Dublin, B proj.

N

0  Kilometres  50

Map 16.   Narrow-gauge railways in Ireland, past and present.
The assistance of Mr H. C. Flood, Chief Engineer of *Bord na Mona* is gratefully acknowledged.

industrial lines were also quite numerous: some of them provided links between factories and main line stations, like the Upperlands horse railway of 1900 (serving Clark's linen factory in Co. Londonderry) while others tapped minerals like the line to Mullaghmore (Co. Sligo) which stimulated stone quarrying and barytes mining. Definitely unique was the private estate railway which connected John Bianconi's farm at Locknasheennagh with the quay at Kildysart (Co. Clare) on the Shannon estuary. The 0.61 m (2 ft) gauge line depended on horse traction (apart from a steam lorry introduced in 1912) and lasted until the owner's death in 1929. However, the most persistent theme in private narrow gauge railway building relates to the winning of peats. Several standard gauge railways have been built over peat bogs, with the aid of drainage and piling, and sometimes this has been preferred to cutting through rocky terrain, as in Connemara, but narrow gauge lines have also been built to facilitate peat cutting and harvesting.

Reed swamp peat was formed in hollows left by the retreating ice at the close of the glacial epoch. This sedge peat gave way to a woody fen peat, which formed an upper layer in response to climatic and vegetational changes, and finally emergence of forest led to formation of sphagnum peat which formed the top of the 'raised bogs'. Such bogs are common in the Irish Midlands Triangle but there is an outpost in Ulster on the edge of Lough Neagh where commercial working has taken place. A different type of peat (blanket bog or mountain bog depending on the topography) is found in the far west where different climatic conditions have resulted in an elimination of pine and birch wood and a complete absence of sphagnum peat. A great deal of bog has over the years been cut for domestic fuel and reclaimed for agricultural and forestry use, but during the nineteenth century there was considerable thought about the possibilities of commercial exploitation of the bogs as a source of power. Surveys indicated the extent of the bogs but none of the various attempts to use peat for briquette manufacture or for distillation products was commercially successful. For a short period narrow gauge railways were built in Co. Kildare to facilitate peat digging for paper-making (Celbridge), packing material and litter (Umeras) and fuel (Derrylea). Most notable was the project at Annaghmore in Ulster. The Annaghmore Turf Railway in Co. Armagh, opened in 1901 to transport peat to the Lagan Navigation from a processing station near Maghery. Electric locomotives, drawing power from the company's own peat-fired power station, were provided in 1907 as the railway system was extended on to the bogs. These dependable machines, once described as travelling hen houses, remained at work until 1957, by which time two diesel replacements handled all the traffic. By this time the peat litter, valuable in agriculture and horticulture, was being taken away by road: there was no connection with the standard gauge railway.

But by this time considerable momentum was being built up in the south.

35. *Railway arch at Carnlough* The bridge was built in the 1850s by the Londonderry family as part of a railway project to take limestone down to the harbour at Carnlough on the Antrim coast.

A promising private initiative was taken in 1924 when a machine was introduced on to the Turraun Bog (Co. Offaly) to produce macerated sod peat for burning in a small power station. Government interest increased as the autarchic element in government policies grew stronger during the 1930s and the Turf Development Board was formed in 1934 to see how far peat could penetrate the country's energy market and reduce dependence on imported fuels. The Turraun Works was taken over and the German method of sod peat production used there was endorsed. Under this method the raw peat is excavated by bucket dredger or 'bagger'. It passes through a macerator and is extruded through a spreader arm which lays it on the bog surface to dry and also cuts each strip into sods. At the same time an alternative Russian method of milled peat production was used in 1935 at Lullymore in Co. Kildare. By this technique an extensive surface is torn up and subsequently harrowed to a depth of 12 mm. The Lullymore venture was started by a private company interested in briquette production and the unit was taken over by the Turf Development Board in 1940. Other bogs had previously been taken over in 1936: a raised bog at Clonsast in Co. Offaly which is still being worked and a small blanket bog at Lyrecrumpane in Co. Kerry, which has now been completely cut over and reclaimed for other uses.

Since the potential of the peat had been quite clearly exposed by this time, especially for a state following a policy of self-sufficiency in energy, the post-war period saw a rapid development of bogs through the agency of the Irish Turf Board (Bord na Mona), established in 1946. More than 50 000 ha. of bogland have been acquired through negotiations with thousands of separate owners. Large continuous areas can therefore be exploited on a rational basis with overall schemes of drainage and cutting in which heavy machinery plays a prominent part. Drainage is crucial for mechanisation: the cutting of drains on the bogs and the execution of arterial works on minor external rivers and streams increases the solid matter available for cutting and increases the bearing value of the bog to the point where machinery can be used even in difficult areas on the bog domes where the depth of younger sphagnum is generally greatest. The output includes briquettes (0.3 m.t.) and moss peat (1.2 m bales), but the bulk of the production consists of ordinary peat (0.9 m.t. machined and 3.2 m.t. milled), most of which is supplied to power stations built on the edge of the bogs to minimise transport costs. The power stations are operated by a separate organisation, the Electricity Supply Board, but the programme has been closely integrated with Bord na Mona's activities. The first were opened in 1950–1 at Allenwood and Portarlington, both relatively close to Dublin and associated with the Ballydermot–Lullymore–Timahoe and Clonsast bogs respectively. In the period 1957–60 came Ferbane, Lanesborough and Rhode associated with Boora (an enlargement of the old

36.  *Working the peat bogs in Donegal* The Bord na Mona peat workings at Glenties in Co. Donegal have their own narrow gauge railway system, connecting the bogs with a distribution depot at the roadhead.

Turraun working), Mountdillon and Derrygreenagh–Croghan respectively. Rounding off the programme was the Bellacorick station in Mayo (1962) on the Oweninny bog and Shannonbridge (1968) in the Midlands on the Blackwater bog.

This means that virtually all the bogs producing more than 100 000 t. of peat per annum have their local power stations. In 1977–8 3.35 m.t. of turf (all but 0.39 m.t. being milled) was supplied to seven power stations with a combined capacity of 427 MW. This compares with a total output (excluding mosspeat) of 4.60 m.t. of which 0.36 m.t. consisted of briquettes. The exceptions are Derringlough, which is geared exclusively to briquetting, and two other bogs which produce moss peat. Moss peat comes from the light mossy growth found in the upper layers of bogs and some special bogs have been exploited for this product where the deposits are particularly heavy. After the failure of earlier attempts in the 1890s the modern demand for soil conditioners, seed propagating material and poultry litter has allowed the first Bord na Mona unit at Kilberry, Co. Kildare (1947) to be followed by Coolnamona, Co. Laois (1965) and a progressive expansion of the bogs which serve these factories. Kilberry has an interesting history with previous attempts at development for peat tar and distillates (1849) and briquettes (1855), the latter scheme reopened 1906 to 1914 with a short railway from the bog to the factory.

The railways are important on all the Bord na Mona bogs for the transport of peat from the bogs to power stations, briquette or moss peat factories and roadside loading points. A light railway has been found the only feasible way of transporting peat. Conveyers are too expensive and temporary roads cannot be laid down without affecting the bog underneath. There is about 1000 km of permanent way while another 250 km of the system consists of temporary track which can be moved around as required (perhaps as much as twelve times each year). Road transport is feasible for carrying peat from small outlying bogs as is already happening at some of the smaller bogs which supply milled peat to Bellacorrick power station in Co. Mayo and for the transport of moss peat for Kilberry and Coolnamona factories (outside their own producing bogs). One large bog is being developed near Monasterevan and will have its own narrow gauge railway although road transport will be used between the bogside and the Kilberry factory. On average there are about 23 metres of railway for every hectare of bog but there is a deviation from this average up to about ten percent either way depending on the compactness of the areas being worked. Basically, each group of bogs has its own system and although some interlinkage may appear in future, as at Clonsast–Derrygreenagh and Ballydermot–Timahoe–Lullymore where some 20 000 ha. of bog would be integrated together, there is no concept of a single integrated Bord na Mona system. Gradients present few problems and are rarely steeper than 1 in 150 on permanent track, although 1 in 50 gradients may arise on temporary track on blanket bog. The most impressive engineering works arise where rivers and canals have to be crossed: the Shannon was crossed above by a 188 m bridge in 1958 and below Shannonbridge (160 m) in 1968 (for Mountdillon and Blackwater groups respectively) while bridges over the Grand Canal (with vertical lift) were built at Allenwood and Rhode in 1952 and 1960 respectively.

For motive power Bord na Mona first tried turf-burning steam locomotives, built by Andrew Barclay. The three steam engines were all disposed of by 1969, but one is still in Ireland working a private steam railway at Shane's Castle, Randalstown, Co. Antrim. Diesel locomotives were found to be more flexible and better suited for running on temporary track. After several diesel locomotives had been tried Bord na Mona designed their own to obtain the best combination of weight, horsepower and tractive effort. Almost eighty of these Hunslet-built 'Wagonmaster' locomotives are now in service. Some wagons and railcars have found their way to Bord na Mona from narrow gauge lines that are now closed but most of the other stock, including aluminium-panelled wagons and management railcars, are purpose-built for the bogs. All the railways are o.91 m gauge except for the early Kilberry system which is o.61 m (2 ft).

At the present time the railways are still developing, particularly at Derryfadda and Littleton where work has started quite recently under the Third Development Programme. However, the various schemes have a short life and considerable areas will soon, like Lyrecrumpane (a mountain bog transferred to the Department of Lands Forestry Division in 1965), become available for restoration. Up to one metre of peat (more in the case of unworkable pockets) is left to facilitate reclamation. Afforestation will account for some of the land but agriculture will also be prominent. Research started in 1955 at Clonsast and Lullymore and has been expanded by the Agricultural Institute which took over responsibility in 1960. The Clonsast experiment was particularly important, involving a narrow belt (some 2.5 km in length) presenting a full range of peat residue and subsoil combinations which can be correlated with the levels of tree growth. At Lullymore, by contrast, the agricultural and horticultural potential of a milled peat cutaway has been explored. The work has been intensified at Lullymore and (since 1964) at Timahoe. Grass seems the most suitable crop at Lullymore and also at Timahoe, where experiments on a sod peat cutaway began in 1970. Deep peat of the woody fen type has been found excellent for vegetable production and projects started at Lullymore (1967) and Derrygreenagh (1970). The market prospects are not too encouraging and it may prove desirable to halt fuel production when the woody fen peat layer is reached so that the horticultural potential can be fully exploited. Meanwhile ornamental shrub production for export (begun experimentally at Lullymore in 1969) may become more profitable. In various ways therefore land-use will change as the peat workings and the power stations eventually close. Already their contribution to the total power output of the republic is falling as additional demand is inevitably met by burning other fuels. And there are growing pressures from agricultural interests to restrict turf cutting so as to retain a wider range of options over reclamation. But although the commercial peat workings are destined to be simply a chapter in the evolution of the Irish landscape and economy it will seem an unusual one for the late twentieth century in being so inextricably bound up with the railways.

# 26

# The Problem of Derelict Railways

One implication of railway closure which received only slight consideration in the early days was the use that was to be made of the redundant installations: buildings and track bed. The closure of some 9000 km of railway between 1948 and 1968 involved a very large area of land, albeit fragmented and somewhat inaccessible. In a densely-populated country such as Britain it is most desirable that any derelict land should be put to good use and redundant railway property is no exception. The land is a valuable asset and naturally British Rail are anxious to capitalise on it when permission to sell is forthcoming from the government. Apart from the special circumstances involved in reversion clauses, which require the return of land to the owners from whom it was taken in the first place, preference has been given to local authorities. And there is an understanding with the N.F.U. that, unless local authorities exercise their option, adjacent landowners will receive favourable consideration. As a result many disused railways have been integrated into the agricultural scene, usually with only slight modifications. Sections may be used as farm roads or else put down to grass to form small enclosures for livestock. Quite commonly the old trackbed is added to adjacent fields, either informally by removing part of the fencing or more radically by taking out all the fencing and perhaps bringing in heavy machinery to eliminate low embankments or shallow cuttings. Bridges afford ready shelter for storage of hay and other materials, and they may be bricked up for use as stables. Unfortunately, the reclamation process operates on a piecemeal basis. Although sections of cuttings can make sheltered livestock pens if drainage is maintained, agricultural use is often difficult when there is a big difference in level between the old railway track and the adjacent land: the percentage of such land may be less than ten percent (Haughley to Laxfield in Suffolk) but frequently exceeds fifty percent. Only special circumstances, usually relating to high land values in urban areas, will justify filling deep cuttings or removing high embankments and such land may therefore remain unused, standing as an inaccessible 'island' of waste.

As regards the urban scene it is worth noting a survey of Liverpool in 1978 which showed that about half the 600 ha. of land used by railways in

1960 had been vacated in the meantime. One third of the vacated land took the form of relatively compact blocks (dockland goods stations and shunting yards) associated with the water front, with the rest (including many narrow strips of former trackbed) distributed widely through the study area in blocks of varying size. Only about forty percent of the vacant land has been redeveloped. Road transport has featured prominently in the reoccupation: Liverpool Inland Containerbase has used the former L.Y.R. complex at Aintree, much of the former L.N.W.R. yard at Garston is used for container transit, while National Carriers has its chief Liverpool depot at the former C.L.C. goods station at Huskisson. Industrial buildings have been placed over the L.N.W.R. Speke Sidings, while housing appears on the C.L.C. Walton Triangle and a caravan site provides a new function at Waterloo Dock goods station. The area remaining derelict is very substantial and although it is perhaps inevitable that the spate of closures in the 1960s should make reoccupation of surplus land a long term problem the lack of an overall plan is unfortunate. Recreational opportunities are considerable but so far only the railway heritage of Edge Hill has attracted serious attention. As part of the celebrations to mark the 150th anniversary of the Liverpool & Manchester Railway a trail was opened to allow visitors to appreciate the challenge facing the builders in reaching the original terminus. The cutting and tunnel which continued to give access to the docks after the switch of passenger trains to Lime Street has not been used by British Rail for some years. The cutting was widened during the 1840s and John Forster's

37. *A bridge without a purpose* The piecemeal nature of the reclamation process is brought into sharp focus by this old railway bridge standing anomalously in a field near Grantown on Spey in the Scottish Highlands.

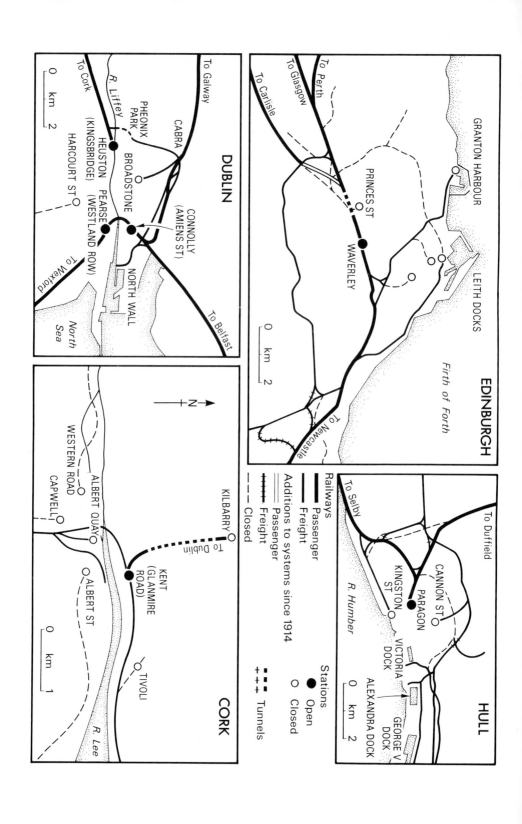

DUBLIN

To Galway
To Cork
R. Liffey
PHEONIX PARK
CABRA
BROADSTONE
HEUSTON (KINGSBRIDGE)
HARCOURT ST
PEARSE (WESTLAND ROW)
CONNOLLY (AMIENS ST)
HARCOURT ST
NORTH WALL
To Wexford
To Belfast
North Sea

0 km 2

EDINBURGH

To Carlisle
To Glasgow
To Perth
GRANTON HARBOUR
PRINCES ST
WAVERLEY
LEITH DOCKS
To Newcastle
Firth of Forth

0 km 2

CORK

WESTERN ROAD
ALBERT QUAY
CAPWELL
ALBERT ST
KENT (GLANMIRE ROAD)
KILBARRY
To Dublin
TIVOLI
R. Lee

N

0 km 1

Railways
Passenger
Freight
Additions to systems since 1914
Passenger
Freight
Closed

Stations
● Open
○ Closed

▪▪▪ Tunnels
+++

HULL

To Selby
To Duffield
R. Humber
KINGSTON ST
CANNON ST
PARAGON
VICTORIA DOCK
ALEXANDRA DOCK
GEORGE V DOCK

0 km 2

Moorish Arch (the first piece of monumental railway architecture) removed in the process. But something of the atmosphere of the original line conveyed by contemporary drawings can be enjoyed through this novel venture. Studies of the Scottish cities of Edinburgh and Glasgow raise similar issues but it is evident that much more importance has been attached to the scope for building new roads. Motorways in Glasgow have used some railway (and also the Monkland Canal) while in Edinburgh there are plans for a new road to Leith, using abandoned lines in the north of the city, and an East Approach Road to relieve the city centre could use the former Innocents line around the southern side of Arthur's Seat. Some lines in Glasgow have been reserved for possible future reopening: the former Kirklee line and the northern circle from Balornock to the Kelvin Valley is still available for a modern suburban railway, while part of the northern circle to Dalmarnock could still be used in conjunction with an outer circle railway for the city.

In all parts of the country the contraction and rationalisation of railways has resulted in a great reduction in the number of stations. This follows from the closure of particular routes but there has also been a great reduction in the number of wayside stations, even on lines that remain open. And in cities there has been some attempt to rationalise services and so concentrate traffic on a smaller number of stations. The examples taken show two cities (Dublin and Cork) where the reduction in the number of stations has come simply through closure of some principal lines and two others (Edinburgh and Hull) where concentration has been possible by building short connecting lines. The Irish cities were mentioned in an earlier chapter when the growth of their railway systems was described. In Dublin there was a distinct lack of railways in the southern half of the city and although the Dublin & South Eastern built a branch into Harcourt Street to stimulate growth in Dundrum and Rathfarnham suburbs the lack of connections with other railways was a drawback which ruled out its survival. No progress was made towards a joint station apart from identification of a possible site at Eustace Street near College Green and rationalisation has come only through the closure of Broadstone in 1936 and Harcourt Street in 1958, both in favour of Pearse (formerly Westland Row). In Cork all services are concentrated on Kent (as Glanmire Road Station is now named) but although this was expedited by the Cork & Youghal's extension of 1859 and the Cork City Railway in 1914 it has taken the closure of services to Bandon, Blarney and Passage to close all the stations south of the river (Albert Quay, Albert Street and Western Road).

Map 17. (*Opposite*)    Rationalisation of railways in Cork, Dublin, Edinburgh and Hull.

At Hull the removal of all passenger services from the lines once forming part of the Hull & Barnsley Railway has necessarily restricted operations to a single station. But in fact a short link on the north-western edge of the city brought about this concentration in 1924. The H.B.R. station at Cannon Street was closed two years later in favour of Paragon Station, built for the North Eastern in 1848 by George T. Andrews in the Italian villa style and enlarged in 1904. In Edinburgh the rationalisation has come since nationalisation. Through the improvement of a former goods branch at Stateford, trains from Carlisle and Carstairs have been diverted from the former Caledonian Railway station of Princes Street on to North British metals and thereby reach Waverley Station. In both cities, however, it is evident that some additional links have been forged for the benefit of freight traffic at Hull docks and the east end of Edinburgh.

Some other rationalisation schemes have not been entirely satisfactory. The closure of Gloucester Eastgate in 1975 and concentration of all services at Central has led to delay of Bristol–Birmingham trains because of the need to reverse, a factor which leads British Rail to divert some of the trains over an avoiding line and thereby reduce the quality of service available to the city. A station site at the junction of the Bristol and South Wales lines

38.  *The changing landscape of Walsingham, Norfolk* The establishment of an Orthodox church here must constitute one of the more unusual cases of railway station conversion.

39. *Railways in the memory* Although the railways have been completely closed down in Melton Constable (Norfolk) the bus shelter bears testimony to the fact that this village was once the centre of the Midland & Great Northern Joint Railway's system.

(Barnwood Junction) would have avoided any delay through reversal and made the station accessible to trains on the avoiding line. It is also worth noting that some comparatively small terminal stations have been rebuilt on new sites which allow more efficient road-rail interchange. Fort William Station has been rebuilt at the northern end of the town and as a result a valuable strip of land at the lochside has been freed for the construction of a relief road. Over in Northern Ireland Londonderry's prominent Waterside Station has been re-sited to allow for road works. The change is a timely one in view of extensive bomb damage but it is good to know that the clock tower, a distinctive feature of the old station (built in 1887) and a local landmark, will be preserved.

Station sites are of special interest because the plot of land involved is usually much less elongated than a strip of normal track and its adaptability is further increased by the road access available and the existence of buildings, including the main station building (often incorporating a house) and goods shed. The special advantages of a station site often result in its acquisition as a separate entity. A wide range of uses of station sites can be readily demonstrated by surveys in almost any part of the country. Most common in north Norfolk are cases where the premises are used as a house

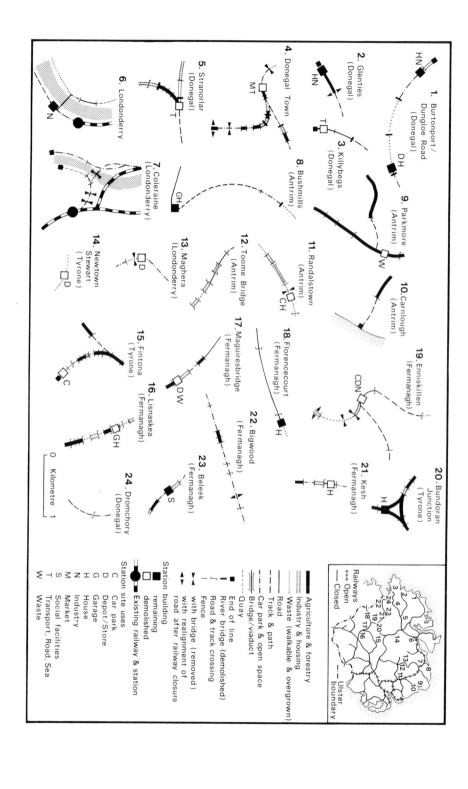

or store; this category includes the delightful example of Knapton and Paston where the whole site has been tastefully landscaped leaving only subtle reminders of the original function of the building. Further cases of new uses producing new landscapes include Trimingham, where the site has been cleared for a new housing scheme, and Corpusty and Saxthorpe Station where an attractive camping site has been laid out by the former Lowestoft Education Committee. At Fakenham (West) the railway atmosphere has been virtually obliterated by an access road to the district sports centre and buildings for a vegetable depot, but part of the platform has been retained as a raised flower bed. Industrial use is evident in some instances but most remarkable is Walsingham where the station building has been converted into an Orthodox church with suitable architectural embellishment!

Some re-use of station sites involves complete or partial demolition of the original buildings. But this is not possible when the station is a listed building which must therefore be preserved. The protection of stations in this way has gathered considerable momentum since the Victorian Society drew up a basic list in the mid-1960s. Finding suitable uses for these buildings can be a protracted business. The most notable example here concerns the former headquarters of the Somerset & Dorset Joint Railway at Bath Green Park (opened in 1870). The magnificent Georgian façade, complementing local tradition, has been associated with various conversion schemes (including hotel, supermarket and swimming pool) since the station closed in 1966. However, preservation is also a feature of the private steam railways which aim not only to provide basic facilities but also to create an atmosphere of authenticity. Competitions for the best preserved station help to create interest even in cases where the railway is no longer used. Thus the Wirral Country Park Station at Hadlow Road retains much of its old character, as does Oakworth on the Keighley & Worth Valley. It is also noteworthy that the celebration of the 150th anniversary of the Liverpool & Manchester Railway has been marked by a useful initiative in Manchester where the old Liverpool Road Station, superseded by Victoria and used for many years as a goods depot, will become an exhibition centre. Renovation of the station began in 1979 with the property in extremely poor condition, but the Liverpool Road Station Society have confidence that the restoration can successfully recreate the image of 1830. The exhibition centre is to have links with the National Railway Museum at York.

An overview of the situation emerges from consideration of various examples taken from Ireland's Ulster province, which covers the whole of Northern Ireland and three counties in the Irish Republic. In a few cases

Map 18. (*Opposite*)   Some derelict railways in Ulster.

where long sections of railway have been used for roads, as at Florencecourt and Maguiresbridge (the latter involving a section of some five kilometres north-westwards towards Lisbellaw). But generally the railway track is divided into small compartments, many of them involving agricultural use with the former railway land merging with adjacent fields through removal of hedges. Some farm tracks have also made use of railway track bed. Considerable areas remain as waste land and it is evident that in the damper west, notably Donegal, the rapid growth of vegetation has rendered such sections virtually impenetrable. Otherwise the waste land can be used for informal recreation. In Enniskillen and Londonderry a section of old railway has been formally converted into a walkway, but such developments are rather rare in Ireland so far. Urban development consists largely of some road widening, car park provision and development of housing or industrial premises. The station sites also show a generally low intensity of use. The station buildings sometimes survive as dwelling houses (notably Bundoran Junction) with space occasionally used for a garage business (Bushmills and Lisnaskea). Storage (often in connection with road maintenance) is a prominent function (Maghera and Newtown Stewart) and several Donegal stations have been used for other forms of transport: harbour expansion at Killybegs and a container terminal at Stranorlar.

# 27

# Conversion of Railways into Roads

One particularly positive approach to the re-use of surplus railway property lies in the redevelopment of entire stretches of railway so that the whole section is re-integrated with the rest of the working landscape instead of remaining an anomalous relict feature. As previously indicated, considerable 'linear use' arises through use of old railways as farm tracks. But it is also feasible in several instances to build new public roads wholly or partially on former railways. Indeed, in 1957 T. I. Lloyd proposed a wholesale shutdown of railways so that 'the entire unprofitable railway system' could be converted into a modern road network of reserved roads set aside for fast-flowing traffic. Stations would be cleared away to become open spaces where the reserved roads could connect with the minor roads for local distribution. The idea was launched (before Britain's motorway programme had got under way) in a bid to save money and avoid the strong opposition that would inevitably arise through acquisition of agricultural land to build entirely new roads. However, there were serious objections: how would transport be organised in the transition between railways closing and roads opening; how could single and double track railways provide the space needed for four- or six-lane motorways without costly development; how could public transport on the roads provide levels of comfort, efficiency and reliability associated with the railway? Consequently the proposal has not been implemented, although some recent research continues to advocate conversion on commuter lines: six studies were made in the London area, representing the widest range of railway passenger traffic, and in each case it was found that the community would benefit from replacing the trains with buses and lorries and converting railway formation into public road. Feasibility studies were also undertaken in Nottingham with a view to converting twenty-five kilometres of disused railway into a concrete busway at a cost of some fifteen million pounds. But despite its advantage of cheapness compared with a suburban rail system and the advantage of collecting passengers on the streets in the city centre, the rise in fuel costs is leading to counter-proposals that railways should be retained, and in some cases reopened, in order to avoid costly new investment in extra roads.

So far, there has been a piecemeal reduction of the railway system and in certain cases old trackbed has been suitably aligned to allow road development to make use of it. Railway closures have not taken place with any specific form of conversion in mind and land has usually been left derelict for a period of years before the possibility of a road scheme arose. Some motorways were built in advance of major rail closures and in Leicestershire the M1 runs for several kilometres wastefully alongside the now derelict Great Central main line. However, in Scotland the much later completion of the M90 to Perth has made it possible to use much of the track of the former North British Railway through Glenfarg and Arngask. And in many cases the closure of railways has led to an almost immediate provision of additional facilities for road transport, notably through the use of space for car parking and the conversion of certain bridges. At both Connel (Argyll and Bute) in the Scottish Highlands and Sutton Bridge in Lincolnshire the bridges once shared by rail and road traffic are now available exclusively for the latter. In Londonderry where Craigavon Bridge had a lower deck for rail traffic and an upper deck for road both levels are now used by road traffic. Otherwise road developments have emerged more gradually. Realignment of trunk roads has sometimes made considerable use of old railways as with the 'Heads of the Valleys' road in South Wales. Frequently, extra land is required to provide a carriageway of adequate width but a new coastal road in Southport demonstrates that a twenty-four foot (7.3 m) road can be constructed at a low cost with hardly any additional purchase of land.

Particularly common is the bypass situation where an old railway touching the edge of a small town may correspond very closely to a desired line suggested by traffic engineers for a bypass. Several schemes have been completed successfully, although difficulty arises when the growth of the town (subsequent to the opening of the railway) has led to urban development on both sides of the line. The bypass then becomes an internal relief road and although it merely perpetuates a long-standing line of severance the risk of additional noise and pollution may generate local opposition to conversion. Finally, there are cases of private road developments. The proposal by Dunlop to use a seven kilometre section of the old Leicester–Rugby line as a high speed tyre testing facility has not been followed up, but china clay is shipped from Fowey thanks to the creation of private road access to the port along the former railway alignment from Par. On the whole the rate of progress has not been rapid and although the Railway Conversion League was able to enumerate a long list of projects at the start of the 1970s the majority involved sections shorter than three kilometres and only a small number of them had been completed at the time.

An unusually large number of conversions have been made in East Anglia. Many of the schemes affect only short stretches of railway and

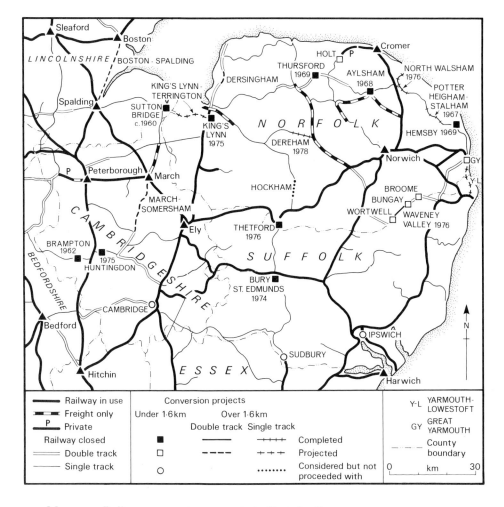

Map 19.   Railway conversion to roads in East Anglia.

consist of bypasses for towns like Bury St Edmunds, King's Lynn and Thetford, where derelict track has been conveniently aligned for these projects. But much longer conversions have been made in Norfolk in the North Walsham, Dereham and Lowestoft areas. In the former case the Stalham–Potter Heigham section of the old Midland & Great Northern Railway was converted more than a decade ago (the first scheme in East Anglia): station buildings were removed, although Stalham remains as a local authority road depot. A further section of this railway was converted in 1976, giving access to North Walsham and at the same time providing a route through the heart of the town on to the Mundesley road. At Dereham, on the other hand, it is an old Great Eastern route that is involved in a scheme to improve traffic flow on the King's Lynn–Norwich road. The Waveney Valley line, leading westwards from Lowestoft, has been converted for a short distance, part of a scheme that will eventually affect the whole section between Broome and Wortwell.

The line between Great Yarmouth and Lowestoft is an outstanding candidate for future conversion, like the King's Lynn–Terrington and March–Somersham sections. The time scale for some of these projects is considerable however: Cambridgeshire County Council hope to build a new road from March to Chatteris (bypassing Wimblington, Doddington and Chatteris) within the next few years, but the extension to Somersham is not expected before the late 1980s. It is all a question of demand: roads cannot be made out of railways just because the physical conditions are suitable. At Hockham the use of a section of old Thetford–Swaffham railway would make for a somewhat shorter journey between Thetford and Watten (the direct link having been closed by the Army training area), but traffic likely to benefit was thought to be too small to justify the expense, unlike the situation at Dersingham where Hunstanton traffic will be diverted in future. Having said this it is apparent that East Anglia has been able to make considerable progress. Although there are few schemes for building new major roads, numerous *ad hoc* improvements to the existing system are needed to cater for the expanding towns, like Bury St Edmunds, and to cope with the very heavy summer traffic to the coastal resorts. So planners have been looking for new road alignments in several parts of the region and old railways have been used wherever possible. Comprehensive road schemes for long stretches of railway are not to be expected but with the continuing growth of road traffic East Anglia's impressive conversion record seems likely to be maintained.

# 28

# Recreational Uses for Derelict Railways

In a major report dealing with derelict railways J. H. Appleton discussed their recreational potential but noted some prejudice against old railway routes by walkers who preferred 'prehistoric trackways, ridgeways and other paths of respectable pedigree'. Certainly the image of a working railway may discourage ready acceptance of derelict trackbed as a basis for leisure activity, and some sections can be distinctly monotonous. However, old railways can be tidied up to project a sense of pastoral calm, while the frequent alternation of cutting and embankment 'provides a variety which is the very essence of the picturesque as expounded by its protagonists in the late eighteenth century'. Even in long cuttings thoughtful tree planting can increase interest. Discussing the potential of the Deeside Railway for recreational purposes E. T. Parham describes the climb out of Banchory 'through a series of cuttings flanked by young coniferous plantations. The banks carry heather and bilberry and there has been heavy invasion of birch. There is a sense of quiet and isolation.' And the section at the Loch of Auchlossan was commended as 'an interesting self-contained visual unit with agricultural land at the lower levels and forest and moorland round the rim'. Value for holiday chalets and caravans was noted while the educational function in bringing out changes in scenery and rural economy was stressed. Yet even where a route has little scenic merit its development as a footpath or bridleway may be justified in connection with existing paths or, more particularly, M. Dower's concept of greenways to link areas of major recreational value. There is an urban equivalent to this idea through the linear park as pursued on the Potteries Loop in Stoke-on-Trent and along the Derwent Valley south of Consett in Co. Durham.

The potential can only be realised at considerable cost however. Trackbed is an expensive item, to say nothing of the repair of bridges, installation of access points (usually former station sites) and basic facilities. Maintenance will result in continuing liabilities. In many cases the option of recreational development hardly exists since the land may be sold off in small sections to individual farmers. Although local authorities are approached at an early stage their powers and responsibilities over conservation and the enjoyment of the countryside were limited before the Countryside Act of 1968. Greater interest has sometimes been expressed in subsequent years, as indicated by the survey of disused railways carried out by Northamptonshire's County Planning Officer. Many possibilities were considered, but less than ten percent of the total length of derelict trackbed was thought worthy of further study. Few tracks offered compelling scenic attractions, while low level of usage of existing rights of way (footpaths and bridleways) made it difficult to anticipate heavy demand. Heavy mainten-ance costs encouraged greater priority for canal towpaths and country parks. About twenty kilometres of track (divided between nine sites) were considered worthy of further investigation because they included some of the more interesting features and, in conjunction with public rights of way, offered scope for walking, cycling and horse-riding circuits. Yet in the end action has only been taken in one instance where the former Blisworth–Peterborough line runs beside Thrapston gravel pits.

Progress in the adjacent county of Leicestershire has also been disappointing. Several sections are used as farm tracks and some of them have a recreational value through shooting or horse riding. The potential of certain cutting sections (at Scalford, Shenton and Thurnby) for nature reserves has been appreciated. But nothing has been done to provide any facilities for public recreation. Since the landscape value is not compelling, and several sections of derelict trackbed near the towns can be used informally for recreation, the local authority decided not to make any purchases when the option was presented to them. But it is unfortunate that the potential of certain lines round Coalville has not been appreciated in view of the associations with famous canal and railway engineers. Earthworks relating to the tramways of the ill-fated Charnwood Forest Canal are still quite fresh around Thringstone while the remains of the lower part of the Ticknall Tramway are very clear both in the fields south of Ashby and on the approach to Staunton Harold. Even more important, however, are the inclines on the Leicester & Swannington Railway, particularly the one at Swannington which is now thickly overgrown. Although there may hardly be the scope for promoting the Stephensons in quite the way that Thomas Telford has been remembered by the people of Shropshire there is a basis in Swannington Incline (along with Calcutta Colliery and Moira Furnace) for a conservation programme that would meet local recreational needs and also harmonise with the local authority aim to exploit the region's industrial heritage and image as a contribution to the development of tourism in the East Midlands. The Leicestershire & Swannington line, which opened the 'railway age' in Leicestershire is still basically a going concern, as most of the coal mines along the route continue to flourish. But it would be appropriate if the celebration of its 150th anniversary could be

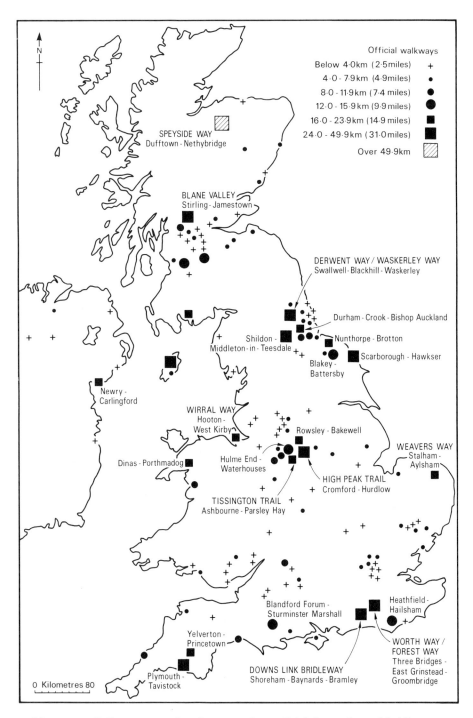

Map 20a.   Railway conversion for recreation: official footpaths and bridle ways.
Projected paths are included.

marked by a belated recognition of its status as a historic monument.

However, it should not be overlooked that in many other parts of the British Isles derelict railways have been converted for recreational purposes. The map shows approximately 150 walks now established or definitely planned on old railways and there is still time for others to be provided. Several organisations are active in promoting the idea, including one rambling group ('Railway Ramblers') which specialises in railway walking. Of the walks presently established almost three quarters are shorter than eight kilometres (5 miles) in length. Those longer walks which are at least twelve kilometres (7.5 miles) long may be described regionally as follows. Devon proposes walks on the Plymouth–Tavistock and Yelverton–Princetown branches, while Dorset plans a bridleway along the Somerset & Dorset between Blandford Forum and Sturminster Marshall. In Sussex the Forest Way and Worth Way together already produce a path from Three Bridges through East Grinstead to Groombridge, while the Downs Link Path has been provided along the old railway line from Shoreham to Baynards Tunnel on to Bramley in Surrey. And another Sussex project will connect Heathfield with Hailsham. The Wye Valley in Gwent can be followed by the railway path from Tintern to Monmouth. Further north comes the Welsh Highland Railway path in Gwynedd (extending gradually from Dinas to Porthmadog), the Wirral Way in Merseyside (Hooton–West Kirby) and the Weavers Way in Norfolk (Stalham–Aylsham). But the Peak District offers quite a range of paths: the Derbyshire walks along the High Peak and Tissington Trails should be supplemented in future by the Rowsley–Bakewell section of the Midland Railway, while back in the 1930s Staffordshire provided the first long-distance railway conversion with the Manifold Valley between Hulme End and Waterhouses.

For the North York Moors there is a coastal section from Scarborough to Hawsker Bottoms and an upland walk by the Ingleby Incline to Blakey and Rosedale, while Cleveland has a project for the section from Nunthorpe through Guisborough to Brotton. Durham has been particularly enterprising however. In conjunction with Tyne & Wear Authority a path leads from the Tyne at Swalwell by the Derwent Valley to Blackhill (Consett) with a further trail over the moors to Waskerley and Stanhope. A connection is planned for Durham by the Lanchester Valley. Durham already has paths to Bishop Auckland (Bishop–Brandon walk) and Crook (Deerness Valley). Finally there is a project in Durham to connect Shildon with Bishop Auckland, Barnard Castle and Middleton-in-Teesdale. The Isle of Man has footpaths on sections of the St John's–Ramsey line. Scotland's longest paths are planned mainly in Strathclyde at Lesmahagow (Stonehouse to Auldton Heights), Kilmarnock (Hurlford to Priestland) and from James-town near Dumbarton along the Blane Valley to Stirling in the Central

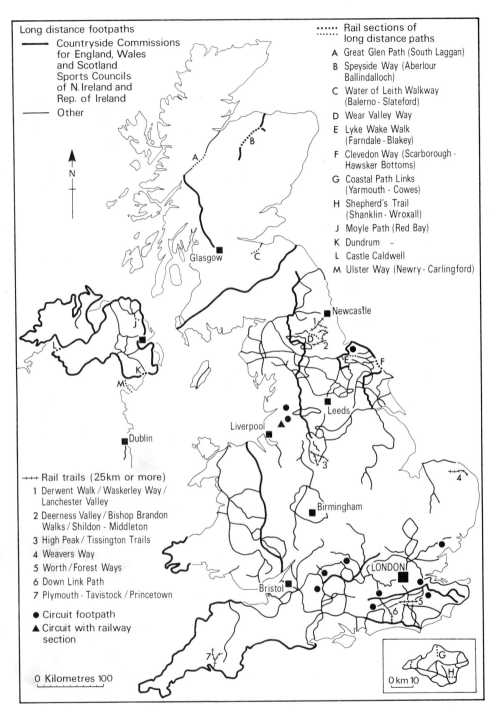

Long distance footpaths
——— Countryside Commissions for England, Wales and Scotland Sports Councils of N. Ireland and Rep. of Ireland
——— Other

⋯⋯⋯ Rail sections of long distance paths
A Great Glen Path (South Laggan)
B Speyside Way (Aberlour Ballindalloch)
C Water of Leith Walkway (Balerno - Slateford)
D Wear Valley Way
E Lyke Wake Walk (Farndale - Blakey)
F Clevedon Way (Scarborough - Hawsker Bottoms)
G Coastal Path Links (Yarmouth - Cowes)
H Shepherd's Trail (Shanklin - Wroxall)
J Moyle Path (Red Bay)
K Dundrum -
L Castle Caldwell
M Ulster Way (Newry - Carlingford)

N

Glasgow

Newcastle

Leeds

Liverpool

Dublin

+++ Rail trails (25km or more)
1 Derwent Walk / Waskerley Way / Lanchester Valley
2 Deerness Valley / Bishop Brandon Walks / Shildon - Middleton
3 High Peak / Tissington Trails
4 Weavers Way
5 Worth / Forest Ways
6 Down Link Path
7 Plymouth - Tavistock / Princetown

● Circuit footpath
▲ Circuit with railway section

Birmingham

LONDON

Bristol

0 Kilometres 100

0 km 10

Map 20b.  Railway conversion for recreation: incorporation of derelict railways into long-distance footpaths. Projected paths are included.

40. *Welsh Highland* One of the bridges on the Welsh Highland Railway in Gwynedd restored for pedestrian use.

Region. But a section of the Dumfries–Stranraer railway is also earmarked (Mossdale to Gatehouse of Fleet) while the Speyside Way in the Grampian Region involves the railway route from Dufftown to Nethybridge which seems destined to become the longest railway walk in the British Isles.

The list is quite impressive, but it must be remembered that many are still in the planning stage. Furthermore, railways as yet provide only a very small part of the rapidly growing system of long distance paths. Sections of railway are sometimes integrated, as has already happened with the Speyside Way and may happen in future with the projected Great Glen Path. But for the most part the railway paths stand alone and they are only shown on Map 20 when they are more than twenty-four kilometres (15 miles) long. Nevertheless this is not to disparage the notable achievement to date. A particularly imaginative project is the Wirral Country Park which provides recreation in a scenically attractive area on the edge of a great conurbation. The railway between Hooton and West Kirby was completely closed in 1962 and it seemed only a matter of time before it disappeared into history. The drains became choked and part of the track became waterlogged while elsewhere brambles and gorse took over. Station buildings decayed, a number of bridges were dismantled and British Rail began to sell off portions of the line.

However, the idea of a country park for the Wirral coast had been discussed by Wirral Green Belt Council when passenger services ceased in 1956 and Cheshire County Council came forward with a formal proposal in 1968. It was not an idea that appealed to many local people, especially those with property backing on to the railway. At the very least privacy would be threatened, to say nothing of the risk of vandalism. Yet the demands for recreation could not be overlooked (especially in view of the success of Tissington Trail in 1971), but it is a tribute to the planners and wardens that local opinion has become wholly reconciled with the scheme. Continuity was restored by providing ramps or wooden spans where bridges had been removed – the entire track bed was cleared of undergrowth to allow for riding and walking, to say nothing of the botanical and geological interest of certain sites. Neston Cutting is particularly rewarding and a special nature trail brings out the botanical features. Because of the distinctive drainage characteristics the south wall is permanently damp while the north wall is dry. Mosses and ferns are prominent on the damp ground while lichens dominate the dry ground opposite. More than a hundred species have been counted in the cutting with less than a quarter common to both sides. Without the Country Park scheme the cutting would now be quite inaccessible, since initial local authority plans envisaged a main sewer running through the cutting with the ground then levelled off by tipping! Finally, it is pleasing that the stations have not been overlooked. The administration of the park is based at Thurstaston while other sites are used for information, car parking and conveniences. But Hadlow Road, the first station out from Hooton, has been carefully restored so as to appear as it did in the last years of the passenger service, complete with posters and advertisements and all the trappings right down to the trolleys, scales and milk churns.

# 29

# Preserved Railways

Railway preservation covers a very wide variety of activities extending from the efforts of the individual enthusiast who displays treasured possessions on his mantelpiece through to projects by large organised groups to restore locomotives, rolling stock and sundry acquisitions. The ultimate stage is reached when substantial sections of track are taken over for the running of steam trains, involving vintage locomotives and coaches. And it is with this comprehensive activity that this chapter is mainly concerned. However, since the steam railway is probably inspired primarily by an affection for the steam locomotive it is necessary to comment briefly on the interest in locomotive preservation. The effort has been a rather disjointed one beginning much too late to ensure that a truly representative selection of nineteenth-century designs was preserved. Of the four companies of the grouping only the L.N.E.R. showed a clear awareness of its heritage and the railway museum at York (greatly enlarged in 1975 as the National Railway Museum) was a most commendable enterprise. There was no great increase in interest after nationalisation, although James Ness, who managed the Scottish Region for a time, ensured the survival of representative engines from four of the old Scottish companies (Caledonian, Great North of Scotland, Highland and North British).

But private interest has been very substantial in the post-war period, with considerable momentum arising from the efforts of Alan Pegler who arranged many successful special workings by veteran locomotives and purchased the former L.N.E.R. Pacific *Flying Scotsman*. This style of preservation continued until 1967 when British Rail imposed a ban on the working of steam specials. Happily the policy was later revised to allow for steam working on selected lines in Britain and similar arrangements have been made in Ireland. The 'Portrush Flyer' has operated since 1973 from Belfast by Northern Ireland Railways, using locomotives and coaches maintained by the Railway Preservation Society of Ireland at Whitehead, Co. Antrim: the name recalls an express of the 1930s, one of several which ran into the famous seaside and golfing resort. Interest continues to grow and, in Britain, B.R. themselves now operate steam trains for enthusiasts, notably on the circuit from York through Leeds and Harrogate. But the temporary ban did serve to increase interest in entirely private railway ventures and the number of projects has increased rapidly over the past fifteen years. Indeed, so great has demand become that there is now a distinct shortage of engines suitable for preservation and without the foresight of Messrs Woodhams of Barry, in accumulating a large collection of steam locomotives at their scrap yard in South Wales, the problem would already be serious. Even so, more thought may soon have to be given to diesel and electric locomotives: some are already genuine vintage models and so are eminently desirable candidates, quite apart from the advantages of economical working and reduced pressure on the stock of steam locomotives. Yet in any case a ceiling will be reached in terms of both money-raising to meet the cost of purchase and replacement parts and free skilled labour to carry out the preservation work.

Many locomotives retained purely for display purposes in museums would be incapable of hauling trains. But others can be steamed and are used either to work in a confined railway yard or to take more vigorous exercise on lengths of preserved railway which may extend from just a few kilometres to almost thirty on the North York Moors Railway. In the latter cases there may occasionally be a public service provided, but the principal objectives lie in the desire of members to preserve steam railways as working systems and share their enjoyment at working the trains with members of the public at large. The voluntary labour of the members, along with money taken through ticket sales, publications and fund-raising efforts makes the projects viable. But it should be added that help has come through the Light Railways Act (passed in 1896), which sanctions relatively inexpensive operating procedures, and also through grants which some private companies have received from tourist organisations to accelerate development and provide recreational activity in a busy holiday area. Even so, financial viability can by no means be taken for granted and a distinction may be drawn between over-ambitious projects launched by enthusiasts and more rational schemes that the public can reasonably support. The former may evolve into the latter, as in East Anglia, where the initial idea for a private Leicester–Yarmouth service on the former Midland & Great Northern Joint line crystallised into the North Norfolk Railway operating from Sheringham to Weybourne in 1965.

The principal preserved railways are quite widely distributed. Although choice is inevitably restricted to lines closed by British Rail yet still available for purchase as a unit, the results have been very satisfactory with individual projects having a substantial catchment in terms of both permanently resident population and tourists. The balance will certainly fluctuate with a heavy tourist emphasis on the Speyside Railway in Scotland and a steadier demand on the Great Central Railway (Main Line Steam) in Leicestershire. Leicestershire is rather unusual in having two preserved railways in close

41.  *Severn Valley scene* A visit to the workshops of one of the railway preservation societies (here the Severn Valley railway at Bridgnorth) indicates the scale of the task and the importance of voluntary labour.

proximity since the former main line between Loughborough and Rothley is complemented by the Shackerstone Railway Society, taking a section of the Midland–L.N.W.R. joint line from Shackerstone to Market Bosworth (not to mention the delightful narrow gauge line laid in the rectory garden at Cadeby and an industrial locomotive preservation scheme at Cottesmore).

The first closed branch line of British Railways to reopen as a private preserved railway was the Bluebell Line in 1960 between Sheffield Park and Horsted Keynes in Sussex. But by this time there were several other preserved railways in operation including the Festiniog and Talyllyn railways in Wales. These two slate railways form part of a group of 'Great Little Trains of Wales' which have become a prominent feature in the Welsh tourist industry. The idea that tourists might support a rural railway was tried in the 1930s when the Great Western Railway modernised its Vale of

42. *Main Line Steam action* A B1 4–6–0 locomotive leaves Loughborough (Central) with a train for Rothley on Main Line Steam Trust's 'Great Central Railway' in Leicestershire.

Rheidol branch (Aberystwyth to Devil's Bridge) and promoted it as a tourist attraction: the venture was successful and the railway continued to flourish on reopening in 1945 after wartime closure. Meanwhile other narrow gauge lines tried to survive on the basis of a dwindling freight traffic but closure thereby became inevitable: Festiniog in 1946, Corris in 1948, Welshpool & Llanfair in 1956, Padarn in 1961 and Penrhyn in 1962. However, the Talyllyn survived. Built in 1866 to serve the Bryneglwys quarries, it continued to operate until 1950 when the death of the owner, Sir Haydn Jones, brought its future into grave doubt. The late L. T. C. Rolt conceived of a railway service supported by a preservation society and this has proved a happy solution, enabling the railway to continue in operation, in the traditional style, and provide pleasure for large numbers of holidaymakers. An extension to Nant Gwernol was opened in 1976, taking the line above Abergynolwyn towards the now derelict slate quarries.

The same idea was adopted for the Festiniog Railway which was partially reopened in 1955. In 1982 after years of work in track clearance and in rebuilding the upper section, to avoid the reservoir which flooded part of the original track bed, railway contact was regained between Porthmadog and Blaenau Ffestiniog. Links with the past are retained through the availability of Fairlie double-boiler locomotives, although some engines have been inevitably brought in from outside (notably *Blanche* and *Linda* from the Penrhyn Railway). The Welshpool & Llanfair was partially reopened in 1963 and a section of the Padarn Railway has been relayed as the narrow gauge Llanberis Lake Railway, which opened in 1971. It forms an appropriate complement to the workshops of the Dinorwic Quarry Company which have been preserved by the Welsh National Museum. Finally there are plans to reopen a section of the Welsh Highland Railway built as recently as 1923 but closed only fourteen years later. At the time of writing services operate over just one kilometre of the line from Porthmadog to Pen-y-Mount. Further detail on the Welsh railways (particularly the Festiniog) is given in the next chapter.

Although every preserved steam railway has its special points of interest the North York Moors line is particularly attractive because of its fine scenic route and the close cooperation between the railway and the national park authorities. For the original scheme for a preserved railway in 1967 involved only ten kilometres from Grosmont to Ellerbeck. Although there was support from Grosmont village and from the local authority (North Riding County Council) interested in the park, there was no way that substantial local authority support could be given until the 1968 Transport Act. In 1971 the matter was resolved in favour of the whole twenty-nine kilometres from Grosmont to Pickering. North Riding County Council negotiated with B.R. for purchase of the track from Ellerbeck to Pickering and leased it back to

Map 21. (*Opposite*)   Aspects of railway preservation.

NOTES 1. There are now approximately 1200 preserved locomotives: 900 standard gauge and 300 narrow gauge. Altogether nearly three-quarters of the preserved engines are steam locomotives (the rest diesel, petrol or electric) but less than forty per cent were formerly owned by public companies (the rest being 'industrial' locos).

2. To avoid confusion in the Porthmadog area of Wales the locomotives of the Narrow Gauge Railway Centre (Blaenau Ffestiniog) and Welsh Highland Railway (Porthmadog) are combined with those of the Festiniog Railway.

3. Routes on which steam trains are operated by B.R. were all available for steam working in 1976 and 1981, except for Perth–Aviemore which was available in 1981 only.

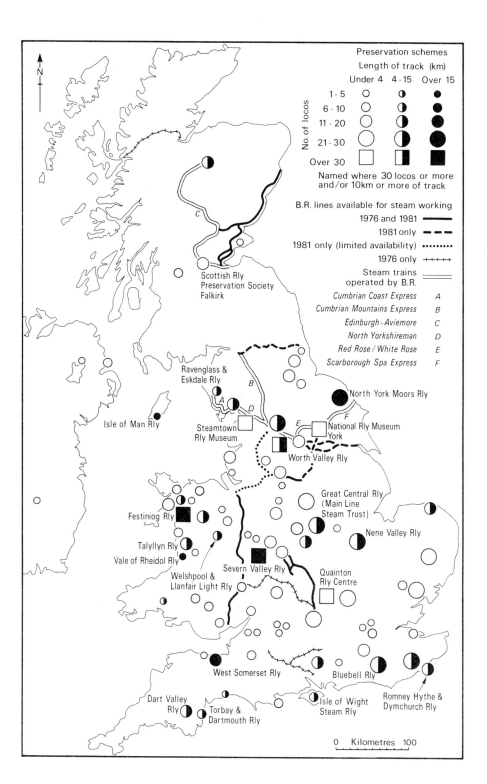

Preservation schemes
Length of track (km)

| | Under 4 | 4 - 15 | Over 15 |
|---|---|---|---|
| No. of locos | | | |
| 1 - 5 | ○ | ◑ | ● |
| 6 - 10 | ○ | ◑ | ● |
| 11 - 20 | ○ | ◑ | ● |
| 21 - 30 | ○ | ◑ | ● |
| Over 30 | ☐ | ◨ | ■ |

Named where 30 locos or more
and/or 10km or more of track

B.R. lines available for steam working

| 1976 and 1981 | ———— |
|---|---|
| 1981 only | – – – – |
| 1981 only (limited availability) | ·········· |
| 1976 only | +++++ |
| Steam trains operated by B.R. | ═══ |

Cumbrian Coast Express          A
Cumbrian Mountains Express      B
Edinburgh - Aviemore            C
North Yorkshireman              D
Red Rose / White Rose           E
Scarborough Spa Express         F

Scottish Rly
Preservation Society
Falkirk

Ravenglass &
Eskdale Rly

Isle of Man Rly

Steamtown
Rly Museum

North York Moors Rly

National Rly Museum
York

Worth Valley Rly

Festiniog Rly

Great Central Rly
(Main Line
Steam Trust)

Talyllyn Rly
Vale of Rheidol Rly

Nene Valley Rly

Welshpool &
Llanfair Light Rly

Severn Valley Rly

Quainton
Rly Centre

West Somerset Rly

Bluebell Rly

Romney Hythe &
Dymchurch Rly

Dart Valley
Rly

Torbay &
Dartmouth Rly

Isle of Wight
Steam Rly

0    Kilometres    100

43.   *Snowdon Mountain Railway* One of few railways in Britain built essentially for leisure and recreation. Using the rack and pinion system the Snowdown Railway is now one of the outstanding 'Great Little Trains of Wales'.

the North York Moors Railway. The society's efforts have been further encouraged by financial assistance from the English Tourist Board through a 'tourist incentive payment'. The scenic attraction of the area, culminating in Newton Dale (originally cut by meltwater from a glacial lake in Eskdale), has been greatly enhanced by the Forestry Commission's maturing plantations. The railway was seen to be accessible from a wide area and provided an environmentally-acceptable means of transporting people into and through this attractive, yet sensitive area. An intensive service is maintained during the summer months and an interesting range of locomotives is available: the initial North Eastern and L.N.E.R. flavour has been diluted to spread the wear and keep steam traction available for a longer period. Furthermore, diesel traction has been introduced, both locomotives and multiple units. While the latter have been marketed as a positive attraction (National Park Scenic Cruise) the main interest lies in cheaper motive power for services that are lightly-used and as standby against fire risk or steam failure.

  A feature of the North York Moors Railway is the effort made, through help from the Countryside Commission and the North York Moors National Park, to provide the public with information about the development of the railway and its historical associations with the area through which it passes. A variety of media are being used including display panels at stations, pamphlets offered for sale and a small audio-visual facility at Pickering dealing with wildlife and railway history. Curiously, one of the men closely connected with the railway in its early years, the Whitby solicitor Henry Belcher, also believed in keeping the public informed. He produced a classic tourist guide book on the scenery of the Whitby & Pickering Railway and this includes some fine engravings by George Dodgson: 'so universal and so decided was the admiration expressed at the beauty of scenery' thrown open to travellers 'that the idea of having an illustrated description of the railway was at once adopted'. Belcher incidentally was prime mover in the plan to build an Anglican church at Grosmont in 1839 and special trains were run from Whitby to support a bazaar in aid of funds. When he died in 1854 a full lancet window was erected in the church in his memory and this can still be seen in the present enlarged church opened in 1875. The railway certainly had tourist potential in the Vale of Goathland, 'hitherto unvisited and almost unknown', 'and in the wild and desolate scenery of Newton Dale where railway building was complicated by broken and boggy ground'. The moorland village of Goathland became an inland spa: it was an ideal walking centre for wealthy Victorians and Edwardians and its buildings still show a clear stamp of this period. In the 1930s day excursions were run through Newton Dale from West Yorkshire cities although after the war the private car displaced much of this traffic and the line was finally abandoned by British Rail in 1965.

The railway was first conceived by the people of Whitby as a means of stopping the decline of their town which was suffering from a sharp decline in its coastal shipping trade. Better overland communications were sought and since moorland roads were inadequate, while a canal was not feasible, George Stephenson was asked in 1831 to build an 'inexpensive way for horse-drawn carriages'. An act of parliament was obtained in 1833 and the line opened three years later. It brought an immediate boost to Whitby's trade since shopkeepers in the Pickering area received their orders by sea to Whitby and by rail from there. However, Pickering subsequently became linked with York and the Whitby–Pickering line was drawn into the national system. This led to early modernisation. In view of the initial use of horse power (the first trains took two-and-a-half hours for the 38.6 km) gradients had to be gentle, with major differences in level overcome by the installation of inclines. One incline of 1.4 km was needed between Grosmont and Goathland where the land rises sharply along the Eller Beck Valley. In the days of horse traction the incline involved 'no interruption to the average speed of travelling' since the five minutes needed to haul a single coach up the incline compared favourably with the average speed for the line as a whole. But with steam locomotives hauling longer trains delays were considerable, not to mention the operating problems through the need to have locomotives at either end of the incline. The line was taken over by

George Hudson's York & North Midland Railway in 1845 and converted to steam locomotive operation. The short 110 m tunnel at Grosmont through Lease Rigg, giving access to the Vale of Goathland, was rebored (the original tunnel is now used for access to the new locomotive shed of 1973, where incidentally a viewing platform for visitors has been installed). Bridges built by Stephenson, using Baltic fir, were replaced in stone and permanent station buildings were provided. In addition the northern approach to the Beck Hole incline was straightened.

A further improvement was made in 1865 when the incline was eliminated by a deviation railway which involves a 1 in 49 gradient from Grosmont to Goathland. The old alignment is only joined about one kilometre south of Goathland however and so a new station building was needed in the village. The present Goathland Station is a fine North Eastern period piece of 1865 with hardly any subsequent alteration. The incline, with a gradient of 1 in 5, can still be followed and a footpath has been laid out along it: the walk provides views of the old Bank Top Station and railway cottages as well as the cottage at the foot of the incline. There are also clear signs of iron working which brought many people into the area in the late nineteenth century and in particular brought about an enlargement of Grosmont and a rebuilding of the church. Henry Belcher asserted in 1836 that iron ores of Goathland Vale 'promise much advantage to the railway whether from the mere transit and exportation of the ore itself or from the profitable establishment of blast furnaces in the district which possesses so many natural advantages for the purpose'. The northern approach to the incline remained open after 1864 for the iron ore traffic as far as Beck Hole and an autocar service was provided from Whitby until 1914. Cottages built to house the workers at Beck Hole ironworks have been demolished but the Esk Valley mine cottages still stand adjacent to the railway (lacking road access until recently). A remarkably distinct and intimate relationship between the railway and its landscape greatly enhances the appeal of Britain's longest preserved railway.

# 30

# Railway Preservation in North Wales

It is an impressive indication of the way in which industrial history has become a respectable tourist preoccupation to see how the rapid postwar decline of Welsh slate quarrying has been followed by schemes of preservation. Competition from Continental slates and from other roofing materials has meant that twentieth-century housing booms have exerted only a limited effect on the industry's fortunes. New uses for slate (in flooring and fireplace units) and the development of materials like 'Penrhyn Grout' (a binding material for road construction made from ground slate mixed with bitumen) have not prevented massive rationalisation which leaves Penrhyn to dominate the modest industry that survives in North Wales. However, the closure of Dinorwic in 1969 was followed up quickly by the opening of the North Wales Quarrying Museum in 1972. This is housed in the old quarry workshops near Llanberis and provides a striking insight on the old quarry industry, including a dependence on water power expressed through the 1.2 km cast iron pipe leading from Llanberis Waterfall supplying a 15.4 m diameter water wheel (replaced by a Pelton Wheel in 1925). At Blaenau Ffestiniog drastic closures have taken place. However, the Llechwedd–Maenofferen–Bowydd amalgamation has allowed some continued working at Bowydd while the old Llechwedd Quarries were reopened to tourists in 1972. Battery locomotives now haul trainloads of tourists through the famous caverns.

The same transition has been made on the railways. A previous chapter outlined the development of the quarry lines. Some had appeared only after the standard gauge railways had penetrated into North Wales and from the start were feeders to the main railway companies and used steam locomotives. But others were earlier developments and used horse traction to take slate to the ports. The construction of the main line railways led to problems of adaptation which were solved with great distinction: despite a very narrow gauge (around 0.60 m or 2 ft in the majority of cases) steam locomotives were introduced and a common carrier function was assumed for passengers and goods. During the present century, however, the railways tended to become simply freight carriers and slowly deteriorated with the fall in slate traffic. There has been a transfer to road vehicles which as far as Blaenau Ffestiniog is concerned was complete in 1962 when the last shipment was made to British Rail's Llandudno Junction line. The facilities at Minffordd remained until 1972 but slate was taken there from Blaenau by road.

However, the railways have not disappeared: the old Cambrian line to Pwllheli retains a passenger service as does the Conwy Valley line from Llandudno Junction, and although the G.W.R. line from Bala was closed in 1961 and the trackbed partially submerged for the Llyn Celyn reservoir scheme, the opening of the nuclear power station at Trawsfyndd in 1963 secured the northern end of this branch which now has a physical connection with the Conwy Valley line to allow the removal of uranium element rods. The narrow gauge railways have also shown a sturdy capacity for survival and a further phase has now started in which passenger traffic, in the form of the summer tourist trade, is now dominant. The inspiration came primarily from the Talyllyn. The closure of Bryneglwys Quarries in 1948 finalised a move that had actually been contemplated back in 1910, but only for the Liberal candidate (later M.P.) for Merioneth constituency to step in and negotiate purchase of the business in order to safeguard employment. However, he could really do no more to develop the quarries than the previous tenants since there was no basis for new capital investment: the dwindling reserves of high quality slate were picked out while safety margins narrowed. But the enterprise was able to survive into the steam preservation era and the Talyllyn Railway is unique in providing the atmosphere of a mid-nineteenth-century railway that never experienced modernisation or extension: such was the marginality of the whole Bryneglwys enterprise. The railway was kept open initially to provide a public transport service but the death of Sir Haydn Jones in 1950 led to a great uncertainty which was eventually resolved by the formation of a preservation society. Locomotives and rolling stock have been brought in from other railways, like the Corris Railways (closed in 1948 after flood damage to the bridge in Machynlleth) which adopted the same gauge of 0.68 m. But they have conformed to the established blend and contribute to the perpetuation of the such classic railway landscapes as the crossing of Dolgoch Falls and the threading of the Nant Gwernol ravine. It is unfortunate that the quarries have not featured in the preservation programme, though the extension of the railway to Nant Gwernol takes the railway into the ravine and it is an easy walk along the valley to the derelict quarries that provided the *raison d'être* for one of the country's most popular pleasure railways.

The Talyllyn Railway is not the only slate-carrying line to survive. The Penrhyn Railway closed completely in 1962, after losing its workmen's trains in 1951, but a railway museum opened at Penrhyn Castle in 1965. The Padarn Railway lost its remaining slate train in 1961 (workmen's trains had ceased in 1947) but a section of the line from Dinorwic Quarry has been relaid along the side of the lake (from the old workshops of Gilfachddu to Penllyn) although the gauge is narrower than the original. However, the new gauge is practically similar to the one previously used within the quarries and so the Llanberis Lake Railway was able to take over a good deal of old equipment including the locomotive *Dolbadarn* which hauled the inaugural train in 1971. Much more substantial is the Festiniog Railway which has been rescued from years of dereliction by the most imaginative restoration scheme to have been implemented in the British Isles so far. After surviving for many years thanks to its links with the quarries of Blaenau at one end and with the Cambrian Railways (later G.W.R.) at the other, the line closed to passengers in 1939 and for freight in 1946. Traffic was light and the years of wartime neglect left the system in a critically rundown state. However, enthusiasts came together in 1951 to consider restoration and after legal matters had been cleared up work could begin on reopening the first section of railway along the Cob in 1955. Three years later services were running on through Minffordd and Penrhyndeudraeth as far as Tan-y-Bwlch (12.1 km) which provided a scenically interesting journey over a worthwhile distance with road access at each end.

After years of consolidation the services were extended to Dduallt in 1968 but only to encounter a major frustration arising from the flooding of part of the old trackbed above the Moelwyn Tunnel as part of a pumped storage hydro-electricity scheme. Electric schemes are as much a part of the Ffestiniog landscape as are the railways and developments have been put in hand since the late nineteenth century. Llyn Bowydd, which lies beside the old quarry line to Manod, was harnessed to supply a small generator for Maeneroffen Quarry, typical of the small schemes which had capacities less than one megawatt. Special power companies built larger installations primarily to augment supplies to larger quarries: Dolwen station below Blaenau started supplying power in 1900 and eventually achieved a capacity of two megawatts while a generation later Maentwrog station opened with 23 MW (1934). But since that time the development of a grid system has reduced the need for small conventional hydro stations and diverted interest to pumped storage schemes which can soak up surplus power at offpeak times and make substantial supplies available for short periods of maximum demand. The Tanygrisiau station completed in 1963 can supply 360 MW for short periods as water runs down from a small upper reservoir (the enlarged Llyn Stwlam) to the main storage lake, known as Llyn Ystradau. The enlargement of the latter meant the flooding of a kilometre of railway trackbed and, through the sealing of Moelwyn Tunnel, blockage of easy access to Ffestiniog. Yet when compensation was belatedly awarded it yielded little more than £100 000. Although the power station project was among the first to include detailed consultations on amenity matters the implications of the scheme for the Festiniog Railway were largely overlooked. It is a reflection of the way in which the conservation movement has broadened in little more than a decade.

The compensation received was only a modest contribution to the cost of an elaborate diversion scheme which had provided a new track on the northern side of the reservoir and access from Dduallt by a new tunnel which is reached by means of a spiral: a huge circle which gains 10.5 m in height. The spiral opened in 1975 and trains started regular working through Moelwyn Tunnel to a temporary railhead beside the reservoir in 1977. With the help of a job creation project the deviation line has been completed to rejoin the original Festiniog route at Tanygrisiau. Completion through to Blaenau is now assured and this will increase the tourist patronage and also provide a railway link between the British Rail stations at either end of the line. The distinct possibility that the incline connecting the Festiniog Railway with the Llechwedd Quarries might be restored was realised in 1979.

The Festiniog Railway has attracted tourists to Porthmadog to the extent of making a significant contribution to its summer trade and one which is recognised in the town and in local government. Hence there is considerable optimism about the effect that the restoration of services to Blaenau

44. *Reconstruction on the Festiniog* A section of newly constructed track which takes the Festiniog Railway above Llyn Ystradau and assures the return of the railway to Blaenau Ffestiniog.

Ffestiniog will have on the old slate town in the hills. Local opinion has campaigned strongly for a station in the centre of the town so that visitors will feel inclined to patronise local shops. Rather than use the site adjacent to the present British Rail station (which is too far from the centre) or the old Festiniog terminus of Diffwys (which is too cramped to accommodate long trains) land will be cleared round the old G.W.R. station. British Rail will also use the new station which was opened in 1982, thanks to generous financial assistance from national and local government.

A critical element in the work to reopen the Festiniog Railway has been availability of substantial workshop space at Boston Lodge. New coaches are being built there and locomotives overhauled. The latter include strangers such as *Blanche*, which hails from the Penrhyn Railway, but there is strong continuity not only in the continued existence of *Prince*, one of the original steam locomotives of 1863, but the Fairlie double-boilered locomotive *Merddin Emrys* built at Boston Lodge in 1879 and rebuilt there on three occasions before being inherited by the modern company. A brand new Fairlie locomotive was produced in 1979 with the name *Earl of Merioneth*. This is oil burning, like all the other Festiniog Railway locomotives. Rather than rebuild the first locomotive to carry this name it was decided to preserve the historic engine (which will now be displayed in its original condition) and build an entirely new *Fairlie* incorporating various modern refinements.

# Bibliography

## 1. A GENERAL REVIEW

A great deal of the background information on the topics dealt with in this book may be gleaned from the histories of the various railway companies. Regarding the major companies of the pre-grouping period the following may be cited: *Barry* (D. S. Barrie – Tarrant Hinton, Oakwood Press 1978); *Brecon & Merthyr* (D. S. Barrie – Lingfield, Oakwood Press 1957); *Caledonian* (O. S. Nock – London, Ian Allan 1961); *Cambrian Railways* (R. Christiansen and R. W. Miller – Newton Abbot, David & Charles 1967–8 2 vols.); *Cheshire Lines Committee* (R. P. Griffiths – Tarrant Hinton, Oakwood Press 1978); *Dublin & South Eastern* (W. E. Shepherd – Newton Abbot, David & Charles 1974); *Great Central* (G. Dow – London, Locomotive Publishing Co. 1959–65 3 vols.); *Great Eastern* (C. J. Allen – London, Ian Allan 1955); *Glasgow & South Western* (C. Highet – Lingfield, Oakwood Press 1965); *Great Eastern* (C. J. Allen – London, Ian Allan 1955); *Great Northern* (J. Wrottesley – London, Batsford 1979 2 vols.); *Great North of Scotland* (M. Barclay-Harvey – London, Locomotive Publishing Co. 1940); *Highland* (H. A. Vallance – London, Stockwell 1938); *Hull & Barnsley* (K. Hoole ed. – Newton Abbot, David & Charles 1972); *Lancashire & Yorkshire* (J. Marshall – Newton Abbot, David & Charles 1969–72 3 vols.); *London Brighton & South Coast* (J. H. Turner – London, Batsford 1977–9 3 vols.); *London & North Western* (O. S. Nock – London, Ian Allan 1960); *London & South Western* (R. A. Williams – Newton Abbot, David & Charles 1968–73 2 vols.); *Midland* (C. E. Stretton – London, Methuen 1901); *North British* (J. Thomas – Newton Abbot, David & Charles 1969–75 2 vols.); *North London* (M. Robbins – Lingfield, Oakwood Press 1976); *Northern Counties* (*Ireland*) J. R. L. Currie – Newton Abbot, David & Charles 1973–4 2 vols.); *North Eastern* (W. W. Tomlinson, revised by K. Hoole – Newton Abbot, David & Charles 1967); *North Staffordshire* (R. Christiansen and R. W. Miller – Newton Abbot, David & Charles 1971); *Rhymney* (D. S. Barrie – South Godstone, Oakwood Press 1952); *Somerset & Dorset* (D. S. Barrie – Tarrant Hinton, Oakwood Press 1978); *South Eastern & Chatham* (O. S. Nock – London, Ian Allan 1961); *Taff Vale* (D. S. Barrie – Sidcup, Oakwood Press 1939).

Many other histories, dealing with the minor railways, have been published, especially by David & Charles and Oakwood Press. Histories of the 'big four' companies of the period 1923–1948 include: *Great Western* (E. T. Macdermott, C. R. Clinker and O. S. Nock – London, Ian Allan 1964–7 3 vols.); *London & North Eastern* (C. J. Allen – London, Ian Allan 1966); *Southern* (C. F. D. Marshall – London, Ian Allan 1963 2 vols.).

Regional histories are largely restricted to the David & Charles series on the *Regional history of the railways of Britain* available as follows: *I West Country* (D. St. J. Thomas 1960); *II Southern England* (H. P. White 1961); *III Greater London* (H. P. White 1963); *IV North East* (K. Hoole 1974); *V Eastern Counties* (D. I. Gordon 1968); *VI Scotland – Lowlands and Borders* (J. Thomas 1971); *VII West Midlands* (R. Christiansen 1973); *VIII South and West Yorkshire* (D. Joy 1975); *IX East Midlands* (R. Leleux 1976); *X North West* (G. O. Holt 1978); *XI North and Mid Wales* (P. E. Baughan 1980); *XII South Wales* (D. S. M. Barrie 1980); *XIII Thames & Severn* (R. Christiansen 1980). The same publisher is also promoting a series of regional texts on *Forgotten railways*. The following are available so far: *East Midlands* (P. H. Anderson 1973); *North East England* (K. Hoole 1973); *Chilterns and Cotswolds* (R. Davies and M. D. Grant 1975); *Scotland* (J. Thomas 1976); *North and Mid Wales* (R. Christiansen 1976); *South East England* (H. P. White 1976); *East Anglia* (R. S. Joby 1977); *South Wales* (J. H. R. Page 1979). Other contributions include E. Course on *Railways of Southern England* (London, Batsford 1973–6 3 vols.); G. Whittle on *Railways in the Consett area* (Newton Abbot, David & Charles 1971) and a series by K. Hoole on *Railways in Yorkshire* (Clapham, Dalesman Books) which began in 1971. Scotland is dealt with by W. Ackworth *The Railways of Scotland: their present position* (London, John Murray 1890) and O. S. Nock *Scottish Railways* (London, Nelson 1950). For Ireland, work includes M. H. C. Baker, *Irish railways since 1916* (London, Ian Allan 1972); H. C. Casserley, *Outline of Irish railway history* (Newton Abbot, David & Charles 1974); J. C. Conroy, *A history of railways in Ireland* (London, Longmans Green 1928); T. Middlemass *Irish standard gauge railways* (Newton Abbot, David & Charles 1981). There are several books on the railways of London including T. C. Barker and M. Robbins, *A history of London Transport* (London, George Allen & Unwin 1975–6 2 vols.); J. R. Day, *The story of London's underground* (London, London Transport 1966); A. A. Jackson, *London's termini* (Newton Abbot, David & Charles 1969); A. J. Jackson, *London's local railways* (Newton Abbot, David & Charles 1978) and R. H. G. Thomas, *London's first railway: London & Greenwich* (London, Batsford 1972). Atlases include S. Baker, *Railway atlas of Britain* (Oxford, Oxford Publishing Co. 1977) and S. M. Hajducki, *A railway atlas of Ireland* (Newton Abbot, David & Charles 1974).